MASTERING THE GRAIN MARKETS
How Profits Are Really Made

by Elaine Kub

MASTERING THE GRAIN MARKETS: How Profits Are Really Made

Kub Asset Advisory, Inc.
Omaha, Nebraska 68022

Library of Congress Cataloging in Publication Data:
Kub, Elaine
      Mastering the Grain Markets: How Profits Are Really Made
      Includes Index.
      ISBN 978-1477582961

      2012911523

ISBN   1477582967   978-1477582961

Printed and bound in the United States of America by CreateSpace
Cover art copyright © 2013 Elaine Kub

www.masteringthegrainmarkets.com

To the memory of

the inimitable Mark Pearson (1957 to 2012)

who was a strong hero for agriculture,

and a magnificent inspiration to me.

CONTENTS

CHAPTER 1
The Philosophy of Commodity Profits

The South Dakota prairie, where I grew up, was formed as Ice Age glaciers retreated two million years ago. In these glaciers' wake, a mantle of mineral-rich deposits was left behind, including clay soil and rocks of all shapes and sizes. And I mean lots of rocks ... from big brown or pink or gray granite boulders, to smooth, fist-sized sedimentary stones, to irregular chunks of multi-colored quartzite.

The rocks tell an interesting story about where and how the glaciers moved and melted, but to a prairie pioneer like my great-grandfather Albert Kub, they were more a nuisance than a neat geological guide. Imagine cutting into the thick-rooted prairie with a moldboard plow in 1902, only to have each step interrupted by bulky chunks of rock tumbling up out of the soil. The plow's blade would strike stone and get bent or dulled, or be stopped altogether if it hit a big enough boulder. It was a significantly bigger challenge than his forebears faced farming in the fine sandy loam of Bohemia.

So from the freshly-tilled soil, South Dakota pioneers would pick out all the rocks by hand and cart them away from the fields. Some of this task would just have been tedious: lifting little 25-pound rocks, one after another. But I still can't figure out how they unearthed some of the bigger boulders back then without heavy equipment. Eventually, the stones would be dumped unceremoniously into big piles, which were strategically located in the low-lying sloughs where they couldn't be seen from the road. The rockier a field was, the more challenging it would be to raise a crop, and the less it would be worth. Therefore, the bigger the rock pile, the less a farmer would want his neighbors to see it. We have a family story about Grandpa getting chewed out by Great-Grandpa because he was sent out to clear a field of rocks and ended up building a rock pile fifty feet from the main county road.

Rock picking is a never-ending battle, because each time a field gets tilled even today, "new" rocks are uncovered and brought to the surface. I don't have to stretch my imagination too far to envision the drudgery of picking all those rocks one by one out of a field.

Modern tillage, planting, and harvesting equipment is generally able to work past all but the biggest rocks, but a hay baler which combs the ground picking up all the little things it can find – leaves of grass and hay, grasshoppers, rocks – is rather more sensitive to these Ice Age souvenirs. So my sister and I used to be sent out each year to the fifty-acre alfalfa field to clear away interminable quantities of rocks. There weren't as many rocks then as there would have been back in 1902, but it was still unpleasant.

Trust me, all of these details are relevant in some way to my experience as a 21st century farmer. The soil type affects what kind of crops can be grown and how productive those crops will be; the pioneers' efforts inspire and guide management decisions about the land's fertility. That will all be a part of this book, but the most important thing I want to mention about those rocks is how they illustrate a trading method that is critical to the grain markets: arbitrage.

Omaha, Nebraska, where I live now, is perched on the silty clay hills just west of the Missouri River. No rocks scattered around. So when a homeowner in some fresh, new West Omaha subdivision wants to build a retaining wall or line a driveway with decorative stone, they go to a gardening center and plunk down $60 per ton for some rocks. If they want particularly attractive rocks, maybe they end up paying a little more.

Well, if someone had told my eight-year-old self that all those stupid rocks I picked up out of the dry dirt and heaved onto the trailer had been worth nearly $1 a piece … I don't know if that would have made the task more or less frustrating. Probably more frustrating, because I certainly wouldn't have been able to sell those rocks for $60 per ton in South Dakota. That would be like selling sand to a Bedouin or saltwater to a sailor. The rocks are only worth something where they are scarce.

A person could, however, acquire those rocks for free in South Dakota, put the money and effort into transporting them nearly 500 miles, and turn around and sell those same "free" rocks to someone in Omaha for $60 per ton. Now, that's a trade. That's arbitrage.

....

Knowledge as Money

Grain trading hasn't always been as exciting as it is today, but it has always been challenging; and for as long as humans have been growing crops, it has always been vital to our life on earth. The earliest agricultural activity can be traced back to 9,000 B.C. on the banks of the Euphrates or 8,000 B.C. in the Andes. Farming and grain trading weren't the first things mankind ever did, but they were certainly in the top five. And they are as critical now as they ever were.

Demand for feed grains, in particular, is expected to double between 2010 and 2040 as the world's population grows not only in size, but in the sophistication of its diet – away from staple grains or starches and toward more protein and meats, which are produced by animals who are fed grain. To ensure these needs are fairly met with sufficient production, that the grain gets efficiently transported where it needs to go, and that it eventually gets sold to the consumers who need it most, is all going to require a lot of sophisticated knowledge and hard work from a lot of people. In short, it's going to require grain traders.

While I've always romanticized the agriculture industry, once I grew out of childhood and moved off the farm, it became apparent to me that not everyone else felt the same awe and admiration for grain market participants. When I left business school for the "real world," not all my classmates in California were too impressed by my choice to work in the grain markets and move to (of all places) Nebraska. But commodities trading – a fast-changing, tangible and math-driven pursuit – was a siren call to me. Agriculture was already becoming a sexier topic back then, and I predict it will continue to be a strong, exciting field to work in as recognition grows for the critical importance of keeping our expanding world fed, peaceful, and prosperous.

If you already have some exposure to the grain markets – for instance, if you are a farmer or a grain consumer – it's already evident to you that successful grain trading is vital to your business. If you are just now exploring the possibilities of the grain markets, it will become clear that knowing about all the markets' functions will help you make money with your trades.

But there's a fundamental difference between the way you're probably used to making money and the way money is made in commodity markets. In most minds, the response to "what earns profit?" is probably "the creation of some economic value." The service of painting a house is an activity that creates value for someone, and that person will pay for that value, and the painter will make a profit. Manufacturing creates a value greater than the sum of its raw materials, and manufacturers earn profit from their customers.

However, if I sold those $0 rocks from South Dakota for $60 per ton somewhere else, I wouldn't have *created* any economic value, although I would have transferred the ownership of those rocks to the buyers who most highly valued them. In other words, I would have just traded some rocks. My profit was earned simply by recognizing where two values were different, then buying low and selling high.

Grain trading is a very special and exciting variety of trading, but at its heart, it's not much different than trading rocks or baseball cards or used cars. Farmers do create (grow) products with fresh economic value, but they must also wisely trade their crops. The success of their trading or of any other grain trader's decisions will hinge on how much they know about the market and how well they use that knowledge to identify buy low / sell high opportunities.

Investment occurs when an investor has a certain amount of capital, which she would like to turn into a larger amount of capital at some point in the future. She will therefore put that money into an economic asset today, with no intention of consuming that asset, but rather of receiving periodic income from that asset or of later divesting of that asset at a profit. An investor has a lot of alternatives when selecting an asset, and will sometimes gravitate toward an asset with the highest expected return. However, between two assets with the same expected return, the investor is likely to choose the asset that has a lower expected risk of loss. Similarly, between two assets with the same expected risk of loss, the investor will choose the one that has a higher expected return (the Mean-Variance Rule). This is why "safe" assets, like Certificates of Deposit at your local bank, don't pay very exciting profits, and why the assets which promise a lot of profit typically display very volatile performance.

So of all the things in which you can invest your money, what could you do? Consider the simplest examples. If you're an 8-year-old with $5 in your pocket that you'd like to turn into $50, you can take your capital down to the grocery store and buy lemons and sugar. Put together with some plant expense (a folding table) and some marketing (a sign saying "Lemonade - 50¢"), you'll have a business. One hundred cups of lemonade later, you'll have your $45 in profits, a 900% return.

If you're a 22-year-old with $5,000 in a 401k retirement plan, your first instinct will be to follow this same pattern of value creation. You'll probably invest the money in shares of companies that do roughly the same thing as your lemonade stand – they purchase inputs (raw materials, labor) and produce something with those inputs to create more value than the sum of the parts. Even companies that don't produce any product and just produce a service (marketing, consulting, legal advice, etc.) are theoretically creating more value with their processes than the sum of the parts that make them (an office with a computer network and people). By purchasing those stocks, you're effectively giving them a portion of the first $5 for the lemonade stand and hoping in return to receive a portion of the final $45 profit.

Making money in the commodity markets doesn't work that way. The model would be more like another 8-year-old offering to buy the first kid's whole inventory of prepared lemonade for $30, then turning around and repackaging it and offering it on a more advantageous sidewalk for $1 per cup. Let's say that kid's profits would be $60 ($100 minus the initial $30 investment and $10 of transportation costs to get the prepared lemonade to the new market). The second kid never actually *created* any new value, she just identified an underpriced product and figured out how to sell it for more money. She conducted an **arbitrage**, perhaps between a shady sidewalk where people weren't very thirsty and a sunny sidewalk where passers-by were happy to shell out a dollar for a cup of warm lemonade from a cute kid.

A lot of money can be made in the grain markets with similar arbitrage trades – perhaps by identifying a time when grain seems underpriced and predicting a later time when the price will be higher. Perhaps by identifying a type of grain that seems overpriced when a different type of cheaper grain can be used as a substitute. Perhaps by identifying a specific buyer who is more willing to pay for grain at a high price than the buyers somewhere else. There are many, many dimensions used to arbitrage grain.

The methods available to you for grain trading will depend on who you are. Pretty much any person with some available cash (or a way to get some) can make trades in the commodity futures and options market and mechanically it's very similar to trading stocks, so most people will find it a pretty straightforward process. Whether or not it is wise for them to engage in the process is another matter.

If you have a unique access point to the grain markets (you own a grain elevator or work for a company that does, or you own some farmland or maybe just some farming equipment), you will not only have opportunities to trade grain for profit, you can also directly engage in value creation.

Whatever your case, the better educated you are about the tradecraft of everyone else in the industry, the more you will be able to identify trading opportunities. Certainly you *can* use technical trading techniques or any other broad market strategies or schemes to analyze grain price levels and hope for profit. But the real fortunes of the grain markets – the multi-billion dollar international grain trading houses, the multi-generational family farms, the lasting hedge funds with stable returns and low risk-to-reward ratios – are all paying attention to the more complicated details about how grain is grown, moved to market, and how it's demanded by end users. They're identifying arbitrage opportunities of all types: between geographies, between quality levels, or even between the different trading mechanisms through which you can buy and sell grain.

Real proficiency at this is rare. Expertise in the grain industry – like the grain itself – is usually stored in vertical silos of specialization. Separated by thick concrete walls, any one type of expertise is usually kept from comingling with other types in other silos. Futures brokers don't always know much about crop production. Ethanol plant managers don't always have time to keep track of how geopolitical events affect grain prices. An options trader in Chicago may be able to take advantage of miniscule changes in the vega on a March corn call, but not know a thing about how that corn came into being or how it will be used. On the other side of the coin, a farmer may be knowledgeable about the latest genetic seed technology and how best to design the irrigation system on his farm, but may not know what the vega on a March corn call is ... or that it even exists ... or how best to manipulate it and achieve better, more stable revenue from his corn.

At the risk of sounding melodramatic, some of this information is the kind of stuff the big, successful grain companies don't want you to know. Dan Morgan pegged it correctly in his 1979 book, *Merchants of Grain*: there is a "traditional and well-protected secrecy of grain companies" which allows them not only to defend their competitive advantages from each other, but also to some extent to keep farmers and end users in the dark about how much money is being left on the table with each trade. Certainly, it benefits private grain companies to keep the broader investment community away from competing in their industry. Farmers, quite on the other side of the secrecy spectrum, profess loudly every day that they would love investors to know and respond more quickly to the market factors that affect production.

Regardless of its diplomatic wisdom or lack thereof, this book aims to break down those silos. I think every grain industry participant could improve his profits by knowing just a little bit more about his customers' business, or his customers' customers' businesses. I won't offer an in-depth discussion of the underlying parameters of options pricing or the intricacies of irrigation system design. Rather, I will simply de-mystify the entire scope of the grain trading process, so that anyone who chooses to participate in the industry will have a basic idea of how grain is traded at every stage.

Volatility

....

The film studio of Iowa Public Television is mostly silent and dark each Friday afternoon, with the accumulated shadows of decades of fundraising drives and political roundtables huddling in the furthest corners of its cavernous space. But one pool of light falls from sophisticated lamps onto a set piece – a wooden table with two chairs – and a few people sit around tapping on their smartphones, waiting. There are two professional cameramen, an intern, and a commodities market analyst frantically memorizing the week's closing prices for soybeans, cotton, and hogs. A program producer ambles in and as he opens the door all heads turn, because everybody – including the producer – is wondering: "Where is Mark?"

At the appointed hour Mark Pearson arrives, and if the darkness itself doesn't lift, the silence certainly does. "Well, hellloooo!"His presence is as thriving and flourishing as his person, which is a figure dear and familiar to a million public television viewers in 27 states – farmers, ranchers, bankers, traders, equipment dealers, ethanol plant managers, and everyone else who happens to flip through the re-runs on Saturday morning and find *Market to Market*.

On this particular Friday, the stock market closed up a couple percentage points and Mark is in fine cheerful form, telling tales of his travels that week: speaking engagements stretching across the Corn Belt from North Platte, Nebraska to Monmouth, Illinois. All eyes are on him as he does the read-through of the night's script. When there's a pause for some editing, he turns to Scotty, the cameraman, and says, "Hey, Scotty, so my neighbor Earl was going into the kitchen the other day and he asks his wife, Irma, if she wanted anything. Irma says: 'Well, Earl, you gotta write this down now. You're getting so forgetful anymore. Bring me a bowl of strawberries with some whipped cream ... and *don't forget the cream*. Write that down or you'll forget.' So Earl shuffles off to the kitchen and putters around for a while and then he comes back out with two plates of waffles and eggs. 'Here ya go, dear,' he says to Irma. And she says, 'Earl! I told you not to forget the syrup!'"

Scotty laughs. Everybody laughs. Mark could tell a story about paint drying on a John Deere tractor and have every person in the room smiling and nodding and laughing. But the instant the camera light blinks on, Mark-the-quipster disappears and Mark-the-eminent-pundit springs to life. He drills the analyst: "How big will India's cotton crop be?" "Should corn farmers be buying puts right now?" "Is the Russian drought fully priced into the wheat market yet?" "Will South Korean demand drive up cattle prices?"

All those farmers, ranchers, and bankers turn on their television sets every Friday night to hear not only the feature stories about the latest USDA decisions or ethanol legislation or urban food deserts, but also to get a sense about what might happen to the prices of wheat, corn, soybeans, cotton, live cattle, feeder cattle, hogs, and other commodities in the coming days, weeks, and months. In the agriculture industry, an industry where your annual income can shift by 7% on any given market day, it's hardly surprising that the markets loom over participants like demi-gods – fickle, vacillating, sometimes unjust. But always, always interesting.

....

The choice to trade commodities rather than to use your capital for investing in stocks or bonds or any other asset is more than just a philosophical one. Trading grains will be experientially different for you, because of one ubiquitous hallmark of the grain markets: volatility.

If a person could have just owned "grain" over the past forty years (let's just assume an equally-weighted index of corn, wheat, and soybeans based on Chicago futures prices), the value of that asset would have increased 356% during that time. That wouldn't have come close to beating the stock market (the S&P 500 grew 1,209% during that same period), but that's the least of the reasons why it wouldn't have been a particularly appealing investment. Hedge funds use metrics like a worst drawdown or a Sharpe ratio (reward divided by risk) to compare assets' performances and measure how safe an investor's money would be. In that theoretical "grain" asset, the worst drawdown was a whopping 55% from the April 1996 high to the August 1998 low, with other, similarly astounding drawdowns occurring with disturbing regularity throughout history. The annualized return over the past 40 years would have been 3.85%, and the Sharpe ratio would have been a disastrous -0.0265 (using the Fed Funds rate to compare grain returns against a theoretical risk-free investment). That's really bad, from an investment perspective. One definitely wants one's money to be in an asset with a Sharpe ratio higher than 1.0, meaning the asset offers relatively more reward than risk, and the higher the better. What these statistics tell us is that grains have historically *not* been a particularly rewarding *nor* a particularly safe place to park investment money.

But the unattractive volatility and wild drawdowns aren't necessarily the results of flaws in the grain markets, and it isn't completely reasonable to expect grain, as an investment class, to behave like a well-managed equity fund. Volatility and drawdowns are just what happens when you have a desperately demanded (i.e. inelastic) product produced once or twice a year around the globe, subject to that globe's capricious weather one year, then suddenly over-produced the next year.

In the stock market or in real estate markets, analysts can speak of "bubbles." For a market to be in a **bubble,** it must be trading at a price that is higher than the real, underlying value of the asset. As long as investors can figure out the real, underlying value of an asset, bubbles typically don't happen. So it would be pretty hard to have a bubble form in lemonade, for instance. If you went to one store and the lemonade seemed too expensive, you'd just go find it at another store for a cheaper price. Blue chip stocks of large, stable, well-known companies are also unlikely to form bubbles – most investors are fully aware of how much capital, how much debt, and how much earnings are represented in those stock prices. Companies with less familiar business models (like the internet start-ups of the 1990's) certainly can attract excited buyers willing to pay stock prices above the real value of the company, because nobody could really define the "real" value of the company. Real estate has a similar problem – until you actually try to sell a specific property on the open market, how can you guess what its value is? How do you account for that unknown value on your balance sheet?

Grain, however, doesn't have that problem. There is always a known, underlying "real" value of the grain being traded, because there is constantly someone out there needing it and willing to pay a market price for it, whether that buyer is a livestock feeder, a flour mill, or an ethanol plant. It may be complicated to distill all the millions of individual grain trades happening around the world into one benchmark asset price, but it's not impossible.

That doesn't necessarily keep grain prices from violently spiking, then violently falling. If put on a chart and set in front of a stock trader, a grain market's natural price patterns would look an awful lot like bubbles forming and bursting in a repeated, historical fashion.

The wheat price in England went from just above $2.25 per bushel in 1807 to a record of $3.85 per bushel in 1812 (a 71% rise). By 1815, it had collapsed back down to $2.00 per bushel.[1] Similarly, U.S. wheat traded in Chicago experienced a brief peak at $3.50 per bushel in 1919, easily $2.00 per bushel higher than its 'average' prices just a few years before and for decades after. The years leading up to that time were known as the "Golden Age" of farming, and agriculture producers spent many subsequent decades seeking parity with those income levels.[2]

In more recent times, Chicago wheat prices experienced volatile peaks about once every decade since the 70's; Chicago corn prices spiked in 1974, 1988, 1996, and 2008; Chicago soybean prices saw brief highs in 1973 and other similar years as corn. What has been causing these crazy short-term rallies throughout history?

Simply: the fundamental needs of human survival. The 1807 peak coincided with the Napoleonic Wars, and all other 19th century price spikes occurred when wars limited the movement of grain out of shipping ports to demand centers. The big 1919 peak occurred because America had become the one big source of grain while the Allied Powers were tied up in the First World War. When massive starvation struck Russia during and after their 1917 revolution, the U.S. government's commitment to foreign aid drove up domestic grain prices. The fiery highs of the 1970's were again caused by a Russian spark – in a world facing global grain shortages during the 1972-73 crop year, the Soviet Union suddenly switched from not trading with the capitalist world to buying 30 million metric tons of grain (mostly from the U.S.). That was well over half of all the commercially exported grain in the world that year. The 1988 peak and the 1996 peak were caused by shortages of U.S. production.

The global scramble to source grain amid a shortage is frantic while it lasts, but all those price spikes had the same cure: new production. Within a year or two, there was always better weather in the world's grain-growing regions, and massive production motivated by the high prices themselves. A fresh glut of supply in the next growing season almost always cures a grain market's frantic bullishness. These are annually-produced crops, after all, and farmers can choose to grow relatively less grain when prices are low and relatively more grain when prices are high.

Because of that well-established economic pattern, the 1807, the 1919, the 1973, the 1988, and the 1996 price spikes never stuck around for very long. But the 2008 price spike was something new. It occurred while U.S. production prospects were actually normal and alongside spikes in many other commodities, meaning that it was a demand-driven rally rather than a supply-driven rally. As a signifier of consumers' new willingness to pay higher prices, demand-driven rallies tend to be more lasting. And that may be the case for grains – although 2008 grain prices plummeted back to 2006 levels before the end of the year, they have since moved back to mid-2008 levels and remained there for over two years and into 2014, which is a very different pattern than what we usually expect from supply shortages.

No matter how you expect grain prices to move in the future, the beauty of commodities trading is that all this volatility isn't necessarily a bad thing. When stock prices rise, pretty much everybody is happy – retirees, everybody with a 401K, pension fund managers, stock brokers, and the operators of the companies themselves. When stock prices fall, there is a very small population of traders who were foolhardy enough to short sell stock, and those are the only people who don't feel their heart sinking on those "bad" days. In commodity markets, there are no "bad" days. There is as much pleasure felt when prices fall and raw materials become cheaper for a buyer as there is when prices rise and income grows for producers. Think about crude oil and gasoline – Middle Eastern princes benefit when prices rise, but as far as your own pocket is concerned, drastic drops in fuel prices are a delight.

Similarly, investors in the grain market can as easily make a profit when prices fall as when they rise. If they're very clever, they can do both: ride a price spike with a long position, then turn around and make the same money twice when the chart eventually collapses. In that sense, the grain markets' volatility is one of their most treasured features, but it emphasizes the importance of understanding the underlying factors that cause such movement.

The Almost-Myth of Non-Correlation

Harry Markowitz, aside from being a brilliant, warm, and engaging lecturer (I took his 'Portfolio Theory' class in business school), is also the 1990 joint winner of the Nobel Memorial Prize in Economic Sciences. He earned that distinction for applying matrix mathematics to the stock market; specifically, for developing the theory of optimal mean-variance portfolios in 1952.[3] To grossly oversimplify, that means he was able to mathematically prove that if an investor carefully selects a full portfolio of many assets with known returns and known risks, the net tradeoff of the risk and return of that particular portfolio can be measurably better than any one of the portfolio's parts. This was a fundamental breakthrough in financial theory, and Markowitz is justly considered the father of modern portfolio theory.

So ever since Markowitz worked with Paul Samuelson, Robert Merton, and Michael Goodkin in 1968 to develop the first known **hedge fund** for computerized arbitrage trading, the investment world has put a lot of effort into not just selecting good investments, but in selecting *groups* of assets that complement each other as an entire portfolio and offer investors the optimum mix of risk and reward they're seeking.

It's pretty standard if you walk into any random investment advisor's office that the advisor might tell you to put your capital into a mix of "aggressive" small-cap stocks, maybe a stock index, and some "safe" bonds. The exact distribution of your money into relatively safer or relatively riskier assets will depend on your age, your investment goals, and your own personal risk appetite. The whole justification for that distribution is portfolio theory. The investment advisor may believe one specific consumer goods company is going to be the best investment opportunity for the next twenty years, but if you just dump 100% your capital into that company's stock, you face the risk of losing 100% of that capital if that one company goes bankrupt. The saying is, 'Don't put all your eggs in one basket,' and as well as being a philosophically sound strategy, it's also a mathematically superior strategy.

Here's where the grain markets fit in – there are degrees of individuality for every stock and every bond available for selection in an investor's portfolio, but really, when the stock market plummets, most of the individual stock selections tend to plummet at the same time. And when the bond markets underperform, they tend to underperform as a group. The stock market and the bond market have significantly different performance patterns, but the more independent asset classes you can get your hands on, the better able you will be to optimize your portfolio's risk-to-return ratio.

Thus – the appetite for real estate, fancy Exchange Traded Funds (**ETFs**), and of course, commodities. The idea is that commodities, as an asset class, have little to no **correlation** to the stock market, and non-correlation is the holy grail of portfolio management. If you have half your money in one asset (let's say a stock index) and half your money in another asset (let's say corn), and whenever stock prices fall, corn prices don't necessarily behave the same way, you would feel that the risk of a net loss in your portfolio would be reduced. One asset class may profit while the other posts losses.

Perfect positive correlation (+1.0) occurs when two data streams both rise and fall in exact scale and synchronicity. Perfect negative correlation (-1.0) occurs when one data stream falls whenever the other rises. Even if two assets are directly related as substitutes (e.g. the price of Tropicana lemonade and the price of Minute Maid lemonade), there is always some slippage and delay between the two price streams moving together. There are some assets which directly affect each other negatively (e.g. the price of the U.S. dollar and the global price of crude oil, which is denominated in dollars), but even these never display perfect negative correlation.

Overall, it's desirable to find some investment assets that might do well while the rest of your portfolio is struggling, therefore limiting your risk of aggregate loss at any one point in time. So if commodities in general or grains in particular really do have non-correlation or negative correlation to the stock market, it's no wonder they've attracted so much investor attention.

As it happens, however, the correlation between the monthly returns of the S&P 500 Index (a benchmark for stock prices) and the monthly returns of the Goldman Sachs Commodity Index (a benchmark for commodity prices) from 1995 to 2012 is actually positive: +0.27. When calculating the correlation between assets, it's critical not to use the asset values themselves, but rather to use the periodic change in the assets' values (the returns) to keep all comparisons apples-to-apples and avoid spurious correlation.

If we just look at grain (using that theoretical evenly-weighted index of corn, wheat, and soybean prices in Chicago) and go even farther back from 1972 to 2012, the correlation of the two return streams is still positive: +0.10. Those correlations are still relatively close to zero, in a portfolio selection sense, making commodities in general and grains in particular seem like desirable additions to a portfolio's mean-variance matrix.

More recently, however, a wrench has been thrown into the otherwise smooth operation of a well-diversified portfolio. From 2007 to 2012, the correlation between commodities' returns (as indicated by the GSCI) and stock returns (as indicated by the S&P 500) was as strong as +0.62. The correlation between grains' returns and stock returns was also quite strong: +0.42. This was a real pickle for investors. At roughly the same time that the stocks portion of their portfolios was bleeding value from October 2007 to March 2009, commodities were also taking a nosedive from July 2008 to February 2009. So much for uncorrelated assets stabilizing a portfolio.

In fact, so much for the myth of uncorrelated assets at all. In today's world of globalized finance, when investors start to lose money in one asset class (stocks), those losses can trigger massive rounds of selling in completely unrelated markets (commodities) just to cover the original losses, regardless of the underlying economic justification for that selling. Exacerbating this trend in 2008 was the fact that every market's bearishness was a result of global recession, which meant that real consumption of physical goods (commodities) truly was diminished at the same time the prospects for growth in company shares diminished.

Also, the investors who got into commodities to begin with were doing so specifically to seek out returns, and once their priorities switched from seeking return to minimizing risk, there was no longer as great an appetite for commodity investments. That's a pattern that is going to haunt global markets for a very long time, and possibly forever. As long as all the same investors are participating in all the same markets, all those markets are going to experience all the same bullishness or bearishness of sentiment at all the same times. On the most extreme days, you can look at a quote screen and tell in a glance whether it's a "risk on" or a "risk off" trading session. Markets that tend to rise on risk-seeking days are stocks, especially mid-cap and small-cap stocks, and consumer commodities, like crude oil and the grains. Markets that tend to see increased investment on risk-fearing days are the U.S. dollar, bonds, and gold. Previous relationships, like a negative correlation between crude oil and stocks, have been destroyed by this new pattern.

So some would argue that the late 2000's also destroyed the very reputation of portfolio theory and of my favorite professor. That argument, however, would fail to consider the most important detail of mean-variance portfolio optimization. To get accurate results, you must use assets with known probabilities of risk and return. Unfortunately, nobody *really* knows the probability of future risk and return in upcoming months and years. Typically, people just use historical probabilities as a proxy for what might happen in the future. Even worse, people usually assume potential returns will occur according to a **Normal** statistical distribution, which underemphasizes the potential for extreme results. Both approaches, especially in tandem, are a recipe for mathematical disaster.

Which is indeed to say, there is no such thing as "accurate" results from portfolio optimization. There are poor guesses or very good guesses, but they are all guesses, and Markowitz never claimed anything other than that. No one can predict what will happen in the future. It may be that a nicely diversified portfolio, with positions in a lot of interesting assets, will give you some confidence that you might not lose all your capital all at the same time, but it can never fully guarantee you won't experience loss, even major loss.

For the purposes of my topic - grain trading - the takeaway is that commodity markets in general and grain markets in particular are, for one thing volatile, and for another thing not even reliably volatile in ways that can always be counted on to help your investing goals. I believe you should approach each grain trade as an expression of some underlying idea about the supply and demand of grain, rather than as some theoretical tool for investing.

The Players of the Game

....

Springtime wind across the flatness of northern Iowa is like the ocean surf against a reef: roaring, immensely powerful, and brutally, brutally constant. Crazy-making constant. Joe Smith chewed his gum and watched some scraps of last year's corn stalks get whipped across his farthest, newest farm. The Williams' boy had washed out after five years of overextended equipment loans and poor crops. So Joe had offered the elder Mrs. Williams more rent per acre than either he or any of his neighbors had ever dreamed of paying for un-tiled ground fifteen miles from any grain storage. To make the economics of expensive new equipment and ever-increasing seed prices make sense, it is every farmer's mission to expand to any extra ground he can find. He suspected the Williams boy had left the fields with deep ruts and compaction, although there wouldn't have been much he could have done to avoid that. The boy had been trying to make farming work as a side job to his regular gig with the phone company, but that meant disking and planting and fertilizing and spraying whenever he could fit it in on the weekends, which may not have always been the best dry days for the soil.

Dryness was not a problem now. Joe couldn't remember a winter that had been so dry. His dad said it had felt like this in 1977, but Joe had only been ten years old then and didn't remember that the county's corn production dropped to a third of its usual level and posted an average yield worse than any since the 40's. In the years since the 1977 drought, Joe had gone from kid to farmer in a path familiar to many in the industry: his childhood had involved many hours of riding jump seat with his dad in various tractors and sprayers and combines; the best Christmas present he ever received was the professional tool set his parents gave him when he was fifteen; his post-secondary education in diesel mechanics was undertaken with only two goals in mind – to drink as much beer as humanly possible, and to get back to the farm. Since then, Joe had smelled the fresh-waking soil every spring and heard the ducks cheer on every harvest. He couldn't figure out how all the shopkeepers and insurance salesmen in Des Moines could always tell he was a farmer, but having spent the majority of his adult life outside in the sun and the weather, Joe had that windblown complexion which couldn't be disguised by simply changing out of a seed cap and putting on a nice shirt.

When the last two droughts had hit central Iowa, in 1988 and 1993, Joe had just been starting out, working for his dad for an hourly wage rather than putting capital of his own into the venture. He certainly remembered the anxious tragedy that played out in his family's household those summers, but didn't fully grasp the financial implications. Now, if the current dry weather pattern didn't break, Joe would get a firsthand opportunity to see whether or not today's seed technology could be vigorous enough to withstand a real, honest-to-goodness drought ... and how his crops' performance would affect his own family's checking account for the next several years. On the other hand, if the rain turned on right now, in April, and kept up pretty steadily through July, the corn would be fine.

Well, not *right* now ... Joe still had to get everything planted, and he was antsy to get started doing just that. As he stepped out of his truck, the wind savagely snatched the door away from Joe's grasp. The temperature wasn't particularly cold, but the wind chill had kept everyone bundled in jackets and caps for the past week. It didn't feel like it would be warm enough yet to give little corn seedlings a chance in the world, but wind chill can be so deceiving. Joe figured the soil might be warmer than you'd think, and he plunged the thick aluminum stake of his soil thermometer into the ground beneath his feet. It took a fair amount of wrangling to get it far enough down into the hard, dry soil. Then he scurried back into his truck, shook off the cold with one fierce shiver, and settled back down to wait for the thermometer to get a reading.

Joe thought to himself – sure, the soil temperature reading may come back and say it's time to plant, but what good was warm soil going to do for little corn seeds who would have no water to drink? It would take an incredible amount of faith in nature, perhaps even faith in God, for Joe to bury hundreds of thousands of dollars of seed, seed treatment, and fertilizer into the dirt, with such seemingly poor odds for those dollars to grow into real plants, which would then just go on to face all the new weather challenges of summer and fall. He shook his head and picked up his cell phone to call his banker.

Rodney Brune was part banker, part farmer, part vintage car enthusiast, part soil scientist, part student of the human psyche. Those last two qualifications were especially useful to the first one, because Brune's banking involved a lot of loan-making to humans who were mortgaging various plots of soil. He was a cheerful and intellectually curious old soul, and he loved nothing better than when one of his customers picked up the phone to call him, rather than forcing the transaction to take place the other way around.

It took him two seconds after his secretary called "Joe Smith on line one for ya, Rod!" to have his newspaper folded away and have his mind entirely focused on everything he knew about Joe's operation. Brune picked up his telephone and rumbled, "Hello there, son – how are things out west today?"

"Oh, I'm actually up at that Williams farm I'm renting this year."

"Oh, very good. Getting ready to plant I would guess. I got my wheat in just last night. Dry as a bone south of town, anyway."

"Well, that's sort of why I'm calling. What's gonna happen if this damn weather never changes and I don't pay you back this year?"

....

There are a variety of people who all hold some stake in the grain markets. There are of course the people who produce the grain (farmers) and the people or companies who consume the grain (end users), but also a full cast of traders (merchandisers, speculators, investors), supportive industry professionals (bankers, seed salesmen, equipment dealers), and tertiary participants (investors in agricultural land or equity investors in agricultural companies).

Of these participants, farmers are the ones with the most risk. The risks they take on each year aren't optional. They can either plant grain or not plant grain, and because they will always have to pay rent, a mortgage, or at least taxes on their land, the no-go decision is effectively impossible to select. Being an eternal optimist, a farmer will always plant the seed and hope that the weather delivers what he needs. The only time I've ever seen fields go unplanted was when too much spring rain made planting physically impossible, and that led to a heartbreaking summer of driving past dismal fallow fields. Ever since we've figured out how to do it, the entire history of the human race has been an example of farmers planting, planting, planting, unless war or an act of God kept us from it.

So by definition, if a farmer must farm, he is placing his entire livelihood at the mercy of weather and grain prices each and every year. It's true that end users of grain also face great risk – what if they can't get their hands on the critical input for their business? But they have the benefit of diversified providers; if one farmer's crop fails one year, that's it for the farmer; but the flour mill that would have received his grain can probably go get similar grain from a different farmer, perhaps even from a different country. Everybody else in the industry – the grain traders, the bankers, the speculative investors – can choose what proportion of their total capital to place at risk in the volatile grain markets, and trim or extend that proportion at any time.

If the reader of this book has a goal to fully understand the grain markets and develop some instincts for picking trading opportunities, it will behoove that reader to develop some empathy for the mission of the farmer and the end users of his grain. "Farming" is a term that could apply to a lot of things, including growing some tomatoes in your backyard and selling a few of them to your neighbor. In this book, however, I'm limiting the discussion of farming specifically to **grain** production.

To some degree, any one type of grain is fairly substitutable for any other type of grain. Wheat can be fed to livestock instead of corn, which is the most common feedstock in the United States. Really, any edible substance can be run through a spectrophotometer at a lab to determine its protein, fiber, energy content, etc. You could get a standardized analysis for dandelions' nutrient content, and if it was economical to feed dandelions to livestock or use them for any other commercial purpose, they could be (and would be) commoditized and commercially grown, stored, and traded, too. Livestock feeders actually do use sugar beet pulp, leftover Oreo cookies, and cottonseed meal, among other unlikely things, as parts of their feeding programs because those substances, like grain, are edible and contain energy. And if Oreo cookies are substitutable for corn, then obviously each type of grain is roughly substitutable for other types of grain.

This interchangeability is why you hear about wood chips or grass species, like miscanthus, being used to produce cellulosic **ethanol** – there is energy contained in all organic substances, even in plants' inedible cellulose. Whatever part of the plant we process to glean the energy, we use that energy to live (we eat it) or to carry out our lives here on earth (we turn it into power). Grain is the ultimate form of solar energy, transformed by a plant into a tangible substance.

When we talk about "grain," we are usually referring to a dry, edible seed. Even though the actual definition – the seed or fruit of a cereal grass – would limit the term "grain" to only corn, sorghum (a.k.a. milo), wheat, barley, rye, oats, rice, or one of the ancient cereals like triticale or amaranth, in this book, I'm going to talk about grain as any **commodity** seed used for its energy. This will therefore allow me to include soybeans (which are actually a **legume**), canola, and sunflowers, which by rights should be placed in their own little basket labeled "**oilseeds**." Since I'm talking broadly about trading agriculture commodities, rather than about nutrition or agronomy, they're all going to fit the bill and be lumped in together with my "grains." Corn, soybeans, and wheat are the three biggest crops grown in America by volume, so they'll be getting the most attention in this book about grain trading.

The more general term "commodity," by the way, refers to a mass-produced, standardized, unspecialized product. If "it" is a commodity, there is a lot of "it", and all of "it" looks and feels and smells and behaves just like all the rest of "it," – any one sample of "it" would be interchangeable with any other sample of "it." Plain white copier paper is a commodity (every page is the same and can be interchanged with any other), but hand-crafted artisan paper with little flowers in it isn't a commodity.

Think of gasoline. When your car's fuel tank gets low, you know you can pull up to any gas station in the country and buy a standard product that will perform as you expect it to perform in your car's engine. True, there are variations in octane. If you were an energy trader, you could arbitrage 89 octane gasoline against 92 octane gasoline, for instance, but even these variations are standardized across all vendors. That standardization allows easy comparison – which gas station is charging the least amount for same comparable product? – and therefore, it allows efficient trade.

When you go to a farmers' market, the ears of sweet corn on various vendors' tables are not all interchangeable, and therefore they're not commoditized. Each vendor is selling a **value-added** product. He can tell you face-to-face what makes his corn better than the corn at the next table (a better variety, a different color or flavor, more care, better weather at his particular field). So that's not commodity corn, and it's not very efficient to trade.

If it's not a commodity grain, it's not what this book is about. This book is about the corn, wheat, soybeans and other grain that's grown commercially on a large scale all across the country each year, dried down and brought to market as trillions of nearly-identical kernels of grain.

Just like commoditized gasoline can be separated into octane categories, grain samples can also be different or specialized in some way, like white corn (for tortillas, chips, etc.) or high-protein wheat. But while a sample of food-grade white corn will be different than a sample of No. 2 Yellow field corn, each sample of food-grade white corn will be roughly interchangeable, according to standardized grading variations, with every other sample of food-grade white corn.

Entire market structures have evolved to facilitate the trading of these grains. The Liverpool Corn Exchange opened in 1806 and was the first of its kind in the western world. It was established during the Industrial Revolution, when a worldwide grain market developed to move grain from the fields of rural England and Poland to the burgeoning urban population centers. The growing international grain brokerage community needed an official mechanism to organize cash grain trade, keep track of prices, and maintain contract standards.[4] And that's how the **exchange**, the institution of organized grain trade as we know it today, was born.

Just about anybody can trade commodity grain through a futures exchange. Corn, soybeans, soft red winter wheat, hard red winter wheat, hard red spring wheat, oats, and rice are all grain markets that are large enough to support active futures trading in the United States. If there's a futures market for a type of grain, it must have standardized contracts and the grain itself must be commoditized. But there are commoditized grains which don't have futures markets: rye, sorghum, sunflowers, etc. I just want to clarify that they're still commodities, because they can still be standardized. This will be important if you should ever start to trade one of those grain markets – remember that the basic trading mechanisms should be mostly the same as trading corn, wheat, etc.

There are also other commodities whose own markets peripherally affect the grain markets. The price of crude oil can be related to the price of corn, for instance, because both commodities can be used to provide energy for transportation. But the mechanics of trading physical crude oil are different than the mechanics of trading physical grain (notice I didn't say the mechanics of trading crude oil *futures* are materially different than trading grain *futures* ... because they aren't). All the non-grain commodity markets are going to remain outside the scope of what this book is trying to illuminate.

There are some other commodities which are indeed agriculture crops, but aren't grain: cotton, sugar beets, or alfalfa hay, for instance. These are somewhat relevant to grain trading as discussed in this book. The first marketing decision made in any grain market occurs when a farmer chooses which crop to grow on his land. Because cotton, sugar beets, hay, rye, rice, poppies, pumpkins, corn, sorghum, soybeans, sunflowers, wheat, peanuts, and miscanthus all compete for ground to grow on, it's important to think about them even if they all aren't strictly "grains."

I hope at the end of this book, you'll feel confident to go make great grain trades. But I also suspect you will begin to feel a love for the agriculture industry itself. No other industry is so fundamentally tied to our human nature. It is *creative* in the truest sense of the word - by growing plants, we *create* and sustain life. And no other industry ties the global population together so inescapably. All life on earth depends on agriculture, and how well we distribute agriculture's products - *how well we trade grain* - determines how Earth's population gains access to its most fundamental needs.

CHAPTER 2
Contracting a Fair Trade

....

Mack, the company executive who was in charge of training new traders, even had to go buy Jason a pair of work boots because the kid didn't previously own any and he'd already discovered the beauty of asking for things through expense reports. The company credit card was also paying for a two weeks' stay at the Soo Paw Motel in Upton, Kansas, which looked to Jason like something out of a 1950's horror film, especially with the wheat harvesters' beat-up old pickup trucks parked in front of five of the motel's six room doors. His own shiny red Mazda Miata pulled up in front of the last one.

It was July in North Central Kansas, and if the weather wasn't that much different than Jason's native Chicago – humid, hot, windy – the environment certainly was. Once he got over the indignity of having to stay at the Soo Paw, and then got over the fact there was no Chipotle or Jimmy John's at which to buy his lunch (he was going to have to buy supplies at the little grocery store on Main Street … and cook … for himself … in his motel room), all he had left to do was come to terms with his job for the next two weeks. The company had sent him to Upton ostensibly to "help out" with wheat harvest, but mostly so he could learn about running an elevator. Fortunately, his new place of work was easy to find; the only building in town over 25 feet tall was the Upton elevator.

As he drove across the railroad tracks and turned down the elevator's gravel driveway, Jason noticed the place seemed to hum with a mysterious energy and purpose. What could there possibly be to *do* here that they're so excited about? A dozen semi-trucks, joined by five smaller farm trucks, were parked in a line down the right side of the driveway. Dust was billowing out of the dumping station at the elevator's mouth and basically out of its every pore. It took a few seconds for Jason to steel his nerves and decide to actually get out of his car, but he liked the idea of being a commodity trader and he liked his new employers, so he did.

Lenny, the elevator manager, immediately put Jason and his pretty new steel-toed boots to work unloading trucks. This meant thirteen-hour days bent over at the waist cranking various trucks' rusty trap doors open and breathing in the dust and chaff that sailed up from their contents. Jason also got a taste of working in the scale house, frantically weighing each incoming truck and issuing its detailed paperwork as fast as he could. He got to answer the phones from farmers wondering about dumping hours, contesting grain discounts, and asking about prices. He even got to spend one 97-degree day at the top of the un-air-conditioned elevator's headhouse, pulling the levers to direct incoming grain into one bin or another. All his efforts managed to earn him the nickname "Chicago" from the rest of the elevator employees. He assumed it was because they were impressed by how much he knew about the world; they were actually identifying a certain urbane delicacy which showed through each physical task.

On the morning of the fifth day of his stint in Upton, Jason called the elevator and asked to speak to Lenny. "Hey, Lenny, I think I'm going to take a personal day today." God, he was sore. Every muscle in his body ached. It was going to be lovely to just stay in his shabby little hotel room and watch TV with the air conditioner window unit cranked all the way up.

"Excuse me, *what*?" Lenny was the most notoriously violent-tempered and vulgar-mouthed elevator manager in the company. After a good five minutes of ass-chewing, and then a desperate call from Jason to Mack, who actually took Lenny's side and ... ahem, *encouraged* Jason to go back to work, the kid finally did. He pulled on his now-scruffy work boots and ambled into the elevator at eight thirty in the morning. Fifty trucks full of warm, sweet, newly harvested wheat had already been unloaded.

The tipping point came on Tuesday of Jason's second week in Upton. He had just arrived at the scalehouse, and every single one of the first four farmers who came in to get their paperwork was fretting like an old wet hen. There are still so many fields to harvest! Protein is terrible this year! And there's a hail storm coming. Almost certainly, the thunderclouds forecast to build up that afternoon would turn green and drop epic torrents of hail – what the farmers called "the white combine." It was comical to Jason how worked up and paranoid and whiny and silly those farmers were being.

So he asked Sarah, the girl weighing the trucks and printing out the paperwork at the scalehouse, what would happen if it did hail that afternoon. "Oh, I wish these guys wouldn't even mention hail … it would be terrible! The whole crop would be gone."

"Gone?"

"Wiped out. Destroyed. When hail comes, it just shreds the plants in the field and you can't harvest anything."

Jason felt a glimmer of hope in his tired, angry heart. "Ha! Awesome! I hope it does hail today. God! Not another truck to unload, not another whiny farmer to have to listen to. Oh man, I hope it hails today. I hope it hails *right now*."

And that was the moment the people of the Upton, Kansas elevator stopped thinking of "Chicago" as their harmless little bumbling city-boy, and started to really dislike him. He had picked the wrong audience for his treatise on the benefits of a harvest-ending hail storm. Sarah, who had learned a thing or two from Lenny in the ways of foul-mouthed ass-chewing, reduced Jason to a tattered, spittle-covered mass. She took on the persona of an Amazon warrior princess defending her people, and everything they worked for all year, and everything they stood for. How dare he even think of wishing their success would blow away like the trailing clouds of a storm!

Deep down, Jason's attitude about the kind of people who would choose to live and farm and work in Upton, Kansas never really changed. But he was able to make it through the next four days at the elevator by keeping his head down and his mouth shut. Mack gave him his next assignment: at company headquarters, learning all the rest there was to learn about grain trading.

………

Virtually all the grain traded all over the world since the beginning of time, and therefore most of the food consumed in the world since the beginning of time, has passed through the hands of people like the people in the story above. Farmers worried about storms and willing to sit in line on hot, windy days to bring their product to market. Grain company employees moving that grain along a supply chain. All unite to convey life-giving grain to those who need it. Even for the very end-most consumer, the person eating Frosted Mini-Wheats for breakfast, understanding the origins of the trading process could help a person understand the grain market as a whole.

I think most people, if asked where their Frosted Mini-Wheats came from, might think the process goes something like this: A farmer wearing denim bib overalls goes to his field and plants and grows some wheat. Then somehow, and presumably more efficiently than shocking it Little-House-On-the-Prairie-style, he harvests it and puts it on a truck. He drives that truck to the Kelloggs factory, where somebody writes him a check for the grain and he goes on his merry way. That check represents the farmer's and the factory's grain "trade," for which the price was set by some spastic guys in funny-colored jackets in Chicago. Anyway, once it was traded off, the wheat goes directly into some fancy shredder thingie, gets coated with some sugar, and shoved in a box. The next day, it shows up at your local grocery store.

In reality, the grain trading process is no less magical, but it is much more complex. Imagine if every end user of grain had to buy the grain directly from a farmer. We'd see huge caravans of grain trucks driven by farmers as they moved their corn from a field in Iowa to an export shipping port in New Orleans. It would be a wildly inefficient use of everyone's time. The farmer needs to be farming, not spending days on the highway. And the exporter needs to have a more predictable source of incoming grain than just hoping some farm trucks show up when there's an empty ocean vessel handy.

The need for an efficient system of handling grain first came up in fifteenth century Japan, when feudal lords received their income from peasants as rice. For the same reasons we experience today, it was more efficient for the peasant farmers to deliver their rice to a local warehouse and get back to the field quickly than to make an arduous journey to the city where the feudal lord lived. So merchants and brokers evolved to handle the rice in local warehouses, trade and transport it to the urban centers where it was needed, and manage the feudal lords' holdings by issuing coins and receipts.[1]

At the Elevator

Today, the grain industry still needs merchants and brokers. There are some instances when a farmer will bring his grain directly to a local end user, like an ethanol plant or a cattle feedyard, but more commonly he will deliver it to a local grain **elevator**. "Elevator" is the term for those rural skyscrapers you see in photographs of small towns ... basically big buildings which aggregate and store grain. They're called elevators because they contain mechanical systems to "elevate" grain up to the headhouse at the top of the elevator, usually with a series of little buckets on a vertically-moving chain.[2] Once the grain has been elevated, it can be directed into the proper storage bin.

Actually, the term "elevator" can be archaic these days when so much grain is stored in big individual bins, silos, and piles, but for our purposes, any major grain storage structure – or any organization that owns such a structure and buys grain commercially from farmers – will be called an elevator. The employees who work at an elevator buying and selling its grain are called **merchandisers**. The term merchandiser can apply to a much broader population of grain traders, but for now, we'll just deal with the guy sitting behind a desk at the local elevator.

If a farmer brings in a truckload of grain without previously arranging a price, the elevator (or ethanol plant, or mill, or whatever) can "**spot**" out the load. That means they will just pay for the grain at that day's posted price. It's the most basic grain trade, but it should be noted that even in that instance, the farmer isn't going to walk out the door immediately with cash in his pocket. Even for spot loads, the merchandisers must write up a contract with the farmer to officially document the trade, and the elevator's bookkeepers must go through a full settlement process to account for the grain coming in and how it affects the elevator's overall inventory, and for the payment going out based on the contract.

A cash grain contract itself is a lot more complex than just saying "Springfield Farmers Co-op will pay Joe Smith $3,000 for one truckload of grain" but that does cover some of the most important items. A more complete list would be:

CONTRACT ENTRY	EXAMPLE
Contract number	**PW 8752**
Who is the buyer (and contact info)	Springfield Farmers Co-op
Who is the seller (and contact info)	**Joe Smith**
Date of the contract	August 16
Quantity being traded	**5,000 bushels**
Commodity being traded	Hard red winter wheat
Category	**12% protein**
Category discounts / premiums	$0.15 premium each percentage point higher than 12% protein; $0.25 discount each percentage point lower than 12% protein
Pricing mechanism	**Spot price**
Price	$6.00 per bushel
Price basing point	**Delivered to Springfield Co-op**
Delivery period	August 16
Weights & Grades governing contract	**Destination weights & grades**
Trade rules governing contract	NGFA trade rules and arbitration
Contract terms	**Must be free of infestation**
Payment terms	Springfield Co-op will issue a check at Seller's request upon completion of delivery provided that Seller has signed this contract.
Contract remarks	**Hold payment until after Jan 1**
Signatures and dates	"Joe Smith 8/16"
Statement of Grain Terms	**Seller warrants that on the delivery dates and on the ending shipment date the grain shall be free from any security interest or lien, and that Seller shall pass to Buyer good and marketable title to the grain. (etc.)**

Some parts of the cash grain contract are standard on every one of the merchandising company's contracts, and some parts are specific to each trade, usually first handwritten by the merchandiser, then printed up officially and sent to the seller. Even the handwritten copy represents a completed trade, however. Once a contract number has been exchanged, the trade is final – i.e. the price and terms won't change.

Measuring conventions

That doesn't mean Joe Smith is going to receive a check for exactly $30,000 from this trade, though. First of all, the chance of Joe bringing in exactly 5,000.000 bushels is impossibly small. A bushel is a measure of volume, equivalent to 9.3 gallons. In practice, however, grain is actually purchased, managed, and used according to its weight in pounds or tons. If Joe brings in five truckloads of hard red winter wheat to fill this contract, he's not going to be able to magically fill each truck with exactly 1,000 bushels unless he has an extremely sensitive and sophisticated scale out on his farm ... and a lot of time on his hands. So let's say the five trucks each carry 57,460 lbs of wheat, 56,980 lbs, 57,120 lbs, 56,860 lbs, and 57,040 lbs, respectively, for a total of 285,460 lbs of wheat.

Springfield Farmers Co-op will pay for the wheat at the contracted per-bushel price by assuming a standard 60 lbs of wheat per bushel. That's known as the **test weight**, which is effectively a standard measure of density for each type of grain. The test weight for corn is 56 lbs per bushel, but for wheat and soybeans it's 60 lbs per bushel, so the five trucks in our example carried the mathematical equivalent of 4,758 bushels (285,460 ÷ 60) of wheat, and the Co-op would pay Joe Smith $28,548 for the contract (4,758 x $6), if there are no other premiums or discounts.

If you had a way to actually measure the volume of wheat carried on those trucks, it may not have been exactly 4,758 bushels (44,249 gallons). The wheat itself probably had a test weight something more or less than 60 lbs per bushel. Lighter grain gets discounted because it's less efficient for end users to handle, but in this example, let's assume Joe Smith had some good quality wheat that was close enough to the correct test weight not to be discounted.

In that case, to "settle" the contract, a bookkeeper at the elevator would have to collect the five **scale tickets** generated by the incoming loads and match them to the contract. A scale ticket contains all the data about a sample of grain, for instance:

INBOUND
TICKET # 140 0049584
Springfield Farmers Co-op, Springfield IA -– NOT NEGOTIABLE –-

Customer: Joe Smith   **Contract #:** Pw 8752
Timestamp: 8/16/11 10:12   **Vehicle ID:** Red #3579
Gross Wt: 81,580 lbs   **Tare Wt:** 24,120 lbs (driver on)
Net wt: 57,460 lbs
Est Cash Bushels: 957.67   **Cash Price:** $6.00
Test weight: 60.1 lbs
Moisture: 14.5%
Shrunk or broken (damaged) kernels: 0.8
Foreign material: 0.5
Dockage: 1.2
Protein: 11%

Inspector/ Weigher: Sarah
Remarks: Have a nice day!
Steinway Grain Analyzer SL95 Version 8.0 – INSPECTION NOT VALID FOR PURPOSES OF THE UNITED STATES GRAIN STANDARDS ACT.

So for this load, Joe's payout wouldn't have been discounted for poor test weight, but it would have received a discount for the protein of his wheat. Each time a truck showed up at the elevator, an employee would have taken two random samples of the wheat in the truck and tested them for various quality factors: the test weight, the moisture of the grain, what proportion of the samples had damaged kernels (perhaps from insects), what proportion of the samples was made up of foreign non-grain material (like dust or bits of insects), what proportion of the samples was made up of non-wheat dockage material (like weed seeds, chaff, etc.), and – critically for wheat – what percentage of the grain itself was protein. In this example, the co-op based their price for Joe Smith's wheat on the assumption it would be 12% protein. If his five trucks came in and tested 11% protein, the Co-op would discount 25 cents per bushel, according to the contract, and cut him a total check for $27,358.50 (4,759 bushels times $5.75 per bushel).

That's because there was nothing else really wrong with his grain; significant insect damage or foreign materials could also trigger discounts. Remember on the example contract, the merchandiser bought this grain according to "destination weights and grades." That means Joe Smith agreed to agree with how the

Co-op (the destination) weighed his trucks and how they measured the quality of his grain. If he had some reason to think the Co-op had a bad scale or tended to grade its incoming grain unfairly, he could have requested official grading from GIPSA to govern the contract. GIPSA is the Grain Inspection, Packers and Stockyards Administration, a division of the United States Department of Agriculture (**USDA**).[3] Such a request would have meant he'd have to either take his trucks to a GIPSA office (and there aren't that many; the state with the most is Illinois, with only eight) to get sampled, or pay for the samples taken by the Co-op employees to be sent to a GIPSA office.

As you can imagine, official grading isn't very frequently used to settle individual truckloads of grain. The GIPSA offices do grade with vigorous accuracy, and their testing machines yield final official results, but elevators already calibrate their own testing equipment to match GIPSA's measurements, because it's crucially important they do so.

There are many critical tasks in an elevator, but the first one is arguably the most important: grading the grain correctly. This is so an accurate inventory can be maintained. A processor like an ethanol plant or feed mill that directly takes in truckloads of grain needs to know the measurements of that grain (moisture, damage, etc.) to know how to calibrate their processing equipment. But even more importantly, an elevator which is just storing the grain before selling it to some other company must know the qualities of the grain it has in each bin.

Mix & Blend

That's where some of the greatest opportunities in cash grain merchandising can occur. The "**mix & blend**" process is how merchandisers create value in an otherwise low-margin trading environment. Basically, they buy grain at a discount because of various grading factors (e.g. low protein in wheat, high heat damage in corn, or a high proportion of shrunk and broken kernels in soybeans) then, by mixing it with better grain, they can average out the grading factors and sell the whole quantity of grain on the market without discounts.

That's the theory, anyway. A merchandiser can hatch the most clever, profitable plan to mix & blend grain, but it may not always be possible or convenient for the **facilities operators** to physically mix the grain the way the merchandiser has in mind. It may not be possible for the **originators** to actually find the grain necessary for the plan. Sometimes merchandisers who identify trading opportunities are also the same employees who "originate" the grain (communicate with farmer clients to buy as many bushels as possible), but sometimes a grain company will split the two functions, and that can make their sometimes conflicting priorities even more apparent. Sure the originator can buy 50,000 bushels of soybeans, but where is the facilities staff supposed to put them if the elevator is already full? Perhaps the originator is only able to buy high-moisture corn, but the merchandiser has no customer to whom he can sell high-moisture corn. Perhaps the merchandiser calculates that wheat with 11% protein is only worth a certain price, but the originator can't convince anyone to provide them with wheat at that price. Mix & blend opportunities are frequently more challenging to implement than they are to identify.

The math behind mix & blend just involves building a matrix of weighted averages. For instance, if you mixed 1,000 bushels of wheat with 11.5% protein and 58 lb test weight; 1,000 bushels of wheat with 12.0% protein and 60 lb test weight; and 1,000 bushels of wheat with 12.5% protein and 62 lb test weight, you would end up with 3,000 bushels of 12.0% protein wheat with 60 lb test weight.

However, the practical application of knowing how to segregate an elevator's bins by which categories, knowing which bins to mix with others, and then physically mixing the grain correctly is a sort of magical alchemy that only a few elevator superintendents can do with true mastery. So for a merchandiser to work with elevator operations staff who can pull it off well is a competitive advantage in the market, as is a thorough knowledge of where to buy deeply discounted grain and where to sell lower graded grain for the least punitive discounts.

Because unfortunately, every elevator is going to end up with some poor quality grain. Every grain storage system of every design in every country in the world throughout history has at some point failed to keep all its grain in perfect condition. To illustrate this, let's think about some of the worst case scenarios.

A farmer in Africa, as you can imagine, may not have a lot of access to buy shiny new aluminum bins with diesel-powered augers to lift the grain inside, or electric sweeps to gather the grain up off the floor, or gas-powered grain dryers to bring the grain's moisture down to an ideal level for long-term storage. Typically, if you want to store corn for six to twelve months, you want it to have 14% moisture or less and to remain at relatively cool temperatures throughout its storage.[4] Higher moisture levels make it susceptible to heating up, decaying, or attracting pests like insects, rodents, birds, fungi and microbes. If you've never shoveled wet, moldy, mousy-smelling grain that's hot and crusted over and teeming with bugs in a dark, dusty grain bin somewhere … I don't recommend it. Cows, chickens, and ethanol plants don't really like it, either.

Back to our African farmer, let's say she had to harvest her maize (corn) by hand at 20% moisture because there were too many rainstorms at harvest. She doesn't have a shiny aluminum bin to put it in, or a modern local elevator to take it to, because she lives in sub-Saharan Africa. Instead, she'll store it for future use throughout the year in the same way humans have been storing grain for 11,000 years … in homemade structures. Hand-woven or mud-plastered granary rooms are still used in Africa today, as are hand-built wooden "cribs" to hold corn cobs.[5] To someone who is accustomed to American grain storage techniques, these methods basically just look like convenient ways to gather grain in one spot for the rats and birds and insects and mold spores to find it. And indeed, The World Bank estimates 10% to 20% of sub-Saharan Africa's grain crop gets lost to spoilage each year, which is roughly equivalent to the amount of grain they import, which could feed 48 million people.

I mention that not only because it's a sobering thing to think about, but also because it illustrates the importance of proper grain storage in fundamental human terms. Its importance can also be put in economic terms – if 5% of a bin full of corn is damaged, it still qualifies as Number 2 Yellow Corn (the industry standard), but for each percentage point above 5%, the contracted price for the corn can decrease by 1% or more.

So if the African farmer's grain decays to 30% damaged, for instance, on top of what she's already lost to animals, she may no longer be able to take the grain to town to trade for cash at all. The buyers may not accept grain with that much damage, or even if they did, the discounts may be so steep as to make it not even worth the cost of transporting the grain. It's basically impossible to sort individually damaged kernels from healthy kernels by any mechanical means because, being the same size, shape, and weight, they wouldn't fall through different screens.

And that brings us back to our American grain merchandiser mixing & blending grain. What the African farmer needs is access to a market that can make use of her grain and pay her for it, even if it's not perfect quality. Here in the United States, merchandisers can buy poor-quality grain (at a discount, of course) and, by mixing and blending and knowing their customers' needs, usually make it worth something. There's a limit to these mix & blend opportunities, of course, because the merchandiser must have access to enough good quality grain to dilute the damage, and because his customers only have tolerance for so much of it. A cattle feeder, for instance, won't buy corn with any aflatoxin, a poisonous fungus that can grow in wet grain, but some processing plants can use that corn if their co-products won't be going back into the animal feed market.[6] On the other hand, some corn that would be graded as "heat damaged" (discoloration which usually happens when wet corn is stored and the bin heats up) has nearly the same feed value as undamaged corn, but ethanol plants steeply discount heat damaged corn because it won't produce as much ethanol.[7]

In any of these examples, I don't want to give the impression that our whole grain inventory is stuffed with moldy, damaged grain being pawned off to unsuspecting consumers. For one thing, these damage factors are relatively rare in America where we have excellent grain drying and storage facilities, and there are only a few atypical years when poor weather at harvest makes these issues pop up. For another thing, merchandisers definitely do hold a hard line on some non-negotiable quality factors, like the aflatoxin mentioned previously. Grain that has been "treated" with certain fungicides to be used as seed gets dyed pink, and if that ever shows up in a sample, the whole load of grain absolutely cannot be placed into the food chain. For another rare example, a semi-truck may haul fertilizer pellets sometimes, then go back to hauling grain, and if it doesn't get perfectly cleaned out and even one pellet of fertilizer shows up in the sample, that load of grain would also be rejected and totally worthless in the market.

But these factors illustrate the flexibility of cash grain contracts, and for the little things, like a few kernels of corn with cob rot damage, the mix & blend strategy is an excellent trading tool for cash grain merchandisers. It is just one of the ways they have deeper access than either farmers or speculators to make money on the subtleties in the grain markets. Merchandisers *could* just buy grain with cash grain contracts at one price and try/hope to sell it at a higher price later if the market goes up, but this is generally *not* what they do. Rather, they make smaller profit margins arbitraging the various factors of the cash grain market, like quality, and they rely on moving a high volume of bushels to make their low-margin strategies pay in aggregate.

Farmers, too, can undertake some mix & blend strategies to take advantage of the different prices offered for different quality grains, but it's impossible to do without a multi-compartment grain storage and blending facility, so a lot of people trading grain may not even care about this facet of the markets. Speculators, like hedge funds and retail investors, will generally be using financial proxies that represent grain of a standard quality, rather than true cash grain contracts for individualized loads of grain. They have no good way to "mix & blend" the grain in their portfolio, and therefore can't make money by concerning themselves with the subtle differences between corn from one location and another. There are a few examples of hedge funds who have bought elevators and tried to get into this sector, and there are a few ways a speculator can trade the differences in wheat protein levels, for instance, but more on that later.

Merchandisers

For now, we'll just stick to all the neat things you can do trading cash grain contracts. I said before that the word "merchandiser" can apply to a broad population of traders. A merchandiser can be the kid who grew up on a nearby farm and got a job out of college buying truckloads of grain at the local co-op, or a merchandiser can be a high-ranking executive sitting at a desk in the headquarters of a multi-billion dollar grain company, like Archer Daniels Midland (ADM) or Cargill. Grain companies have merchandisers trading grain of all types and in all sizes of contracts. For instance, a merchandiser writes a cash grain contract – very similar to the truckload example earlier in this chapter – for each Panamax vessel being loaded at our ports with two million bushels of grain to be shipped across the ocean to an export customer.

The term for merchandisers who aren't trading grain out of a physical storage location, but are rather writing cash grain contracts to move grain through the logistics chain from producer to end user, is "cross-country" traders. They may never physically see or touch any of the grain they trade, and however long or short their total position is (i.e. how much net grain they have purchased or committed to sell), the grain never just sits around in an elevator. It's always on the move, being transported by truck or rail or ocean vessel or container.

Some cross-country traders do buy grain from farmers, however. The absolute simplest example of the grain supply chain occurs when a farmer hauls a load of grain directly out of the field where it was harvested (i.e. without ever storing it in a bin or elevator) to a processor, like an ethanol plant. Merchandisers can participate in this process by buying the grain directly from the farmer with a cash contract, and selling the grain to the ethanol plant. They do this because they feel there is an arbitrage opportunity, which is when you can simultaneously buy and sell an asset at two different prices.

Arbitrage

Arbitrage is a beautiful form of low-risk trading. An arbitrage trade is done by simultaneously buying stuff out of one segment of a market and selling stuff into another segment of that same market. For instance: obtaining free rocks from South Dakota and selling them in Nebraska, which is a different geographical segment of the decorative rock market. Another example: short-selling stock in one pharmaceutical company and simultaneously buying stock in another pharmaceutical company. The overall market for pharmaceutical stocks should always move in the same direction, so as one trading position loses money, the other position will gain money (hopefully a little more money than is lost). Similarly, you could buy low-protein wheat and simultaneously sell high protein wheat.

The idea isn't to buy and hold one investment in the hope that you will benefit as its price changes; rather, a successful arbitrage occurs when you identify that one segment of a market is overpriced or underpriced (i.e. recognizing that investors have been too exuberant about the pharmaceutical stock, or that low-protein wheat is currently undervalued) and profiting as that segment's price comes back into line with your expectations. Because you have both bought and sold in the same general market space at the same time, you have very little risk of losing money outright by guessing wrong about the overall direction of the market. You just want the price of your long position to rise relatively more than the price of your short position, or you want the price of your short position to fall relatively more than the price of your long position.

Arbitrage can be the science of identifying and profiting from price differences within a market, and arbitrage can be the art of identifying something that's not worth enough money and turning it into something that's worth lots of money simply by selling it into a different segment of the market. You can use any number of tools to identify and capitalize on arbitrage opportunities – arithmetic, statistics, your own knowledge and experience, or your superior negotiating skills, just to name a few. The different segments of a market can be separated by distance, time, market access, or sensitivity to quality. The markets themselves can be anything; you can arbitrage rocks, lemonade, used cars, financial instruments, human labor, or of course – grain.

Cross-Country Traders

In cross country trading, the most common form of arbitrage is geographical arbitrage. Corn is worth relatively less out in a farmer's field than it is at the front door of an ethanol plant, if for no other reason than it takes time, fuel, and equipment to get it there. Understanding freight availability and freight costs, and having access to great freight providers (truck drivers, rail lines, etc.) is therefore key to the success of a cross country grain trader. Their guideline is to "buy FOB, sell delivered." Buying "FOB" means buying grain "free on board," or writing the cash grain contract so they, the buyer, take ownership at the original location of the grain. There it gets picked up by the freight provider, and the price of the contract is based on that location. The cross country trader will therefore own the grain while it is being transported and then sell it "delivered," i.e. pass ownership on to the next buyer at the destination.

Since the cross country trader has written binding cash grain contracts with whomever is at the origin and at the destination, he knows the price at both those points, and he will make a profit of the difference between the two prices, minus the transportation costs. Transportation costs are his biggest risk.

Geographical arbitrage can be a lot more complex and interesting than just moving corn out of a field to an ethanol plant fifteen miles away. Sticking with corn as the example, corn of the same variety and quality can be worth $1 more per bushel in Texas than it is in Minnesota (or more ... or less ... depending on the market at any given point in time). This is strictly to do with supply and demand. There is a band of land called the "**Corn Belt**" stretching across America's Midwestern lap where the vast majority of corn is grown (think Iowa, Illinois, and Indiana), but only a fraction of the nation's demand is centered there. There are all the cattle feedyards in the Southern Plains that need corn, as well as the ports in the Gulf of Mexico, and other users, all drawing corn.

Now, it's not always (or even frequently) possible to drive a truckload of corn from Hutchinson, Minnesota to Galveston, Texas for less than $1.00 per bushel, but if it was, and if you had the cash and the trading licenses and the trucks to do it, you can see how it would be profitable to buy corn in Minnesota and simultaneously sell it in Texas (arbitrage). You might be able to do this by rail, if the freight rates were favorable.

Especially now that so many ethanol plants have popped up in the Midwest to use – and pay fair market prices for - local corn, it's very rare that such an arbitrage opportunity would actually exist, but this is the kind of thinking cross-country traders go through to identify cash grain trades. They must keep track of local grain market values, fuel prices, the relative economics between truck freight and rail freight and **barge** freight, and a host of other factors ... including the quality factors demanded by their customers.

Quality or protein or any other measurement which can vary between one load of grain and another are all also factors that can make up a successful arbitrage trade. For instance, some elevators don't pay protein premiums for wheat, and even among the ones that do, the premiums themselves differ. So if a cash grain trader can identify and buy high-protein wheat out in the country, somewhere where there isn't much of a market for protein, then sell that same wheat somewhere else and receive large protein premiums for it, he is conducting an arbitrage trade (buying an underpriced asset for a low price and selling it elsewhere for a higher price). Similarly, a cash grain trader can use what he knows about his customers' tolerance for mold or broken kernels or any other quality factor to buy underpriced grain and sell it where it's worth more. Now you get a sense of how valuable it is to fully understand all those nit-picky details about cash grain contracts.

The Grain Supply Chain

What is striking, handy, and magical about this whole process is how each cash grain trade – each movement of each kernel of grain – is done with the exact same style of thinking and trading. A cross country trader buying grain from a farmer's bins could write a contract almost identical to the one from our Joe Smith – Springfield Co-op example, except that it would say "FOB Joe Smith's farm" instead of "Delivered to Springfield Co-op." The same cross country trader could write an almost identical contract if he were buying 100,000 bushels of wheat from Springfield Co-op. He would write a similarly-worded contract to then turn around and sell the wheat to Yeasty Bread Mills in Chicago, except it might be a larger number of bushels and probably delivered by rail. Every cash grain trade is made according to the same style of exacting, fairly-negotiated contract which describes every possible variation of the grain being traded.

Basically anybody (with a **bonded** grain dealers' license) can sell grain to anyone else, if it makes economic sense to do so. These are all private transactions, generally made by privately-owned companies, so it's impossible to know the volume of trades that are made or the volume of grain that moves through each leg of the supply chain, but grain could go through any of these paths:

From grain producers to	- Direct consumers (livestock feeders, etc.) - Elevators (either commercial or co-op) - Processors (ethanol plants, grain mills, etc.) - Cross-country grain traders ("resellers")
From elevators to	- Terminal elevators - Processors - Exporters - Direct consumers - Cross-country grain traders
From terminal elevators to	- Exporters - Processors - Cross-country traders - Direct consumers
From resellers to	- Terminal elevators - Processors - Other resellers - Exporters - Direct consumers

The most common of these paths is probably Grain Producer -> Elevator -> Processor, or Grain Producer -> Elevator -> Terminal Elevator -> Exporter. While for some agriculture commodities (vegetables, organic beef, etc.) the direct route from producer to consumer may be increasingly common, for commodity grains, that's unlikely to ever be a very widely-used logistical path. Think of all we have just learned about mixing and blending to achieve standard quality levels throughout the industry. No single producer can guarantee a standard product to a single consumer at all points in time.

This is the strength of the commodity grain markets – that through their high volume and efficient logistics, they can essentially comingle all grain to deliver a standard quality product through a standard distribution channel.

No matter its path, each movement is surprisingly similar: there is a cash grain contract negotiated between a buyer and seller, then a freight provider – a trucker, a rail company, a barge moving down a river, or a container shipping line – loads up the grain at its origin. A document called a Bill of Lading is assigned to each load, specifying who sold the grain, where and when it was loaded, the details of what exactly was loaded (type of grain, weights, etc.), and to whom the grain is being sold and delivered. The grain gets transported, and at its destination the Bill of Lading is consulted to determine what is on board. The destination weighs and samples the grain to confirm what it's receiving. The scale ticket and the original cash grain contract are used to confirm the trade and trigger payment from the buyer to the seller. This process is similar whether the trade is a truckload of wheat from Joe Smith to his local co-op, or a trainload of soybeans from a St. Louis **terminal elevator** to an exporter in Galveston.

The stakes are higher with a larger quantity of grain being traded, however, simply because of the multiplicative function in the math. If an elevator discounts Joe Smith more steeply than he thinks is fair for his particular quality of wheat, after the first truckload goes through, he can just send the rest of his trucks somewhere else. If a train full of corn (figure 385,000 bushels in a "shuttle" train with 110 cars) is sold to a buyer expecting No. 2 Yellow Corn (5% damage or less), and at the destination it turns out to have 7.1% damage throughout the train, there will be a major loss of capital when the contracted discounts are taken and the final check is settled and written. Correspondingly, larger trades or trades going farther distances are often traded according to official (GIPSA) weights and grades, provided by the government.

Resolving Conflicts

But what happens if a shipment arrives with a different specification than the buyer was expecting? If the buyer isn't an elevator who can just accept the shipment and discount it accordingly, or if the buyer just doesn't have the space and ability to blend the grain into the rest of its inventory, there's a real problem. It may have to reject the shipment, and now there's the question of what to do with the original contract. Can the seller provide a different shipment of grain to fulfill its contract? Or must it buy back out of the contract financially? How are contract disagreements resolved?

Most merchandising work is done over the telephone, but instant messaging and email trades are becoming increasingly frequent. No matter what communication method was used, once that contract is agreed upon, it's final. The seller is legally obligated to provide what he sold when he sold it, and the buyer must accept and pay for what he bought. But as you can imagine, stuff happens. Crops fail, elevator equipment breaks, transportation plans fall apart. In nine hundred ninety-nine of a thousand cases in the grain industry, the buyer and seller will work together to come up with a fair plan to keep everyone relatively content. If there is a dispute, however, the two parties can fall back to the trade rules governing the contract in question.

Typically, cash grain contracts are written to be bound by the National Grain and Feed Association's Trade Rules and Arbitration procedures.[8] In fact, any contract between two members of the **NGFA** (which includes pretty much every grain company, elevator, and grain processor in the United States) is automatically governed by these rules, unless the contract expressly claims otherwise. There are sections for grain trades, feed trades, barge trades, barge freight trades, and rail freight trades.

The long list of rules itself might seem absurdly pedantic to any farmer or futures trader who's otherwise unconcerned with the minutiae of cash grain trading, but each section of the NGFA rules booklet is carefully written to provide the reassurance of authority for every piece of a cash grain trade written between merchandisers. If the company on the other side of a cash grain contract doesn't price their grain in a timely manner or reneges on some agreed-upon fee, there is a generally-accepted method to resolve the issue. The method usually starts with confidential, informal mediation by an NGFA committee, and if that doesn't clear everything up, it can progress through a channel of arbitration hearings, announcement of awards, and appeals.

Accounting - The Long & The Short of It

But it's a very rare grain trade that ends up with a formal dispute. So cash grain traders (merchandisers) can typically rely on the contracts they've written with other parties to be as valuable as cash in hand. Cash grain accounting, therefore, involves accounting for each cash grain contract in many of the same ways a dry goods store accounts for its inventory and sales, or the ways a stock investor accounts for each stock held in his portfolio.

Without getting into the finer points of grain company accounting, particularly because the accounting practices will be different for each grain company, it's still important to mention a merchandiser's "portfolio" in order to give a full picture of the grain markets. Merchandisers trade a "position," not a portfolio, to get the lingo correct. Because an elevator, for instance, both buys grain from farmers and also sells grain to processors, exporters, terminal elevators, other traders, etc., the sum of all their contracts can be either "long" (they have bought more grain than they have sold) or "short"(they have sold more grain than they have bought).

This should be familiar terminology to anyone who's ever been involved in any kind of trading. If you buy Microsoft stock, for instance, you are "long" Microsoft stock. If you sell something, you are "short" in the market for that thing. And yes, you can be short in grains (or any market, for that matter). This is one of the hardest things for new grain traders to understand. They ask: how can I sell something I don't have?

Think about it this way. You're at your family reunion and your rich, somewhat crazy cousin starts talking about how badly he wants a 1970 Chevy Chevelle. Preferably a red one. One that's been really well restored into show condition. Now at this point, you don't currently own a 1970 Chevelle, but you have a pretty good idea where you can get one. So you write a contract with your cousin to sell him one show-quality red 1970 Chevelle for $50,000. You are now "short" the Chevelle market. So you go buy a beat up old chassis and an engine block and whatever else you need and pay your mechanic friend to get it into the proper condition. The whole process costs you maybe $30,000. You deliver it to your cousin and – voila! – you close out your short trade with a $20,000 profit margin.

Those are exactly the steps taken by a merchandiser who doesn't currently own any corn, but who shorts corn to an ethanol plant for instance, and then later buys the necessary amounts from farmers or other traders to fulfill his contracted obligations. He may do some mixing and blending to the corn (like the mechanic friend fixing up the Chevelle), and he has to transport it to the plant (delivery). As far as accounting for the trade goes, when he sells 50,000 bushels, his position is short 50,000 bushels, and each subsequent purchase contract he writes is an offset to his initial short position. If he buys 10,000 bushels from a farmer, his total position would then be short only 40,000 bushels. Ultimately, he will have to "buy in" (offset) the entire position, but the intention behind his original short position in the market was that he felt he could sell the asset at a higher price at one time or to one customer, and then offset his position by buying the same asset for a cheaper price from someone else or at some other time.

The math behind a trading position is just simple addition and subtraction, with long positions (purchases) represented as positive values and short positions (sales) represented in the same units but as negative values. A grain company with several elevators, for instance, can figure out their total market position by summing up each elevator's long or short positions. Likewise, a cross-country trader may have 100 trucks' worth of soybeans sold in one location, but 40 trucks' worth purchased somewhere else. His net position would be short 60 trucks' worth of soybeans.

Because merchandisers can trade a number of different categories of grain, they can even regard their grain market positions as a net sum across many categories. Rather than being just long or short in corn and long or short in soybeans, they can determine how long or short they are in all types of grain, which is important for elevators that are constrained to a certain volume of gross bushels they can store.

'Arbing' a Position

So in some senses, a merchandiser can offset long corn positions with short soybeans positions ... or be long Nebraska soybeans but simultaneously short Missouri soybeans ... or be short 14% protein spring wheat but simultaneously long 10% protein winter wheat, just to name a few examples. Being simultaneously long and short two categories within a market is another form of arbitrage, because the accounting will ultimately work out with one underpriced asset being bought and one overpriced asset being sold.

What makes an arbitrage work is that the *whole* market, within which the two parts of the arbitrage are being traded, should move in the same direction. If the two markets are totally unrelated, like milk prices and Ford stock, for instance, you could buy one and sell the other and they could both move in diverging directions and you could lose money both ways. It's not an arbitrage, because there is no expectation that the two are related or that the prices of one can offset the other.

A good example of an arbitrage would be one that takes place *within* the wheat market (all wheat prices should theoretically move roughly up or down at the same rate). A merchandiser could simultaneously sell 14% protein wheat and buy 10% protein wheat and believe some profit will come from the difference in value between those two categories, no matter if the whole wheat market suddenly shoots higher or lower in price. The math would look something like this:

In April: Sell 1,000 bushels of 14% protein wheat at $7.00 per bushel (+$7,000)
           Buy 1,000 bushels of 10% protein wheat at $4.50 (-$4,500)

In May: Buy back 1,000 bushels of 14% protein wheat at $11.00 (-$11,000)
         Sell the 1,000 bushels of 10% protein wheat at $9.00 (+$9,000)

Result: -$4,000 from the 14% wheat trade, +$4,500 from the 10% wheat trade
Total profit = $500

Two things should stick out at you about that particular example of an arbitrage trade. One: for the amount of capital the merchandiser (or, more realistically, the merchandiser's employer) is sinking into the initial trade, there isn't a really wild amount of profit involved. And even this example is quite exaggerated. I've mentioned before that traditional grain companies tend to operate with relatively low expected margins on each trade, but instead make their profits by trading large volumes. So even if the total profit of this trade was $0.05 per bushel instead of $0.50 per bushel, if you were trading to the tune of 1,000,000 bushels on each side, you'd do ok.

The second thing: this arbitrage worked regardless of the fact that the whole wheat market shot up more than $4 per bushel, and it would have worked even if the whole market had dropped $4 per bushel, because the merchandiser was simultaneously both long *and* short in the market. If he had just sold 1,000 bushels of wheat in April and closed out the trade in May (just the 14% protein part of the arbitrage), he could have lost $4,000 ($4 per bushel). Alternatively, if he had just bought 1,000 bushels of wheat and the whole market dropped $4 per bushel, he would have lost that much. Imagine if that was done one million bushels at a time! That's why grain companies basically never take the risk of being straight long or straight short in the grain markets – it's very risky indeed. And with their ability to handle large numbers of bushels and keep track of all these detailed factors of the cash grain market, they can make safer returns on their capital with these low-risk arbitrage trades.

How Arbitrage Makes Markets Work

The very act of the merchandiser selling the overpriced asset and buying the underpriced asset helped bring his two markets closer together. When there is a large volume of buying interest in a given market, prices move higher (supply and demand). Correspondingly, a large number of sellers can motivate an entire market to move lower. So if enough arbitrageurs identify an overpriced / underpriced situation and do a lot of selling / buying on each side of the trade, the situation will automatically correct itself. That, in fact, is the economic function of an arbitrageur. When the investment bank Goldman Sachs' CEO Lloyd Blankfein unironically claimed his company was doing "God's work" in late 2009, he may have been referring to the fact that traders who sell overpriced assets or buy underpriced assets are helping to bring market prices closer to fair, whatever fair is.[9]

Anyway, how did the fictional merchandiser in this example know to sell the 14% protein wheat and buy the 10% protein wheat, and not the other way around? In a nutshell: because he knew the "spread" (the difference between the two prices, $7 and $4.50) at $2.50 was too large. He was able to identify that 14% protein wheat was overpriced compared with 10% protein wheat and he made his arbitrage trade to take advantage of that fact. Perhaps if the two markets had only been $1 apart, he would have thought the spread was too narrow and made the opposite arbitrage.

There is no way I can write a definitive guideline for what that spread should be at any point in time, because it is all dependent on the supply and demand *at that point in time*. As such, it requires the expertise and constant attention that only specialized merchandisers have. There are merchandisers whose business it is to always know what the wheat protein spreads should be, or what the corn grade spreads should be (quality arbitrage), or what the corn-to-soybean-meal spread should be (inter-market feed arbitrage), or what the Nebraska-to-Missouri corn spread should be (geographical arbitrage). That's how they make their money, and that's how the markets stay efficiently and fairly priced.

Traders' Judgment

But expertise is one thing, and being able to make a decision is another, and being able to expertly negotiate favorable prices for the trade you have in mind is a whole different thing altogether. In a cross-sample of all the grain industry's merchandisers, you would encounter a wide variety of abilities in all these matters. At the end of each day, profit isn't made by just sitting at a desk and making obvious purchases and sales; it's made from taking a risk and being either long or short in a given sector of the market. The merchandiser in our example was short protein (he sold 14% against 10%).

He chose to be short in protein because he was "bearish" on protein. "**Bearish**" is the market term used to describe your viewpoint when you think the prices of a certain asset are going to move lower. "**Bullish**" means you expect the prices of a certain asset to move higher. Because you've already learned that you can sell something (at a relatively high price) before you buy it back, you can see that just because someone is bearish on a market, he doesn't necessarily expect to lose money.

Because of the way a lot of current market coverage and financial education regards the stock market, which has fundamental reasons for continually gaining value over time ... and effectively all its participants benefit when it does gain value, I think people have grown to develop a positive mental association with "bullish" things, and an unhappy mental association with "bearish" things. In commodities, however, prices move up or down with good, fundamental, supply-and-demand reasons all the time, and a trader can make just as much money being bearish and going short in a market as he can by being bullish and going long. The benefits flow in both directions. Think of being bearish in gasoline. Isn't it a positive mental thing when those prices go down and you don't have to pay so much to fill up your car?

Eternal Bulls & Bears

Grain merchandisers, for the most part, get the luxury of choosing whether they are bullish or bearish on a particular market, and going on to establish either long or short positions to reflect their viewpoint. There are some exceptions. A local **cooperative** elevator (a co-op) is owned by the local farmers and is therefore basically obligated to buy their grain whenever they want to sell it. So co-ops, and any other elevators with an eye toward customer service, can find themselves more long in grain than the economics would necessarily motivate them to be. In this, they join most of the other members of the grain markets in sometimes having a position that is more long or short than their bullish or bearish viewpoint recommends. Think about a farmer, for example, with several fields of grain growing in the sunshine. Whether or not he thinks the price of grain is going to rise, he's long grain and he's bullish on grain prices, if for no other reason than he always *hopes* grain prices rise and hopes his income from those growing fields will rise. Actually, given that farming isn't exactly the kind of undertaking one does once and then moves on, a farmer is not only long grain for the current growing season, but also effectively long grain (and bullish) for all the rest of his life, or as long as he intends to continue farming.

Similarly, think of a flour mill. Their business is to buy wheat, grind it into flour, and sell that flour. For all the days that flour mill will be in existence, it will benefit if grain prices grow cheaper and flour prices grow stronger. Of course, grain prices and flour prices probably won't grow cheaper and stronger at the same time, but nevertheless a flour miller is going to *always* want the grain markets to be bearish and *always* want the flour market to be bullish.

Farmers' livelihoods and profits depend on the quantity and quality of each harvest, and on grain prices moving higher (or at least not dropping too low). Efficiently bringing in a harvest and receiving a fair price for it are as dead-serious to each farmer as the movement of stock prices is to the CEO of a Fortune 500 company. The elevator's merchandisers are also dependent on a large harvest to bring in the maximum number of bushels they can accumulate and trade. In fact, anyone who hopes to make money in the grain markets, even by simply speculating on the prices, will benefit from knowing how each harvest progresses and how the grain moves through the market.

CHAPTER 3
A New Dimension: Time

Joe Smith did indeed plant his corn and soybeans in April, dusty as it was. Then just like a clutch quarterback who could always throw a 40-yard Hail Mary pass right when the team needed it most, Nature turned on the faucet in late May. Inches and inches of rain had poured down across Iowa all through the month of June, interspersed with beautiful sunny, humid days. For some reason, every time Joe drove out to scout a corn field when the plants were just a few inches tall, he thought of his own children when they were infants. He could get very close to their fresh, fresh skin and examine every part of their being with a single long look. In that look could be all his hopes and dreams for their future lives, all his awe, and all his curiosity about the challenges they would have to face. At about knee-high, the corn plants reminded him of his own kids as kindergarteners, just heading off to start showing the world the promise of what they could achieve.

But now it was mid-July, and Joe's corn plants were rounding the corner past puberty and singularly focused on sex. Of course, corn plants mostly have sex with themselves (via pollen falling from the top shock down to the ear silks below), sometimes with some interspersing of seed between other plants as the wind carried it, but was that so different than teenagers, really?

Although Joe had always been the kind of guy to half-jokingly threaten his daughter's boyfriends with death and dismemberment each Saturday night, he was actually a huge proponent of corn reproduction. Successful pollination was what allowed each little yellow kernel to come into being and eventually tumble into Joe's combine hopper. Or so he hoped.

He had scouted all his fields this morning, and they were all ready for the big task ahead of them, even the ones that he'd planted latest in early May. But he had also clicked through the various weather apps on his smartphone that morning. There was no rain in the forecast and the daily highs for the next 10 days were expected to reach the high 90's. All that was ok for now – the corn could use its deep roots to siphon June's excess moisture out of the soil, and plants need sunshine for heat as much as they need rain in order to make and store energy.

But Joe's heart sank when he saw the other string of numbers listed on the 10-day forecast: the nightly lows. 72, 75, 73, 77 … too hot. Corn plants spend their summertime days frantically producing energy, but they need cool (and preferably dry) nights to rest and respirate the moisture back out of their leaf surfaces. If they don't get such conditions, the whole process gets stifled. Joe thought everybody pretty well understood that if it gets too hot and dry during July's pollination stages, the corn silks can dessicate and wither away without conceiving new kernels. But he wondered if others realized the disaster that was bearing down on them this year if the corn plants continued to stand green and happy, but too exhausted to reproduce.

So he picked up his phone and called the elevator. The new trainee they had just brought in for a rotation in Iowa answered the phone, somewhat unenthusiastically: "Mungus Grain. Jason."

"Uh, hey there, Jason. I was wondering if Dale was around."

"Dale? Um, nope. Not in yet this morning. Can I help you?"

"Well, this is Joe Smith. I guess can you just tell him I'm a little worried about filling my harvest corn contracts? Or, I don't know. Probably not worried, really … just … could you have him call me back and walk me through what's going to happen if the crop fails and I don't end up with anything to bring in?"

"Uh … I don't know if we can do that …"

"Yeah, well that's why I wanted to talk to Dale."

"I mean, why wouldn't you be able to bring your stuff here as well as anywhere?"

"It's not a matter of the elevator; it's a matter of the grain maybe not getting grown." And then Joe explained to Jason about the problems with pollination on hot nights and didn't hang up the phone until he was confident the kid had actually written down a note with his name and phone number on it for Dale.

The next phone call Jason answered was from Steve, an employee of Edgecast Brokerage, through whom Mungus Grain traded grain contracts on the Chicago Board of Trade. Steve was an actual **floor broker**, a tall guy whose long fingers were well suited for signaling corn lots for sale or purchase among the **pit** of other traders, all swarming around in their brightly colored jackets. Steve had been trying to fill a large spread trade for the Mungus Grain Company for several days, and was finally able to call up and say he'd filled the last few contracts that morning. Plus, he liked to catch up with what was going on out in the country and to share the gossip from the floor in Chicago.

So when Jason, who Steve would have thought was too inexperienced to know the agronomic implications of poor pollination, shared Joe's fears about the upcoming hot nights, Steve definitely filed that away in his quick, efficient mind and already started pondering if some risk premium was justified for the new crop prices. He turned the thought over and over in his head all day like he was polishing a stone, but other than asking the folks in Edgecast's research department to do a little digging and see if the high nighttime temperatures were forecast to be widespread, Steve told no one.

No one, that is, until he met up with his brother Stan at Peanut's Tavern later that Friday. The grain pits close at 2:00 p.m. every day, which facilitates a certain amount of afternoon dipsomania among the participants. Stan Clarke was the Head Trader at Verendrye Capital Management, a Chicago hedge fund that specialized in discretionary trading of the global commodity markets. He made it his business to anticipate every shock to the supply or demand of every grain market all over the world. But the hot nights and poor pollination were news to him ... a very delicious little morsel of news. He cut out after only three Dewar's that afternoon to go pore over mid-term weather forecasts and academic studies from the agronomy departments of seven different land-grant universities.

He was still researching at mid-day on Saturday when his wife drug him out of his home office to attend a neighbor's barbecue. In Chicago, grain traders get treated somewhat like doctors: at any social event, they could always expect to be asked to freely offer thousands of dollars' worth of "advice." Bob Albany was a good sort of neighbor, especially in light of his legendary neighborhood barbecues, so Stan didn't begrudge him a few questions about the prospects for commodity prices. Bob had only recently put a few thousand dollars in a managed trading account to speculate in commodities, and he was still thinking it was going to be as easy as asking Stan for a killer tip. Shouldn't it work like horse racing, where the "insiders" have some secret knowledge to beat the odds?

Fortunately for Bob, Stan was feeling reckless that morning and he really just wanted to get out of the conversation and go get a beer. So he put his hand on Bob's shoulder, looked him in the eye, and said: "Bob, buy December corn." And then he walked away. Bob was initially thrilled, but then he realized his neighbor hadn't told him when to buy, at what price, for how long ... or why.

....

We've talked about trading grain according to what type it is, how good it is, and where it is – now it's time to introduce a new dimension to grain trading: time. With this new dimension comes a new kind of grain contract: the **forward contract**.

Remember that farmers are inherently long in the grain markets for years and years to come – all the years they intend to still be farming. If it's July, for instance, Joe Smith would have planted his corn a few months ago and been watching it grow. Depending how well the weather has supported the corn's growing condition, he might have a pretty good idea how many bushels his corn will yield and therefore how many bushels he will have to bring to market in the fall.

Except in the case of a weather disaster, the corn is basically already *made* and essentially just needs to be picked up and delivered to town in a few months' time, so Joe could write up his own cash grain position like a merchandiser would. For this example, let's say his field is going to yield 24,000 bushels of corn in October. So Joe is long 24,000 bushels ... in October.

Forward Grain Positions

Since he can consider himself long October bushels, he can also offset that long position by selling the corn. All he would have to do is call up his local elevator (or cattle feeder or ethanol plant or whomever) and trade a "forward" cash grain contract with the merchandiser. Refer back to the sample grain contract between Joe and the Springfield Farmers Co-op. There are two entries dealing with time on any cash grain contract: the date the contract is written, and the delivery period. A spot sale has the same contract date and delivery date, but a cash contract for a forward sale could have a contract date sometime in July and have the delivery period written as "October 1 – October 31." Or, because harvest weather is so uncertain, the co-op may be willing to write an October / November contract and the delivery period could be "October 1 – November 30."

Remember the co-op is going to have to account for this purchase in their position, too. If Joe sells them the whole 24,000 bushels for October / November delivery, the co-op's Oct / Nov corn position just grew by 24,000 bushels. Think of the implications of this forward contracting ability: the co-op can be simultaneously long October / November corn and short February / March corn. If that were the case, it would imply they intend to buy a lot of corn at harvest, hold it in their elevator for a few months, then sell it in the spring. That's a pretty typical pattern, but there's no law saying a merchandiser's month-to-month grain position has to be orderly and in line with harvest. The co-op's position could look like:

	Past-due	Jun/Jul	Aug/Sep	Oct/Nov	Dec/Jan	Feb/Mar
Corn bushels	2,000	5,000	-15,000	24,000	-100,000	-300,000

-384,000

Examine how the co-op's forward cash grain position can be long (the positive numbers show they've committed to buy more bushels in a timeframe than they've committed to sell) or short (negative numbers mean they've locked in more sales than purchases), independently in each different timeframe.

For instance, you can see they are long in past-due corn, possibly from an old contract they bought from a farmer who still hasn't delivered the corn to the elevator yet. They have about five trucks' worth of corn bought for the June / July timeframe – probably from farmers who expect to clean out their corn bins in the summer before harvest.

But at some point between now and the end of September, the merchandisers must buy 8,000 more bushels to fulfill their short obligation for 15,000 Aug / Sep bushels. The merchandisers probably made the Aug / Sep sale knowing they would get a little corn coming in as spot loads throughout the summer, and they know they'll need to clear it out before harvest to make space for the new crop of corn. Logically, the 2,000 past-due bushels and the 5,000 Jun / Jul bushels can be used to offset the short, because the elevator will receive them and be able to store them for use in August and September. If the elevator had an existing inventory of corn they were already storing, that could also be used to offset forward sales. In this example, the elevator has no inventory of corn. They must have cleared it all out before June.

After September, the elevator will get into the typical harvest timeframe in their geographical region. Note that whatever they buy for the Oct / Nov position can't be used to physically offset the earlier Aug / Sep sale, because those new crop bushels won't yet be in the elevator's possession.

Shorting a Forward Market

Just as Joe Smith can sell October corn he hasn't fully produced yet, an elevator can sell grain it hasn't really bought yet. The winter and spring sales were made with the confidence that the elevator will be able to buy hundreds of thousands of bushels before those short obligations need to be met, most likely at harvest (October / November).

Joe Smith has already committed to bringing his 24,000 bushels of corn in during that timeframe, and other farmers will likely join him in making forward sales contracts, as well as all the farmers who will bring in their corn at harvest and spot out cash contracts at the current day's price. But until those bushels come in, the math works out to show that, in all, the elevator's merchandisers have a bearish short position in corn of 384,000 bushels, with a lot of their sales committed in the February / March timeframe (in the future). There must have been good prices bid to them for corn delivered in that timeframe.

Think about to whom the co-op must be selling that corn: an ethanol plant? a dairy farm? Whoever the end user is for that corn, they know they're going to need it December, January, February, and March. In fact, if you're an ethanol plant or a dairy farm or basically any other end user of corn, you are going to need to have corn to operate your business every single day of the year. Without feedstock for your fermenting tanks or your dairy cattle, you'd have to shut down.

So in exactly the same way that Joe Smith and every other farmer is perpetually long in the grain markets, the local ethanol plant and every other end user of grain is perpetually short. Even though an ethanol plant's merchandiser will probably never write a forward *sales* contract for corn, he can still represent the plant's anticipated usage as a short position (a negative number) on his own cash grain position. It's a short position in the sense that he has to buy the grain and then 'sell' it to the plant's operating processes. An end user's grain purchase is always an offsetting trade to its inherent, perpetually short grain needs. Once a merchandiser buys grain, using forward contracts, to cover his company's needs for the next few upcoming months, he'll just have to buy more grain for the months after that, and the months after that, in a constant cycle.

Selecting a Timeframe

So for end users, every available timeframe of the market needs to be watched and traded with equal care. Many times, end users don't have a lot of storage space for grain, because they may not want to use up capital to build storage or maybe they just don't want to face the risk of handling grain and keeping it in condition. That makes it more difficult for them to apply inventories from one timeframe to the future needs of an upcoming timeframe. But the seasonality of grain markets creates good buying opportunities in some timeframes and challenging buying environments at other times. An end user's merchandiser really has his work cut out for him watching each timeframe of the market independently, and actively managing his forward cash grain position.

For farmers and local elevators, the physical reality of grain production seasons makes trading activities more obvious in some timeframes than others. If a farmer doesn't have enough storage space on his own farm (usually metal grain bins) to hold an entire harvest's worth of grain, he will obviously have to bring some grain to market in the fall. Logistically, he also has to consider when he's going to market the rest of the grain that's been stored in his bins. Will he be able to access the bins in the middle of winter if there's a lot of snow? Will there be load restrictions on the gravel roads around a farm if wet spring weather makes them too muddy? If he harvested the grain a little wet, how many months can he keep it in the grain bin before it starts to get damaged (hot summer months facilitate mold and grain damage more quickly than cold winter months)? All of these considerations must be planned for; a farmer *can* write a forward contract with his local elevator for any upcoming month he chooses, but he has to consider which timeframe makes the most sense not only for prices, but also for his own logistics.

A Few Complexities

Elevators, the most important storage and throughput tools of the overall grain supply chain, have logistical considerations, too. In the example above, the merchandisers wanted to sell off the entire corn inventory before harvest so they could bring in as many new crop bushels as possible. In theory, an elevator should always be focused on maximizing the number of bushels they receive and handle, because their profit margins will be slim on a per-bushel basis and they need to make up for it in total volume. In reality, merchandisers often have to forgo a perfect logistical solution for customer service issues or the limitations of their facilities.

Merchandisers are also likely to be juggling more than one commodity at a time. Not only are they managing a forward cash grain position for all their corn purchases and sales, but also a similar position for soybeans, oats, milo, sunflowers, several different segregated varieties of wheat ... whatever is being grown locally. Managing the inventory and keeping it in condition may be a job for the elevator superintendent or operations staff, but managing the buying and selling decisions is the job of the merchandiser, who needs to be an expert in each of those markets for every timeframe available for trade. The market for March soybeans might be very hot, but the market for February corn might be offering similar profits. The merchandiser must consider his logistical ability to store both grains past harvest before he can go capitalize on those opportunities, and it may be the case that he only has bin space for one or the other crop.

Hedging the Future

Farmers, too, need to pay attention to market prices in future timeframes. The decision whether to forward contract fall bushels or just spot them out as they're coming out of the field depends entirely on each farmer's individual bullish or bearish opinion. If Joe Smith's neighbor, Gary Green, believes prices will be stronger in the fall, why would he commit himself to selling at summer prices? Meanwhile, if Joe is confident he can make a profit at the prices being offered now, and feels that prices are likely to drop before he gets his corn harvested, he wouldn't want to risk being long in the market. He would want to forward sell his corn now and lock in those profitable prices, as any good businessman would. This is the practice of **hedging**.

A hedge transaction today can be thought of as a substitute for a transaction that is going to happen sometime in the future. Joe knows he's going to sell his physical corn after harvest, but he can write a forward contract today that will represent his not-yet-harvested corn. If prices go down before he actually takes the physical grain to market, he will still receive today's price. On the other, not-so-appealing side of the coin, if prices go up before he takes the physical grain to market, he'll still *only* receive today's price. Disciplined hedgers are willing to forego that uncertain chance of higher prices, because they'd rather have confidence in their profitability today than spend the next several months with the risk of losing everything looming over them.

Hedging is therefore more than just a transfer of grain ownership – it's a transfer of price risk from seller to buyer. Once Joe trades that forward contract with the elevator, the elevator has committed to paying today's price for that grain no matter what. It's the elevator's problem to figure out what they're going to do if the market drops before he brings the grain in and they end up paying $2 over the prevailing market value. Fortunately, both sellers and buyers can make hedges.

You may be familiar with airlines buying years' worth of fuel needs to lock in prices. In that instance, the airline would sign a contract as a substitute for a later purchase and remove the risk of fuel prices rising before they can take ownership of physical fuel needs. That's another example of hedging, from the buyer's perspective. Grain buyers – elevators, feedlots, flour mills, etc. – also do this.

A Price for All Seasons

To make this idea of offering fall corn prices in July clearer, here's what a weekly record of the co-op's corn bids might eventually look like once harvest rolls around. Notice that because their grain position can be broken out into different timeframes, the prices they bid for each of those timeframes can be totally different. July corn and November corn are effectively two different markets, especially because there are two different supply-and-demand situations in the summer (when the previous year's crop is almost all used up) and the fall (when a glut of newly-harvested grain will flood the market):

Co-op Grain Bids	July corn	Aug / Sep corn	Oct/ Nov corn (new crop)
7/15	$5.00	$5.25	$5.50
7/22	$5.05	$5.27	$5.50
7/29	$4.89	$5.19	$5.49
8/5		$5.22	$5.49
8/12		$5.30	$5.47
8/19		$5.32	$5.55
8/26		$5.45	$5.50
9/2		$5.44	$5.45
9/9		$5.49	$5.40
9/16		$5.57	$5.39
9/23		$5.62	$5.30
9/30		$5.65	$5.26
10/7			$5.16
10/14			$5.14
10/21			$5.05
10/28			$5.00

In this example, you can see the whole corn market sank lower during the last three weeks of July. This was true for both **old crop** corn (the corn which was harvested in the previous year and which is still being bid for and used in July, August, and September) and **new crop** corn (the corn which is still growing out in farmers' fields and which will be used in the upcoming year). It's typical on any given day or week that corn bids for all timeframes would move roughly up or down in price together.

However, that's not always the case, as we see in this example. During August and September the old crop bids gradually gained nearly 50 cents. Perhaps the supply of old crop corn was growing scarce in the months leading up to harvest, and buyers had to bid more aggressively to get the corn they needed. But while those old crop bids were moving higher, the new crop bids lost more than twenty cents. They went on to lose another 26 cents before the end of October. Perhaps it was becoming clearer to corn buyers that the crop out in the field was showing excellent prospects for high yields, and because a large new supply was anticipated, the bids fell lower and lower.

Market bearishness about new crop bushels really is a matter of counting one's chickens before they hatch – nobody can say with 100% certainty what quantity of grain will ultimately be harvested before harvest even begins. However, the bearishness is usually justified. Nobody wants to pay too much in May for forward-contracted grain that farmers will eventually have to unload at lower prices once a glut of supply hits the market.

In this example, the **spread** between old crop and new crop corn widened from a positive 25-cent **carry** on July 15 to a negative 39-cent **inverse** by the time harvest got started at the beginning of October. We'll discuss spreads in much more detail later, but for now just be aware that grain prices are typically higher in later (more deferred) timeframes, and subtracting the nearby price from a deferred price will give you either a positive (typical) number or a negative (inverted) number, and we call that number the spread.

Of course, Joe wouldn't have been able to see into the future and know what the co-op would be bidding for corn once harvest actually got started. As it happened, his decision to hedge his 24,000 bushels of corn with a new crop forward contract in July was a good one. He locked in a $5.50 per bushel price for his corn instead of showing up at the elevator with uncontracted corn in October and receiving the spot bid of $5.00 per bushel. It cost him absolutely nothing and he ultimately protected $12,000 of income ($0.50 x 24,000 bushels).

In Hindsight

Then why wouldn't every farmer write these forward contracts? Because again, no one can perfectly predict the future. Remember while Joe was making that forward contract, his neighbor Gary Green was under the belief that new crop corn prices would move higher by fall, perhaps because of poor weather or unrelated macroeconomic reasons. If Gary Green had been right, and new crop corn prices had moved from $5.50 to $6.00 between July and October, he would have been glad he allowed himself the opportunity to receive that higher price. Joe, meanwhile, would have still received just $5.50 per bushel for his corn and effectively lost the opportunity to make an extra $12,000 in income. Joe wrote that forward contract to have a safe, free, guarantee that he would receive a profitable price for his crop, but it did cost him something: opportunity.

I say forward contracts are free, and that's true in the sense that the co-op or ethanol plant or whoever is on the other side of the contract doesn't charge any fee for the contract. However, there are obviously opportunity costs associated with forward contracts, and not just because the market's overall price might change. When Joe called up the merchandiser at the Springfield Farmers Co-op to write that forward contract to sell 24,000 newly harvested bushels, he agreed to sell those bushels to the Springfield Farmers Co-op and only the Springfield Farmers Co-op. It won't matter if, when October rolls around, the Springfield Ethanol Plant is bidding five cents more per bushel than the Co-op is, or if the Mungus Grain Company (25 miles away) is bidding fifty cents better. Joe has locked in the decision to sell those bushels to Springfield Farmers Co-op at that contracted price. So that's another piece of opportunity cost – the lost opportunity to shop around for the best bids at the time of delivery.

A Bushel's Best Home

In fact, that's the very reason why elevators willingly offer forward contracting opportunities to farmers. They take on more risk when they agree to buy grain at a certain price in the future, but remember their profits really come from the small margins they make on handling vast numbers of bushels. They compete with all other elevators and grain users in a geographical area to get their hands on those bushels, and anything they can do to bring in more and more bushels is a boon to their business.

We talked a bit in the previous chapter about how merchandisers use geographical arbitrage opportunities to buy grain where it's lower priced, pay to transport it somewhere where it's higher-priced, and profit from the difference. Farmers need to go through a similar process to decide where to sell their grain. The difference is that they don't have to buy the grain – they can just assume ownership of their future production. But they do have to consider how transportation costs figure in to their sales decisions. Consider Gary Green who didn't forward contract his grain before harvest. Autumn rolls around and he's got several truckloads of corn that he can either take to the Springfield Farmers Co-op (five miles away from his farm), the Springfield Ethanol Plant (10 miles away from his farm), or the Mungus Grain Company (25 miles away from his farm). Here's the decision process he has to go through:

Potential Buyer	Current Bid	Distance	Transportation Cost	Other considerations
Springfield Co-op	$5.00 per bushel	5 miles	$0.0075 per bushel	His brother-in-law is the manager
Springfield Ethanol Plant	$5.05 per bushel	10 miles	$0.0150 per bushel	Trucks have to wait in line 2 hours to unload grain
Mungus Grain Company	$5.50 per bushel	25 miles	$0.0375 per bushel	Sometimes, they are slow to pay

The cost per bushel to transport the grain is figured by first knowing what it costs per mile to move a truckload of grain. In this example, Gary Green is assuming 75 cents per mile for fuel, insurance, and maintenance on his own grain truck, but that's because he will personally drive the grain wherever it needs to go. If he had to hire a commercial trucking company to move the grain for him, it could easily be double or triple that amount, and those rates will change over time.

So to take grain to the Springfield Ethanol Plant, for instance, Gary Green will have to drive his truck 20 miles (10 miles there and 10 miles back), spending $15 per trip ($0.75 * 20 = $15.00). He can evenly allocate that $15 cost among the 1,000 bushels he can fit on his grain truck. Some trucks may hold more or less volume of grain, and if he was hauling a heavier grain, like soybeans which weigh 60 pounds per bushel, the legal load restrictions may also limit the volume of bushels in any given truckload. For a load of 1,000 bushels of corn, however, Gary Green's cost per bushel works out to $0.015 per bushel to haul corn to the ethanol plant.

That may seem like an incredibly small number, but remember that grain is likely to be sold in large volume contracts. If you're contracting 50,000 bushels to one location or another, an extra penny per bushel in shipping costs amounts to an extra $500 saved or lost. So if Gary Green is being a very conscientious businessman, here is how his final decision matrix will look:

Potential Buyer	Bid Delivered to Buyer	Bid "FOB" Green's farm	Decision
Springfield Co-op	$5.00 per bushel	$4.9925	
Springfield Ethanol Plant	$5.05 per bushel	$5.0350	
Mungus Grain Company	$5.50 per bushel	$5.4625	✓

Here again we are using the 'Delivered' and 'FOB' (Free On Board) terminology, even though Gary Green isn't planning to sell his grain FOB off his farm. Instead, here it's just used as part of the conventional language of calculating grain prices, to represent what the grain should be *worth* to him on his own farm. If he couldn't call up a merchandiser at either the Springfield Farmers Co-op or the

Springfield Ethanol Plant and negotiate a better bid than what they're currently showing, a bid that would work out to $5.4625 or better after transportation costs, Gary Green is going to be economically motivated to sell his corn to the Mungus Grain Company.

Why would the merchandisers at Mungus be willing to pay so much more per bushel than their Springfield competition? Maybe they previously sold a train load's worth of corn, and they have to urgently source enough bushels to fill it up. Maybe the corn crop around the Mungus elevator got hailed out and they're not faced with a glut of supply like Springfield is. Maybe their customers are so sick of being paid late that they've had to start bidding aggressively just to buy any grain at all. Those considerations aren't negligible.

If the Mungus bid wasn't so much better than either of the Springfield bids, or if Gary Green was unwilling to drive that far away to deliver his grain, it wouldn't be uncommon for a farmer like him to choose Springfield Farmers Co-op over Springfield Ethanol Plant as the buyer for his grain, even if he will earn the equivalent of 4 ¼ cents less per bushel. Long waits to unload grain are extremely inefficient for farmers' operations, especially at harvest time. Their time – time which could be spent harvesting more grain – is worth more than the 4 ¼ cents per bushel. Also, brother-in-law or not, farmers tend to build and honor relationships with certain grain merchandisers or certain companies and be more willing to sell their bushels to them, even at a less favorable price.

Furthermore, there is an underlying benefit to doing business at a local co-op. Depending on the volume of grain a farmer sells to a co-op, or on the volume of inputs he buys (chemicals, fertilizers, seed, animal feed, etc.), cooperatives distribute cash and /or stock in return for patronage. The stock may be subject to limitations on when it can be sold or how old a patron must be before he sells it. These details, and the specific rates for cooperative distributions, are unique to each individual cooperative. But to the degree that a farmer's annual patronage benefit can be calculated, it should be included in the economic decision of where to sell grain. And that's just from a financial perspective – some farmers will develop an innate loyalty to their local co-op because they are on the board of directors, or because they feel the co-op, being owned by them and their neighbors, is more likely to be acting in local farmers' best interest when pricing grain and inputs.

An Imperfect Mission

It's in keeping with the mission of a co-op to offer a product that can help farmers lay off their risk in the notoriously volatile grain markets. Forward contracts are the cheap, simple way to do that. However, there is only so much risk a co-op (or any elevator or other grain buyer) will be willing to take for the sake of accumulating bushels from their farmer customers. Just as insurance companies can go to re-insurance companies to lay off their risk, grain companies can either choose not to trade if the rewards don't outweigh the risks, or hedge any purchases or sales they themselves have forward contracted.

Farmers, on the other hand, can't possibly lock out *all* their risk for every upcoming year. They may be perpetually long grain in every year they expect to still be farming, but because they'd struggle to find anyone willing to take the other side of forward contracts for any timeframe past the next year's crop, they're unable to offset a huge proportion of their overall lifetime long position.

Forward contracts are nonetheless a critical innovation in grain trading. Unless they could pre-arrange a profitable price from urban grain buyers, ancient Egyptian farmers may not have taken the risk of buying seed, preparing soil, then planting a field and trusting the fickle weather to produce their crops and support a civilization. Similarly, the same rice brokers in fifteenth century feudal Japan, who started warehousing and trading grain, can be credited with formally creating contracts that represented and put a price on upcoming grain production: forward contracts.

Building a Trading Empire

Readers with a certain entrepreneurial mindset will already be thinking of the outstanding arbitrage opportunities made available through forward contracts – opportunities across time, across space, and across all the features of any kind of grain. Perhaps you're already contemplating a trading program and just wondering how you can get your hands on some of those forward contracts. The unfortunate fact is, that unless you yourself are a farmer or a grain merchandiser, you won't have access to trade forward contracts. These are legal contracts representing actual grain and actual cash. If you are an individual investor sitting in your ocean view loft in Miami, what are you going to do with 1,000 bushels of real, physical corn showing up in a grain truck at your building's gate?

Maybe your (admittedly clever) answer is: "Well, I'll just buy some storage space out there in the Corn Belt and run my own little elevator operation." Or: "Well, I'll just do what those cross-country traders do and buy the grain from one source and ship it somewhere else without ever taking possession." That sounds good enough, but the next challenge you'll run into is that such trading is illegal for any entity who isn't a bonded, licensed grain dealer.

States prohibit grain trading or grain transportation by any entity who isn't licensed. For example, "to conduct grain dealer business in Nebraska without a Grain Dealer's License is a Class IV Felony punishable by five years in prison and/or a $10,000 fine."[1] A Grain Dealer's License can be obtained by applying to an individual state's Public Service Commission (or similar department), paying an application fee, disclosing the size of your intended grain trading operation, disclosing all your current financial information (which will be audited), probably undergoing a criminal background check, and then posting a bond based on some percentage of the value of grain you intend to buy. This is all so that you can't take ownership of somebody's grain in that state, then run off without paying for that grain, defrauding the state's citizens.

There are some exceptions – an entity may be federally licensed rather than state licensed, and livestock feeders can usually buy grain without having to go through the licensing process. However, that means an entity who sells grain to an unlicensed feeder faces additional risk if that feeder goes bankrupt. A bankruptcy court will consider that grain seller a creditor, but the state and federal price support programs might not be able to offer recourse to any posted security. There may be state-level indemnification programs to backstop some farmers' and ranchers' losses, but these vary from state to state. In any case, it makes sense for a grain seller to spend a little time investigating the status of any counterparties.

Maybe your ideas for building a trading program that arbitrages high protein spring wheat from the Dakotas against the underpriced protein value of Arkansas soybean meal is so innovative, so filled with profit potential that you really think it makes sense to go get your own grain dealers' license. OK, the *next* challenge you'll run into is that no one will sell anything to you. They might buy grain from you, because there really isn't much risk in agreeing to take physical delivery of a product before you write the seller a check. There is *a lot* of risk, however, in agreeing to turn over physical grain to some unknown, untrusted buyer who may or may not ever cut you a good check, whether that buyer is licensed or not.

The concept of **counterparty risk** is a huge consideration behind every commercial grain trade. Particularly in volatile market conditions, when a wild move in prices can bankrupt any elevator or ethanol plant that doesn't have a sound risk management strategy, grain traders watch their trading counterparts very closely for any accounting signal that they may not be able to pay for the grain they've bought.

So that's another thing about starting your own cash grain trading operation – you'd better have very deep pockets. If you'll be buying from some experienced trading entities and selling to others, assume that you won't be making wild profits on each individual bushel you trade. Rather, you'll be aiming for the same low-margin / high-volume market space currently occupied by every other elevator and grain trading company in business. Now assume you're going to have to buy and fully pay for some of the bushels, before you ever see full payment for the bushels you've turned around and sold. You must be prepared to pay cash up front for a high volume of bushels.

Just for argument's sake, let's say your new, private little trading company is going to start out with a 50,000-bushel corn trade, on which you expect to make 5-cent margins. Let's say corn is running about $5 a bushel at the time of the trade. You could potentially end up paying out a quarter of a million dollars in cash for several weeks before you see your money back, plus the anticipated $2,500 profit. There are easier, safer ways to make a 1% return on a quarter of a million dollars. A savings account comes to mind.

Risky Work and Tricky, Too

I just implied that cash grain trading isn't easy. It's not, and I'm not just talking about developing the analysis and intuition and negotiation skills to identify and execute good trades. I'm talking about the mechanics of doing it, too. You could be the cleverest grain trader in North America, coming up with great, low-risk arbitrage trades with really meaty expected margins. But you also must be able to pick up the phone and get somebody on the other end to trade with you in order to make your ideas work.

It's hard to get people to sell grain to you, and not just because they're concerned about counterparty risk (although that's a big part of it). Especially if you're trying to buy grain from farmers, trust plays a big part in any trade. Ideally, a farmer doesn't like to sell his grain to anyone who doesn't fully understand his operations' challenges, because if something goes wrong, he'd like to be confident that he can communicate to the merchandiser on the other side of his grain contracts and have that person "get it." Personality plays a big part in grain trading: aggressive negotiators may be well suited to some parts of the industry, and other parts of the industry reward good listeners with the background and communication style valued by farmers.

In some cases, it can take a lot of relationship-building to develop a client base from which you can source grain or from which you can receive competitive bids. That 50,000-bushel grain trade you have in mind might take 300 phone calls, or 50 farm visits, or both. Sometimes it's about more than just the price. And sometimes the right number will get you anything you need.

Anyway, if it all sounds like it's prohibitively complex for an individual investor to trade cash grain contracts, that's because it is. Don't despair, though. There's an excellent role for investors to take in the grain markets, too.

CHAPTER 4
Futures Contracts: Everybody's Business

I can picture a certain type of reader who might have picked up this book and skipped straight to this chapter, because they themselves will never have to handle a physical bushel of grain, and all they really want to know is how to bring in some extra commodity-related profits to their investment portfolio. There's no doubt people can – and do – trade grain futures contracts without even giving a moment's thought to what grain *is* or how it's moved around. Heck, some people probably even make money at it. But I maintain you can make better profits, or at least protect yourself from totally unexplained losses, if you develop a firm understanding of the actual trading mechanisms behind those grain investments you want to trade.

The Trouble With Cash Contracts

To get an idea of what a futures contract is and why it exists, first think about what might happen if one or another party defaults on a forward cash contract. Let's say an elevator and a farmer both willingly enter into a forward contract for 100,000 bushels of soybeans to be delivered at harvest in mid-October for $12.00 per bushel. The elevator is happy because it can turn around and re-sell those soybeans to a processor at some profit margin. At a 10-cent profit margin, those 100,000 bushels would represent $10,000 of business for the elevator. Meanwhile, the farmer is happy because he knows what price he will receive for his beans at harvest, and he feels it is a good price – he's happy to lock that in and remove risk from his operation. But both of their happiness depends on the other party to the contract actually making good on what they said they would do.

If the price of soybeans skyrockets to $16 per bushel, the elevator would feel some risk. If the farmer chooses, he *could* physically deliver those 100,000 bushels to some other buyer and receive an extra $400,000 in his pocket (($16-$12) x 100,000). This would be immoral, illegal, and indefensible in a court of law. The elevator would have a record of the farmer signing a contract to deliver it 100,000 bushels of soybeans, and if he doesn't do so, it could sue him. Nonetheless, the risk exists of a counterparty failing to perform on a contract, and it becomes increasingly pertinent if the contract is written in a region or between parties where the legal enforcement of the contract could be a struggle (some intercontinental trades, for instance).

On the other hand, let's say the elevator goes bankrupt and meanwhile the price of soybeans has fallen to $8 per bushel. Now the farmer, through no fault of his own, is suddenly going to have to accept $400,000 less revenue from some other buyer, because the elevator that originally wrote the contract won't be able to pay him anything. A grain buyer going bankrupt creates more complicated problems for its farmer clients than just the default of forward contracts. Consider that the same farmer probably would have had grain in storage at that elevator, for which he might now never be paid, and that the loss of even one grain buyer in his region will reduce the competitiveness of the entire local market.

There may also be situations where a buyer or seller of grain may be forced to default on a contract without it being an ethical failing. Let's say the farmer who sold the elevator 100,000 bushels of soybeans signed the contract in June, when the beans were planted and the weather was nice and everything looked perfectly on track for a record-large crop. Then let's say July and August passed as two straight months of withering heat and zero precipitation. The bean plants all failed to flower, and when harvest time rolled around, there was nothing in the fields to even be harvested. That would obviously be a huge problem for everybody. The farmer has no crop to generate revenue to pay back the creditors who lent him money for seed, chemicals, fuel and labor throughout the summer. The elevator will never see the 100,000 bushels of soybeans it had in turn committed to a processing plant, so it will be on the hook to find other beans to fulfill its own sales contract. Its further problem is that the hot, dry summer probably didn't confine itself to just that one farmer's 2,000 acres. Most likely, the entire region from which it buys grain won't have any crop to sell. Even if it hadn't already placed itself financially on the line to make forward sales elsewhere, it would still be facing an entire year of poor profit. Without bushels, there can be no per-bushel profit margin.

Anyway, the vast, vast majority of forward contracts are willingly and happily written and fulfilled without giving a lot of thought to the risks of default. But anybody who's trading physical grain ought to keep those counterparty risks firmly lodged in the back of his mind. And anybody who's trading grain *futures contracts* ought to be grateful not to deal with such risks, for reasons that will soon become clear.

Buying Out of a Contract

For that biggest crop production risk – weather – there are **crop insurance** products. Farmers purchase these policies before planting, and then if the crop fails, they receive a cash settlement. At the very least, the cash should help repay their lost input costs, but if a large enough policy was purchased, it would also ideally help the farmer maintain his family's annual income and also make him able to financially "buy out" of any forward contracts he may have previously written with a buyer.

In the example above, if he couldn't deliver those 100,000 bushels of soybeans to the elevator, the elevator would be legally obligated to its shareholders to seek financial damages from the famer. He would have to "buy out" of the contract at whatever current market price prevails. In the event of a widespread crop failure, we can assume the prevailing market price would be quite high indeed. Let's say it moved from $12 per bushel in June to $14 per bushel on the October day the farmer walks into the elevator to settle up. He would have to write the elevator a $200,000 check, straight up, in order to reimburse them for the current value of $1,400,000 worth of beans, for which they had agreed to pay $1,200,000. In other words, the elevator was going to lose out on $200,000 of market appreciation if the farmer didn't deliver, so it would have a legal right to seek that value from the famer. Alternatively, it may negotiate an arrangement with the farmer to just deliver that same quantity of beans from next year's harvest, but it's not obligated to be so accommodating. Contractually, it's owed that value *in October,* and any agreement to delay the income will have to be made to the elevator's benefit, not the farmer's.

Actually, at any point in time, at the request of either the buyer or the seller of a forward grain contract, the terms of the contract can always be renegotiated. If one party requests it, it's not the other party's obligation to agree, but that is just the nature of contracts in general, not grain contracts in particular. It is therefore an immutable feature of a forward cash grain contract that once it is entered into, it's awfully hard (and usually not a net advantage) to change your mind and get back out of it. If on June 1ˢᵗ, the farmer wrote the contract to sell his soybeans at harvest for $12, then on June 5ᵗʰ he changed his mind because he thinks the prices will be better later, he *can* call up the elevator and request to buy out of the contract for however much value the market has changed in those four days. But the elevator, whose business it is to always want to buy as many bushels as it can, would have no motivation to agree to the request. Effectively, it could attach any arbitrary "transaction fee" it wants to the renegotiated contract, and if it makes the fees punitive enough, it will discourage the farmer from backing out.

A Larger, More Forgiving Market

More importantly, this is a good introduction to one of the most exciting aspects of the grain markets. If we philosophically isolate the inefficiencies of forward grain contracts to be these issues of **fungibility** (they can't be efficiently traded *out* of because they're not standardized and interchangeable for each other) and **liquidity** (they can't be efficiently traded *out* of because there may be nobody else who's willing to take on your offsetting trade), we can start to imagine what a more efficient grain contract might look like.

Obviously, it would need to allow grain producers and buyers to sell or buy contracts that would lock in a price for grain at some future date, thereby removing price risk from their operations, just like forward grain contracts do. But ideally, it would also be possible to sell or buy such contracts with minimal transaction costs at any time at a fair market price. This would require a massive population of willing market participants, to ensure that somebody, somewhere would always be willing to take the other side of a bid or offer.

Furthermore, it would have to have built-in guards against counterparty risk.

Well, reader, we are in luck. Such a platform of products does indeed already exist, and it is called the **futures** market.

The key feature that makes a futures market more efficient than the practice of forward contracting is standardization. Each cash forward contract is a singularity – it's got a unique number of bushels tied to a precise location; it's trading a specific sample of grain. A futures contract is more of an abstraction – it's a financial contract entered into on behalf of some theoretical standardized grain at some time in the future. That means each futures contract can be exactly like every other futures contract in that particular market (e.g. 5,000 bushels of standard Hard Red Spring Wheat). With the invention of this instrument, the grain markets now had a way to trade a comparable, standardized contract everywhere with everyone, across all geographies and time, regardless of the underlying idiosyncratic physical grain sample that particular futures contract was meant to represent. You can already guess that these futures contracts were invented as a hedging tool. They are more fungible and tradeable than physical grain samples, but the sale or purchase of a futures contract can be used as a financial substitute for the future sale or purchase of equivalent physical grain.

Because they are so nicely tradeable, surely enough people trade them, and not just hedgers. That addresses the liquidity problem – as long as there is a population of willing buyers, sellers, and **market makers** gathered around, it becomes possible to always be able to get in or out of a futures trade, even if it's not at quite the price you want. This is why it's particularly valuable to have **speculators** in the trading population as well as hedgers. The more traders who are willing to buy or sell at independent price levels, the more liquid a market becomes.

And while a farmer might be hesitant to sell 5,000 bushels of physical grain to just any random person on the street who offers to write him a check (remember counterparty risk), someone buying or selling a futures contract can be confident he will receive his full financial profit or loss, because the futures market is all traded through a centralized, anonymous **exchange**. The counterparty who will pay out on a profitable futures trade isn't the other random trader who bought when you sold or sold when you bought; it's the exchange itself. The exchange will also be the entity that collects money from you if your futures trade results in a financial loss.

Commodity Futures

So let's examine the reality of what a grain futures contract really is before you call up your broker and go long five contracts of oats. First of all, that "call up your broker" language should tell you something. You might be familiar with trading stocks and mutual funds and bonds and the like, perhaps as part of a retirement plan. Although the underlying assets are as different as lemons and a lemonade manufacturing company, the mechanism for trading grain futures contracts is similar, in some ways, to trading shares of a company on the stock market.

Shares in a company aren't something you can just go to your local drugstore and pick up. There is really only one place you can trade shares in Verizon, for instance – the New York Stock Exchange (NYSE). An **exchange** is a platform for aggregating all the buying and selling interest in a given market, in order to fairly and efficiently determine that market's price. We've all seen video of aggressive traders in colored jackets frantically buying and selling stocks from each other, or displaying unforgettable consternation on their faces on those days when the market crashes. Those traders are actually 'on the floor' of the NYSE, and through a stock brokerage company, you can have an order to buy or sell stock phoned in directly to those guys. You can also place orders for Verizon stock over the internet, which get traded electronically without ever having a human trader on the floor of the NYSE look at them, but your electronic trade still gets pooled together with all the other trades coming into the exchange, and therefore all trades happen through the same centralized exchange mechanism. Because of that system, there is always one, true, official, publicly known price for a publicly traded company's stock at any given point in time.

Grain futures are financial assets, similar to stocks, traded via exchanges, like the CME Group's **Chicago Board of Trade (CBOT)** or the **Intercontinental Exchange (the ICE),** similar to stock markets. But wait a second. We just got through discussing the many different factors that go into pricing grains. There can't be one, true, official, publicly known price for corn, can there, if high quality corn at the port in Galveston is worth $6.50 per bushel and moldy, light test-weight corn in Minnesota is worth $4.75 per bushel? These exchange-traded grain prices – what are they representing, really? If you call up your **futures broker** and say, "buy corn," what are you going to end up with? A truckload of corn on your front lawn?

No. Futures contracts are **derivatives** of the actual market for their underlying asset, which is to say they represent that asset's price at some point in the, ahem, future. For instance, you can trade stock futures. Wal-Mart stock futures are not actually shares in the Wal-Mart company, but they represent what Wal-Mart shares will be worth in three months, or six months, or whatever. You can also trade futures contracts for U.S. Treasuries, various foreign currencies, stock indexes, and obviously for various physical commodities. A September corn futures contract, for instance, will have a price related to what traders think physical corn will be worth in September.

Turning Grain Futures Into Real Grain

But after reading the previous chapters, now you've got to ask: What will physical corn be worth in September *where? At what quality?* The CBOT and other grain-trading exchanges designate official warehouses to facilitate the physical delivery process that ultimately ties these futures contracts to the cash grain markets they represent. Sticking with the September corn futures contract example, each grain futures contract traded by the exchange has a standardized expiration date – namely, the last trading day before the 15th calendar day of the of the expiration month. So let's say all trading of September corn futures has to stop by the end of the trading session on September 14th. By that time, everyone who still has an open futures position (e.g. bought September futures and never sold out of them), will be able to turn those contracts into real, physical corn.

If a trader was short 5,000 bushels worth of September corn futures, that would mean he was previously representing the sale of 5,000 bushels of physical corn, and now that the delivery timeframe for the September contract has rolled around, he has to offset that short futures position by owning and delivering 5,000 bushels of real corn to a CBOT warehouse somewhere. And if another trader was long 5,000 bushels worth of September corn futures, that would mean she was previously representing the purchase of 5,000 bushels of physical corn, and now that the middle of September has rolled around, she will receive and pay cash for 5,000 bushels of real, actual corn located at that same warehouse. The exchange itself does the matching between those traders who want to deliver cash corn and those who want to receive cash corn, issuing assignments and receipts for the actual, physical corn that was delivered to the warehouse.

As it happens, the warehouse in this process is just one of several exchange-designated elevators. A document called a **warehouse receipt** represents physically delivered grain and can be used to honor a futures contract. The price a deliverer receives for grain is determined by the final settlement price of the futures contract. So one would hope, given the principles of arbitrage, that the final settlement price of the futures contract will be equal to the fair market price for physical grain at the delivery location. And that's why it's important for futures traders to think about the delivery mechanism, even though something like 99 percent of all grain futures contracts are never actually held through expiration and turned in for cash delivery.

At the contract's expiration, futures prices *should* match local cash prices at the delivery warehouses, so even futures investors need to know all the things that affect cash prices. This principle of futures and cash prices matching up at the time of delivery is called **convergence**. Corn futures contracts start trading years before their actual expiration date (e.g. December 2050 contracts will probably start trading in mid-December 2046), so for a long time, the futures prices can be very far apart from the actual local cash grain prices. But the closer a futures contract gets to expiration, the more its price should start to "converge" with the price of cash grain at the delivery point.

Because cash grain prices are different all across the country and the world, and because local supply and demand factors can have an effect on cash grain prices, it's relevant to consider just where it is the grain is being delivered to honor those few futures contracts that are held until expiration. For the grain futures contracts traded at the CBOT – corn, soybeans, oats, and CBOT wheat – the delivery points are any one of the warehouses or shipping stations designated for delivery. These warehouses are located along the Illinois waterway, so we can basically expect grain futures prices to eventually match the cash prices for barge-loaded grain in southern Illinois and Indiana. For the grain futures contracts traded at the Kansas City Board of Trade (hard red winter wheat futures), the delivery points are warehouses in Kansas City, Hutchinson Kansas, Salina or Abilene Kansas, or Wichita Kansas. And for the grain futures contracts traded at the Minneapolis Grain Exchange (hard red spring wheat futures), a trader can honor futures contracts at expiration by using warehouse receipts that represent hard red spring wheat in store at a "regular" elevator in the Minneapolis, St. Paul or Red Wing districts. The grain futures contracts traded at the ICE have no delivery mechanism and are instead cash-settled at expiration according to the price of the matching CBOT futures contract.

U.S. Futures Exchanges

So there isn't just one place you can look to find grain prices. It's anyone's prerogative to set up a new futures trading exchange – as either a physical trading floor or a computer-based order handling protocol, or both. Of course, any new exchange would be scrutinized by the Commodity Futures Trading Commission (the **CFTC**), which is the government regulator of commodity futures and options markets in the United States. It's an independent agency created by Congress and run by Presidentially-appointed commissioners, with the mission to "protect market users and the public from fraud, manipulation, abusive practices and systemic risk related to derivatives that are subject to the Commodity Exchange Act, and to foster open, competitive, and financially sound markets." Its day-to-day business, therefore, is to monitor the exchanges' policies themselves and also the participation by traders. For instance, they implement **position limits** on markets to prevent one or two big traders from "cornering" any given market, and they report the aggregate positions held by hedgers, speculators, and swap dealers in a weekly **Commitments of Traders report**.

So really, as long as a futures exchange is legitimate and not offering fraudulent products, it's free to gather traders together and transact business. There are exchanges that offer futures markets for electricity, emissions, freight, various equity indexes, interest rate products, real estate price indexes, weather ... basically anything you can structure with one, official, standard price point at any given point in time, can be traded as a futures market.

The More, The Merrier

But just because something *can* be traded as a futures market, doesn't mean it *will* be traded as a futures market. I can think of a number of commoditized substances for which there are currently no futures contracts being traded – salt, rocks, copier paper, frozen concentrated lemonade. The biggest challenge exchanges face when they introduce new contracts is convincing traders to use them. Traders like to make their trades through exchanges that have a lot of **volume** and **liquidity.** The greater the number of other traders trying to get an order filled in a market on any given day, the greater the chances that your own order will be able to find a willing counterparty and get filled at an agreeable price.

For instance, the leading Chicago wheat futures contract tends to have 15 times as much daily volume (the number of trades transacted) as the Minneapolis Grain Exchange (MGEX) wheat futures contract. It could happen that a trader who puts in a market buy order for Chicago wheat and a separate buy order for Minneapolis wheat at the same time could have the Chicago order sold to him instantaneously at exactly the price he had in mind. If there were fewer willing sellers in Minneapolis, and their asking prices were farther apart, the trader's buy order at that exchange might get filled two or three cents away from what he had in mind. The tendency for relatively illiquid markets (less populated markets in which it's harder to buy and sell) to have more choppy, volatile price movements becomes especially discouraging when a trader starts to think about having to eventually exit a trade. If there's a panic, in an illiquid market you run the risk of the market collapsing relatively faster without any willing buyers to stop the fall.

We can observe how low liquidity can sometimes become a self-fulfilling prophecy. If there's already a low volume of trade in a given market, new traders might avoid it for fear of illiquidity-related volatility ... and that means the volume of trade stays low ... and that means traders avoid it ... and so on.

For instance, there are many different classes of wheat, and the Minneapolis wheat futures market is a specific derivative of the hard red spring wheat (HRS) physical market, so only HRS wheat can be delivered to honor a Minneapolis wheat futures contract at expiration. Not hard red winter wheat (HRWW) or soft red winter wheat (SRW) or soft white winter wheat (SWW). Meanwhile, the Chicago wheat futures market is a derivative of the more general feed wheat physical market, with less stringent specifications about the class, quality, and protein level of the wheat that can be delivered to warehouses at expiration. Only about 25% of the total U.S. wheat crop is hard red spring wheat, so it makes sense that the MGEX handles only a fraction of the wheat futures trade that the CBOT does. However, higher-protein spring wheat which can be used for human baking responds to a different supply-and-demand situation than the general livestock feed wheat market does, so the MGEX's fraction of wheat futures trade is a reliable fraction, since they're the only ones who offer a contract to follow spring wheat prices specifically.

And that's what they've been able to do – rely on the need for a HRS-specific futures market to support the contracts since 1883. They decided to close down their open outcry pit (where the traders physically stood on the floor and traded amongst each other) in 2008 because they didn't have the volume to make that economically efficient, so now all the MGEX contracts get traded exclusively as electronic trades, but that works fine. An exchange doesn't *need* people shouting at each other; it just needs a mechanism for all the buyers and all the sellers to have their orders seen in the same place at the same time, and for all the trades to get matched up fairly. Computers are great for that. Pit traders will tell you about the advantages of hearing rumors on the floor, or the ways they can use their own physicality to make better trades in the pit than they can on a computer, but that's mostly just something for old pit traders to reminisce about. It's not particularly relevant to most grain market participants today.

Actually Trading Futures

If you don't need to use futures to represent a physical grain position in a delivery warehouse someday, then you, like almost everybody else in the market, will be trading those 99 percent of futures contracts which never get held to expiration and exercised for delivery. Typically, if you take a futures position, you'll get out of it – either for profit or for a loss – before the clock runs out.

With that in mind, you can concentrate on simply profiting in the futures market without fussing with physical grain at all. It's easy to do, really. Open a brokerage account. If you think the price of a grain is going to increase in a certain timeframe, buy that futures contract and then sell it for a higher price later. Collect your profit. If you think the price of a grain is going to decrease in a certain timeframe, sell that futures contract (yes, you can commit to selling something in the future that you don't currently own at the present) and then buy it back for a lower price later. Profit.

But the tricky part, of course, becomes evident if the price doesn't do what you thought it was going to do. The opposite of profit occurs, and it can happen much faster than investors who are accustomed to stocks and bonds are usually prepared for. This heightened risk exists partially because commodity prices tend to be more volatile than the prices of other financial assets, but mostly because of the nature of how futures trading is financed. Trading commodities is a highly **leveraged** activity, and that requires a steep learning curve for the typical investor.

Let's say a speculator, Bob, read somewhere that he should diversify his portfolio into commodities, but decides the most he is willing to risk on commodity trades is a couple thousand dollars. Let's further stipulate that in order to invest in commodities, he would have to buy the actual, physical stuff on the cash market. If corn was priced at $5.00 per bushel, his $2,000 wouldn't buy more than 400 bushels on the cash market – and that's not even enough to fill a semi-truck. It's not even enough to feed 30 cows for a week. And if the price rose 20% - a pretty good rally by most investors' standards – to $6.00 per bushel, Bob would profit exactly 20% (from $2,000 to $2,400).

However, if Bob put about $2,000 toward the purchase of corn *futures* ... i.e. if he traded in financial contracts representing corn rather than trading physical corn itself ... he could gain exposure to 5,000 bushels' worth of corn market movement. If the price went up 20%, his profit would equal the profit of 5,000 bushels gaining a dollar per bushel (his account would go from $2,000 to $7,000). Therefore, leverage would allow Bob to turn a 20% market rally into a 250% profit.

Margin

This is possible because the futures exchange allows traders to buy and sell full-size futures contracts without having to provide cash for the total value of those contracts upfront. They assume, because of statistical probabilities, that corn at $5.00 per bushel is unlikely to gain or fall more than $0.50 per week, for instance. So for a 5,000-bushel corn contract, they may only ask for $2,500 of good-faith money upfront from the trader of that contract. If and when the price moves farther than fifty cents per bushel, the exchange will require the trader to put more money in his account to cover the position's losses. The money itself is called **margin**. You have to provide initial margin for a futures trading position when you first enter a trade, and if the trade starts to lose more than that initial amount, the exchange will require maintenance margin beyond that initial amount. If you fail to provide it, they can close out your trade and hold you liable for any financial losses.

The actual margin rates are set by the exchange, but your brokerage firm (who tracks your trading capital and acts as the go-between for you and the exchange) may ask for more than the exchange's guideline requirements. The requirements themselves can change at any time; the CME, for instance, uses a calculation called Standard Portfolio Analysis of Risk (SPAN) to determine how much value is at risk in any given trade, depending on the underlying value of the assets being traded and the volatility of those markets. This calculation involves a lot of complex statistics about what-if scenarios - they want to have enough capital on hand to cover the potential losses of 99% of possible market outcomes. At the time I'm writing this, the initial margin requirement for a 5,000-bushel corn contract is $2,363, the initial margin for a 5,000-bushel soybean contract is $3,915 (soybeans are more expensive per bushel than corn), and the initial margin for a 5,000-bushel wheat contract through the Chicago Board of Trade is $3,038. If the exchange observes greater volatility in these markets and starts to calculate it needs more capital to be safe from traders defaulting on losing positions, it can (and does) change those requirements frequently at its own discretion.

Sometimes, an increase in the margin requirements will wash out some investors in the market and spark a surge of **liquidation**. For instance, if Bob was holding a long corn futures position and the exchange had $2,363 of his money effectively held in escrow (the margin requirement), and then one morning it announced the margin requirement was raised from $2,363 to $3,000 ... that might exceed the limit Bob was willing to risk on commodities. Maybe he really couldn't afford to cough up the extra margin. In any case, Bob – and a lot of other traders – would all decide they must get out of their corn futures positions. When this happens to large funds with large positions in large enough numbers in any given market, their mass exodus can be quite influential to the underlying price. So margin requirements are important to keep track of – not only because they dictate what kind of positions you yourself can take and what kind of portfolio you can build, but also because changes in these requirements can trigger big market movements.

Daily Trading Limits

Exchanges also set artificial limits on how much the prices of their commodity futures can change during any one trading session, but these decisions must be approved by the CFTC. For instance, corn futures prices aren't presently allowed to move more than 40 cents per day, soybean futures can't change more than 70 cents per day, and wheat futures can't change more than 60 cents per day. (These, too, can change over time.) When I first started working as a grain market analyst, the daily price limit on corn was 20 cents per bushel.

If the price of corn futures closes one day at $5.00 per bushel, and the next day the market opens and everybody frantically wants to buy corn at any price, and very few people are willing to sell corn near $5.00 per bushel, the price at the exchange will move higher and higher. Buyers will first buy from all the sellers willing to sell at $5.00 1/4, and then once there are no more willing sellers at that price, buyers will have to buy at $5.01 ... $5.05 ... then $5.10 ... then $5.20 ... then $5.40 ...

If no one's willing to sell at $5.40, either, because they believe the market is so bullish as to warrant a "true value" of $5.45 corn or $5.60 corn, there will just be a massive backlog of willing buyers stuck at the $5.40 level. Even if someone were willing to sell at, say, $5.41 and lots of people were willing to buy at $5.41, the exchange itself wouldn't allow the transaction at $5.41. That's because of that daily trading limit, which is meant to tamp down irrational market behavior and give everyone some time to think it over before the next trading session begins. On a "locked-limit-up" or "locked-limit-down" day, traders may be able to analyze other derivative markets and get a sense of what price is truly justified by market sentiment, but if that price level is anywhere more than 40 cents away from where the market closed on the previous day, no more trades will be transacted on the exchange beyond that price that day.

An exchange's general goal is to enable efficient price discovery, true, but in these instances they and the CFTC have decided it's ok to sacrifice efficient price discovery for one day in order to prevent otherwise illogical, frantic market movements.

They do give a nod to the need for relatively faster market movements when a contract is in delivery (price movement is unlimited), or on the days immediately after futures contracts get locked limit up or locked limit down. In most grain markets, they change the daily limit the next day to 150% of the original limit. So if wheat is locked limit down one day (loses 60 cents off its price), the exchange recognizes that this signals something drastic has changed about the market's supply and demand, and that traders may need extra room to find a new, fair price. The next day, wheat futures would be allowed to fall (or gain) 90 cents. If they got locked limit down again, the third day they'd be allowed to fall as much as $1.35. And so on.

Maximum Theoretical Loss

Bear in mind that if you were holding a long wheat futures position (you'd bought one wheat futures contract), and the market locked limit down three days in a row, you would lose $14,250 in three days and there would be absolutely nothing you could do about it. ($0.60 + $0.90 + $1.35 = $2.85. And $2.85 x 5,000 bushels = $14,250.) When a market is locked limit down, no one is willing to buy the futures within the day's price range, which means even if you wanted to sell your contract to get out of the market and cut your losses, no one would be willing to buy it from you and offset your position. You'd be stuck. And at the time you entered the trade, you probably thought you only had $3,038 at risk (the initial margin requirement for a wheat futures contract). In fact, if you have a long futures position, your theoretical maximum loss is the entire value from the price where you entered the trade, all the way down to zero. Presumably, grain futures will never be worth $0, but you must be willing and able to account for all that theoretical loss. If you have a short futures position, your maximum loss is technically infinite.

Fortunately, these locked limit moves don't happen very frequently. But the possibility must be mentioned for you to be fully aware of how the futures markets function, and any reputable futures broker will mention that risk to you. When it comes to your maximum theoretical loss, think of it like a nuclear disaster: there may be a very low probability of it happening, but if it does happen, the results would be disastrous.

Leverage

So, there are no guarantees in commodity futures trading. Leverage can be a wonderful thing when it allows you to boost your gains from a relatively small investment, but it also means your losses can accrue faster than you can mitigate them.

To help clarify this concept of leverage, let's say instead of buying a corn futures contract, our example speculator Bob had just bought those 400 bushels of physical corn with his initial $2,000. The worst thing that could happen to him would be the theft or destruction of that corn, after which it would be worth nothing. His investment would go from being worth $2,000 to being worth $0.

Not pleasant ... but a far cry from a leveraged loss of more than three times his initial investment.

Therefore, it's wise to diversify your futures trades and set limits for each individual trade. For one thing, you should have enough capital in your trading account to prevent you from getting totally wiped out, and enough so that the margin requirement for any one trade is only a percentage of your trading capital. For another thing, if you can have several positions in different markets trading at any given point in time, you diversify your exposure and limit the chances of losing capital overall.

The leverage available through the margined investment structure of the futures markets can be your best friend or your worst enemy, but I don't want to discourage you from using futures to accomplish your goals, whatever they are. There are strategies to manage your risk, but you might still conclude that Bob's $2,000 trading limit really isn't very practical from a risk management standpoint. Because of margin requirements, he's basically stuck in one position at a time, with no extra cushion of capital if that one position goes awry. So he better be awfully sure about what he's doing.

Similarly, if Stan Clarke at Verendrye Capital Management was trading with $100 million of capital, you might conclude it would be foolhardy for him to put all of that in a short soybeans position, but perhaps putting $2 million at risk (2% of his risk capital) wouldn't be out of line. There's no hard-and-fast rule about what proportion of your portfolio is wise to risk on any one trade, but the concept needs to be a consideration for all traders, no matter how large their account.

Futures Contract Design

At this point, I hope I've represented the function of the grain futures markets and some of the theory behind how money can be made or lost in these markets, but a good, careful trader will still want more details about the actual *stuff* being traded before he puts money at risk. Remember, if you buy or sell futures you won't actually being buying or selling kernels of grain; rather you'll be buying or selling the right to financially participate in the derivative gains or losses in grain prices.

Beyond the philosophical differences, grain futures contracts are otherwise pretty similar to forward contracts, in that they represent a price for some upcoming grain transaction. Instead of taking place between one buyer and one seller with unique details, futures are traded on an exchange full of many willing buyers and sellers to achieve one consolidated, official price for a commodity, and because of that, futures contracts must be highly standardized. Joe Smith wrote a forward contract to sell 24,000 bushels of corn to his local elevator at harvest for $5.50 per bushel. But if, at the same moment, his neighbor Lindsey sold 100,000 bushels to the ethanol plant for $5.60 per bushel, what does that mean for the price of corn? Maybe the ethanol plant was giving her a better bid for the efficiency of handling a larger quantity of bushels. Maybe the elevator was shading its bid to Joe Smith because his corn always tends to have a lot of foreign material in it. It's impossible to compare two, highly individualized, cash sales contracts and glean one, true market price from them.

The commodity futures exchanges remove that challenge by making every trade a trade for the exact same, standardized contract. Here are the details of what that futures contract looks like for corn:

- 5,000 bushels
- No. 2 yellow corn
- Traded on either the open outcry floor or via the CME Globex electronic platform during normal trading hours.
- Settled by physical delivery

Note how the standardization[1] – it's always 5,000 bushels of good corn – removes the need for a lot of the detail we explored with the cash contracts. No contract terms or discussion of weights & grades is required. A delivery point is implied, but it's always the same for every grain futures contract. The exchange also has a discount schedule to handle variations in the quality of corn that could be physically delivered to a warehouse (No. 1 yellow corn, which has less damage or foreign material than No. 2 yellow corn, receives a 1.5 cent premium per bushel, and No. 3 yellow corn, which is a lower quality product, receives a 1.5 cent discount at delivery), but that's a non-issue to 99.9% of the people who trade these contracts. If you want to trade a corn futures contract, all you need to know is that it represents 5,000 bushels of very basic, standard field corn at a particular point in the future.

Futures' Timeframes

The upcoming timeframe in question depends on which futures contract you trade. Each year, there will be a March corn futures contract and a May, a July, a September, and a December corn futures contract, each of which stop trading on the business day prior to the 15th calendar day of the contract month. So there's no need for individually specifying delivery dates or locations for each trade. It's all standardized. And because these futures contracts are being traded through a centralized exchange, the buyer and the seller of any given contract are anonymous to each other. It doesn't matter who's doing the buying and who's doing the selling – it just matters that one trading party is willing to pay a certain amount of money for the underlying asset during the specified timeframe, and that another trading party would be willing to provide the asset at that price at that time.

Grain futures contracts all have a similar design. Wheat (on all three U.S. exchanges) and soybeans and oats are also traded in 5,000-bushel lots. I always recommend referring directly to an exchange's contract specifications before you start trading something, just so you know what it is you're getting into. Barley, for instance, which is a cereal grain similar to wheat and oats, is traded on the ICE Canada exchange in lots of 20 metric tons each (equivalent to about 920 bushels).

Contracts might also trade in different timeframes than you are expecting. Although corn and wheat each have March, May, July, September, and December contracts, soybeans trade in different timeframes. Below is a table that lays out the abbreviation conventions for grain futures contracts:

Calendar month	Contract month symbols	Corn futures	Soybean futures
January	F		SF_
February	G		
March	H	CH_	SH_
April	J		
May	K	CK_	SK_
June	M		
July	N	CN_	SN_
August	Q		SQ_
September	U	CU_	SU_
October	V		
November	X		SX_
December	Z	CZ_	

That system seems bizarre until you get used to it. We couldn't use a one-letter 'J' abbreviation for June, obviously, because it wouldn't be distinct from a one-letter 'J' abbreviation for July, so the futures trading industry has developed this alphabetical one-letter system instead. CZ3 becomes the abbreviation for corn (C) futures traded with a December (Z) 2013 (3) expiration date. WH4 is the abbreviation for March 2014 wheat futures, MWK4 is the abbreviation for May 2014 Minneapolis Grain Exchange wheat futures, and KWN4 is the abbreviation for July 2014 Kansas City Board of Trade wheat futures. Soybean byproducts trade in the same months as soybean futures, so BOQ4 is the abbreviation for August 2014 soybean oil futures and SMQ4 represents soybean meal futures with the same expiration. The ICE futures that track CBOT expiration months have their own specific abbreviations, as do all futures contracts for all markets. Electronic contracts have different abbreviations than the open outcry contracts.

The collection of active futures contracts isn't just limited to one year at a time. There can be fourteen or more corn futures contracts offered by the exchange at any given moment, stretching across several years, depending on the volume and demand. In October of 2001, for instance, the first corn futures contract that would have reached expiration was the December 2001 contract (CZ1).

Whenever a contract is the closest contract to its expiration date, it's called the **"front-month"** futures contract. When the front-month December 2001 contract expired, the March 2002 contract (CH2) became the front-month contract. The front-month contract may or may not always be the one with the most active open interest and daily trading volume. It usually is, but in the last few weeks before it expires, trading interest in the front-month contract tends to dwindle (and its prices can be choppy). Therefore, the CME uses a "designated lead contract" (with the most interest and volume) to establish the markets' daily settlement prices.

Charts showing a commodity's prices over a long period of time are typically constructed of a continuous series of front-month prices. So the data points on a continuous front-month chart could skip from listing the December contract's price at expiration on December 14th to listing the March contract's daily settlement price on December 15th, but this is still the best – or only – way to show how the value of a commodity has changed throughout many years.

You can trade any available contract month, depending on what you are trying to accomplish. Obviously, farmers who know they will bring their grain to market during a certain timeframe will hedge their sales using the futures contract with the expiration date closest to their intended marketing date, and end users who know they will need a certain amount of grain at a certain time will hedge their needs using the appropriate timeframe. But investors who just want to go long soybeans, for instance, have more leeway in selecting a contract. The front-month contract almost always has the most **open interest** (the market's number of currently held contracts) and daily trading volume, so that can make it relatively easier to get an order filled at an advantageous price level. But if an investor intends to take a position in the futures market and hold it for many months, perhaps he just wants to initiate the position in a **deferred** contract to avoid racking up new transaction charges (commissions, fees, etc.) every time one contract expires and he is forced to "roll" to the next contract.

Rolling futures is the process of moving a futures position from one contract month to the next as a nearby expiration date approaches, and when a large enough volume of this activity happens all at once, it can be a significant event for the market. In particular, **index funds** that place large amounts of investor money into set proportions of a basket of commodity futures roll their positions at specific periods of time. Let's use the S&P GSCI (previously known as the Goldman Sachs Commodity Index) as an example. Thousands of investors, asset managers, and financial institutions who've decided they want to diversify their portfolios with exposure to commodities have put millions of dollars directly into this index fund (and others like it). The index fund uses that capital to take long positions (buy futures contracts) in various commodities, like crude oil, unleaded gasoline, copper, gold, coffee, sugar, live cattle, and of course, the grains, oilseeds, and other agriculture products. A specific, published weighting is designated to each commodity. In 2014, the GSCI structured itself to have 15% of its capital invested in agriculture commodities, broken down even further as:

Wheat (CBOT)	*3.50%*
KC Wheat	*0.74%*
Corn	*4.76%*
Soybeans	*2.75%*
Cotton	*1.00%*
Sugar	*1.47%*
Coffee	*0.58%*
Cocoa	*0.22%*

So for each dollar somebody invests in the GSCI, roughly five cents are tied to a long corn futures position, and the index's purpose is to always have 5% of its performance tied to the price of corn. By default, the GSCI takes those positions in the nearby futures month, but the nearby futures month is always eventually going to expire in a few months' time. Then what?

Let's say that it's November 1st, and the GSCI is holding several thousand long December corn futures contracts. Well, the GSCI roll period is set as the 5th through the 9th business days of each month.[2] So for any commodity contract they hold which is set to expire in the following month, the index must "roll" their position forward. Between November 5th and November 9th, they will sell off all their long December corn futures and buy an equivalent number of March corn futures. They roll their December positions in November because if they waited until December 5th through 9th, the December contract would already be in its delivery period and the index would be at risk of being assigned receipt of millions of bushels of physical corn.

Obviously, the concentrated selling activity in one nearby contract will put downward pressure on those prices, and the simultaneous buying activity in the next deferred contract will exert upward pressure on those prices. So while the index roll doesn't reflect any change in market sentiment for the corn market in general, it certainly can move prices around. If on August 4th, the September corn contract was priced at $5.00 per bushel and the December corn contract was priced at $5.15, we would say the Sep-to-Dec **spread** was 15 cents. By August 9th, assuming the index fund roll pressured the nearby contract lower and the deferred contract higher, let's say September corn futures would be worth $4.95 and December corn futures would be worth $5.20. The spread between them would have widened from 15 cents to 25 cents.

Futures Spreads

That's an incredibly exaggerated example. If the nearby corn spread ever actually did move 10 cents in 5 days, it would confound large sections of the market. More typically, grain spreads stay within a two- to four-cent range for their entire trading period, and for good reason. Notice how in this example, I initially set the December corn futures price 15 cents higher than the September price. That was deliberate – most commodities will tend to have higher deferred prices than the nearby price, to reimburse the market for the costs of storing the physical commodity through a given period of time. This is especially true of the grains, which are only produced annually and therefore must be stored twelve months before new supply becomes available. Commodities like crude oil, which is continually produced, also tend to have relatively higher futures prices as the contract months get more deferred, a situation that is known as "**contango**" or "**carry**." Contango is usually the preferred term of energy traders or commodity speculators, but the grain industry calls its positive futures spread structure "carry" to reflect that we are talking about the costs of "carrying" the grain in storage from one month to the next. The example of 15 cents of carry between September and December is actually pretty realistic. That's three months of storing grain, so it amounts to 5 cents per month –

a decent rule of thumb, but it's a changeable quantity based on sophisticated calculations.

The opposite of contango is "**backwardation**" – i.e. when the nearby futures contracts are priced higher than deferred contracts. If November crude oil was worth $80 per barrel and December crude oil was worth $79.85 per barrel, that market would be in backwardation. But again, in the grain markets, a different terminology is used. If there is no carry and the spreads between the futures contracts are actually negative (e.g. March corn at $5.00 and May corn at $4.95), we say the market is "**inverted**." An inverted grain futures market is a sign of incredible near-term bullishness, usually because of a supply shortage. It's implying that the market won't pay to have the grain stored away for a few months because it so urgently requires the grain *now*. Grain futures markets also become inverted when they expect a glut of new supply at some point in the future (e.g. harvest). So it's not uncommon some years to see July or September corn futures be priced significantly higher than December corn futures, because billions of bushels of newly harvested corn will be available by December.

Old Crop vs New Crop

The difference between September futures and December futures can be summed up with more grain market terminology. In the spring and summer, nearby futures contracts like the May and July are trading the "**old crop**" of grain that was actually raised the previous summer and fall. More deferred contracts, like the ones that are tied to the upcoming December timeframe, and the following March, etc., are trading the "**new crop**" of forthcoming grain.

The spread between old crop and new crop prices is closely watched, but it's not always so clearly differentiated between September and December. There are some years when row crops get planted early in the spring, mature early, then come to the market as a new crop of grain early in the fall; in those years, September futures contracts can trade based on the market's sentiment for new crop supply and demand. The only really clear indicator of the spread between old crop and new crop grain is the July-to-December spread.

Officially, the **marketing year** for corn and soybeans is September 1st to August 31st of each year, so every government projection you see for production and usage categories, like exports, is based on what is expected to happen during that timeframe (rather than during a calendar year). The marketing year for wheat, which is harvested earlier than the row crops, is from July 1st to June 30th of each year.

It's actually very important for you to know and keep track of which marketing year's futures you are trading. If you're a speculator trying to trade based on a fundamental supply-and-demand concern, the situation can be completely different from one crop year to the next. And if you're a farmer or end user using futures to hedge your cash position, the overall price movement of old crop futures can be wildly different from the price movement in new crop futures, so your hedges can totally fall apart if they're not placed in the appropriate futures month.

Abbreviations and Pricing Conventions

You do need to think about the timeframe you're trading, but it's not strictly critical for you to memorize the code letters used to represent each month of the year. It's mostly just the kind of lingo your broker may devolve into in an email. "Bot 3 CK2 @ 6472," for instance, would mean three May 2012 corn futures contracts (equivalent to 15,000 bushels total) were "bought" at $6.47 ¼ per bushel. Grain trades are transacted in quarters of a cent and often quoted in cents (rather than dollars) per bushel, so you might see the futures price represented in any of these various ways:

$6.47	$6.4700	647'0
$6.47 ¼	$6.4725	647'2
$6.47 ½	$6.4750	647'4
$6.47 ¾	$6.4775	647'6

What are actually quarters of a cent are typically quoted as eighths of a cent, so 0, $2/8$, $4/8$, and $6/8$ are mathematically equivalent to 0, ¼, ½, and ¾. Knowing that, and knowing the contract symbol for whichever commodity futures market it is you want to trade, will make your life easier when you use trading software. Because each software package is different, you would probably have to re-learn the whole mess all over again if you switch to a new system. Rather than lay out for you what the symbols are on the software I use, I will just recommend you get familiar with your own, and always be conscious of whether you're trading the contract through the open outcry pit or the electronic exchange system.

Open Outcry vs Electronic Orders

For instance, I could turn now to my futures order entry screen and buy one CZ2 (an open outcry contract for December 2012 corn) and one ZCZ2 (an electronic contract for December 2012 corn). The first order would go from my computer, over the internet, to my prime brokerage's employees on the floor at the Chicago Board of Trade. They would carry out the order in the corn trading pit (the area on the floor that is designated for corn trade) between the hours of 8:30 a.m. and 1:15 p.m. Central Standard Time, and my software would electronically respond back to me the results of their face-to-face trading. However, if I changed my mind about owning that contract in the middle of the night (because of some major geopolitical drama halfway around the world, or for any other reason), I couldn't make an offsetting open outcry trade until the pit opened back up at 8:30 the next morning.

On the other hand, that buy order I put in for an electronic contract would go from my computer, over the internet, into the great mysterious inner workings of the CBOT's computer (their platform is called CME Globex), magically get matched up with a corresponding sell order, and I'd nearly instantaneously receive the results back on my computer. I can trade an electronic grain futures contract any time the open outcry pit is open (called the "side by side" session from 8:30 to 1:15) *or* any time during the electronic session from 7:00 p.m until 7:45 a.m., Sunday through Friday. So that's pretty much *any* time other than the five-plus hours in the afternoon between 1:15 and seven o'clock, or the weekends.

Obviously, allowing as many trades as often as they can receive them is a boon to the exchange, which charges a small fee to process every order it receives. But the ostensible reasoning behind the creation of an overnight electronic trading session was to serve the Asian markets, whose hours of daylight and business are opposite to ours in North America.

You can start to imagine some arbitrage opportunities that may pop up with the subtle differences in trading mechanisms. As a quick example, the price of corn futures at 10:01 a.m. should theoretically be the same everywhere for everyone. However, it's possible for the electronic contract to have a slightly different market price than the pit contract because of the different mix of buy and sell orders coming through each trading platform. This is rare in well-capitalized markets like corn and soybeans, but it can sometimes be witnessed in Kansas City wheat futures or oat futures. Slight momentary differences can also occur between the ICE futures contracts and the identical grain contracts they duplicate on the CBOT.

Pretend you were a trader on the floor of the Kansas City Board of Trade, before it consolidated with Chicago in 2013. If you had wanted to, you could have carried a screen with real-time electronic quotes on it with you to the open outcry hard red winter wheat futures pit. If the bids and asks you heard from the pit were even a fraction different than the market price you saw for an electronic contract, you could buy (if the pit price was too cheap) or sell (if the pit price was too expensive) and benefit each time the two markets moved back to match each other exactly. Simultaneously buying an electronic contract while selling a pit contract is a perfect example of a zero-risk arbitrage. Both markets should move in the exact same direction at all times and there is a known relationship to which they should always eventually adhere – they *should* always match each other exactly. When they do eventually match each other, your profit will be exactly the fractional difference between the two contracts at the time you initiated the trade. However, the only people in a position to do this arbitrage are the floor traders actually standing in the pit, because they can get an open outcry order filled quickly enough to take advantage of the very brief moments when the two prices diverge.

So it's hardly an actionable trading plan for most investors, especially once they factor in the commission costs for each trade. It's just a good example of arbitrage and a way to clarify the differences between electronic and open outcry trades. Which is to say: their only differences are the mechanisms of how the buy or sell orders get communicated to the rest of the market – via a computer signal or via a person physically standing and shouting amidst other traders – and the hours each mechanism is open for trading. Other than that, the contracts themselves are exactly the same and interchangeable with one another. The end experience for someone using the futures market as a hedging tool or investing tool will be identical whether he chooses to enter trades electronically or via the open outcry pit. The final settlement prices of electronic and open outcry contracts will always be equal to each other at the end of each trading session and at expiration. Everything else is the same, too: same contract specifications, same delivery procedures, same timeframes.

The Futures Trading Experience

....

It was hot … too hot to be outside doing anything, and lately Joe's trips to scout his fields had just depressed him. The corn ears were stubby and misshapen from uneven pollination, and the flowering soybeans were probably running out of soil moisture now that the weather had switched back to a dry pattern in August. He had lay awake half the night with a pounding heartbeat and a sick feeling in the pit of his stomach as he added up the various rent checks and bank loans and equipment payments that would come due before the end of the year. If the crops didn't perform and the money didn't come from the crops, where was it going to come from?

Then when he turned on his computer in the morning and looked at futures prices, they seemed outrageously cheap. Didn't anybody in Chicago realize the crop was burning up out here? There would be money to be made with that knowledge, Joe was just sure of it. So he called his broker and told him to buy 5 December corn contracts and 5 November soybean contracts.

There was a lot of sputtering on the other end of the phone line. Phrases like "never a legitimate hedge for a farmer to go long" and "do you realize how much extra risk you're exposing yourself to?" But Joe held his ground. "Just make the trade." And five minutes later, the broker sent an email with the fills:

'Bot 5 ZCZ4 @ 517'2 (ave) and bot 5 ZSX4 @1178'4 (ave)'

Shortly thereafter, some bearish export news about a slowing Chinese economy hit the market and grain prices started dropping. By the end of the day, corn was 20 cents lower and soybeans had dropped 33 cents. Joe logged back on to his brokerage's website and noted he had racked up a $13,000 loss in a matter of a few hours. Looking out the kitchen window at eighty acres of soybeans leaning sideways in the hot wind, he didn't know whether to start drinking Pepto Bismol or whiskey.

....

Regardless of the wisdom of any particular trading idea, all you really need to put a trade in action is that idea, a brokerage account, and some cash. The electronic or person-to-person access to the trading exchange can easily be acquired through a brokerage firm, who will make trades on your behalf and be reimbursed via commission. And it's easy enough to find such a firm – there is a whole population of brokers eager to open new accounts.

As far as selecting the *right* broker, well that's a different matter. To some degree, concerns about counterparty risk should also be on market participants' minds when choosing a brokerage firm. You can conduct some due diligence on a firm's status as a licensed market participant, particularly through the **National Futures Association (NFA)**'s online Background Affiliation Status Information Center (BASIC), which details a firm's history of regulatory and arbitration actions. But that alone won't guarantee a futures broker or brokerage firm won't engage in unethical behavior or outright fraud at some point in the future. The misdeeds of a brokerage firm could range anywhere from encouraging inappropriately risky trades for a retired schoolteacher to completely "misplacing" billions of dollars that should have been in segregated customer accounts. That last example was actually done by a previously well-respected brokerage firm, MF Global, in 2011.

Those rare but disastrous examples of counterparty risk have motivated some market participants to diversify their futures brokerage accounts among more than one firm. Consider any large grain trading company that may have a positive or negative balance of millions of dollars in futures hedges at the end of each market day. If any one brokerage firm goes bankrupt overnight, it would be best to have a minimal amount of one's own cash in that firm's possession. And brokerage accounts don't pay interest on their customers' capital, which is segregated away from the company's own capital, so there is no particular motivation to keep any more cash stuffed away in a brokerage account than is necessary to cover margin costs.

Typically, however, the relationship between a futures market participant and his broker is characterized by trust. Joe Smith, for instance, is busy fixing machinery and checking his crops and doing the day to day business of farming, so he can't be expected to spend hours each day observing and researching the movements of the grain futures markets, even though their movement does have profound impacts on his farming business's revenue. Therefore, he relies on and trusts his broker to be educated about the goings-on of the grain markets at any point in time. Equally, his broker trusts him to be financially accountable for his trades.

Brokerage firms must establish a legal and ethical framework with their customers before opening an account. New account applications will always ask for a lot of detailed personal information from a prospective client, like their annual income and net worth. This has less to do with the brokerage firm wanting to know how much business they could reasonably expect from the client, and more to do with guiding the broker to make appropriate recommendations for the individual. Here's a sample of the language that is shouted in all-caps in a brokerage's Risk Disclosure document. It is meant to discourage people from committing more money to commodity trading than they can afford to lose:

"THE RISK OF LOSS IN TRADING COMMODITIES CAN BE SUBSTANTIAL. YOU SHOULD THEREFORE CAREFULLY CONSIDER WHETHER SUCH TRADING IS SUITABLE FOR YOU IN LIGHT OF YOUR FINANCIAL CONDITION ... IF YOU PURCHASE OR SELL A COMMODITY FUTURE OR SELL A COMMODITY OPTION YOU MAY SUSTAIN A TOTAL LOSS OF THE INITIAL MARGIN FUNDS AND ANY ADDITIONAL FUNDS THAT YOU DEPOSIT WITH YOUR BROKER TO ESTABLISH OR MAINTAIN YOUR POSITION. IF THE MARKET MOVES AGAINST YOUR POSITION, YOU MAY BE CALLED UPON BY YOUR

BROKER TO DEPOSIT A SUBSTANTIAL AMOUNT OF
ADDITIONAL MARGIN FUNDS, ON SHORT NOTICE, IN ORDER
TO MAINTAIN YOUR POSITION. IF YOU DO NOT PROVIDE THE
REQUIRED FUNDS WITHIN THE PRESCRIBED TIME, YOUR
POSITION MAY BE LIQUIDATED AT A LOSS, AND YOU WILL BE
LIABLE FOR ANY RESULTING DEFICIT IN YOUR ACCOUNT ...
UNDER CERTAIN MARKET CONDITIONS, YOU MAY FIND IT
DIFFICULT OR IMPOSSIBLE TO LIQUIDATE A POSITION. THIS
CAN OCCUR, FOR EXAMPLE, WHEN THE MARKET MAKES A
"LIMIT" MOVE ... THE HIGH DEGREE OF LEVERAGE THAT IS
OFTEN OBTAINABLE IN COMMODITY TRADING CAN WORK
AGAINST YOU AS WELL AS FOR YOU. THE USE OF LEVERAGE
CAN LEAD TO LARGE LOSSES AS WELL AS GAINS ... THIS
BRIEF STATEMENT CANNOT DISCLOSE ALL THE RISKS AND
OTHER SIGNIFICANT ASPECTS OF THE COMMODITY
MARKETS."

And of course, there's the classic: "PAST PERFORMANCE IS
NOT NECESSARILY INDICATIVE OF FUTURE RESULTS."

Before those kinds of risks are faced, a broker needs to know
whether or not a client will be able to financially handle them (thus,
the enquiries about income, net worth, and ability to commit funds
for a long period of time) and also whether or not a client will be
able to psychologically and emotionally handle the worst case
scenarios. It's helpful to know how much previous experience a
potential client may have had with trading futures, or even if they've
had some experience in the stock market. A lot of the invasive
questioning and persnickety capital-handling procedures are also
related to the brokerage firm's anti-money laundering legal
obligations.

For instance, to send initial margin money into your account,
you might not write the check directly to your broker, depending on
how that brokerage firm is registered with the CFTC. If a firm or
person is participating in the futures markets on behalf of clients, it
falls into one or more of these registration categories:

- **Futures Commission Merchants (FCMs)** – An FCM is a firm that is set up to handle futures orders from customers and process those orders on the various futures exchanges. They also handle customers' margin money and the proceeds or losses from their trades, so they must keep highly detailed ledgers of all the trades they handle for the CFTC to review, and they must also provide daily statements to each individual customer. Basically all of the prime brokerage houses who participate on the futures exchanges are registered as FCMs.
- **Introducing Brokers (IBs)** – An introducing broker is focused on communication with clients and accepts their orders to buy or sell futures, but the IB itself doesn't execute those trades at the exchange. Rather, it outsources that function to an FCM. The IB also doesn't play any direct role in the handling of client capital; that, too, is done by an FCM.
- **Commodity Trading Advisors (CTAs)** – A CTA not only handles futures trades on behalf of clients, it may also charge those clients directly for giving advice on what trades to make.
- **Commodity Pool Operators (CPOs)** – A CPO amasses funds from a number of participants, to be aggregated and invested in commodity futures and options trades. Sometimes, this is done under the framework of a limited partnership (LP).
- **Associated Persons (APs)** – An AP is any individual who's involved in handling customers and customer orders in the futures market, on behalf of a registered FCM, IB, CTA or CPO.

As an example, the broker Joe Smith called to make his corn and soybean trade may have been some guy registered as an AP with an IB, doing business through an FCM who has direct participation at the CME. All of which are registered with the NFA and the CFTC. When Joe, the customer, wants to place a futures trade, he calls his broker, but the organization that actually handles his trading capital and shepherds the order through the exchange and sends Joe a statement at the end of the day could be a separate organization – a large international bank, an independent firm that specializes in clearing financial trades, or perhaps even a large grain company that has diversified into financial trading as well.

Back to selecting which firm or broker to trust with your business, maybe you'll base your decision on a referral. Maybe you'll select one from a list of firms on an exchange website. Maybe you'll hear a broker be quoted on the radio someday and like the way he communicates. Maybe you'll just sign up with the broker who is geographically closest to you, although beyond the building of trust and rapport, customers and brokers can easily get by without any face-to-face interactions. You'll find most of your transactions being done via the telephone or with well-documented internet communication.

However – and with whomever – you choose to gain access to exchange-traded futures contracts, the actual experience of making trades can be as simple or as complex, as laid-back or as electrifying, as you choose. There is a whole range of tools and strategies you can use or forgo, all depending on what kind of trades you want to make.

Making Confident Trades

....

Bob Albany's brother-in-law had spent the entire Christmas dinner bragging about doubling his money by trading commodities. He recounted each natural gas call spread with excruciating detail, each platinum-gold spread with the glee of a savant. You would have thought he was Warren Buffet taking questions at the annual Berkshire Hathaway shareholders meeting ... except no one was asking him any questions. The man was an assembly line worker at a lightbulb factory, for heaven's sake.

Still, even though Bob was pretty sure his wife's brother had conveniently left out a few stories about failed trades, the man's evangelism did have a ring of truth about it. So for several months, Bob had pondered the idea. He envisioned himself becoming so filthy rich from clever commodity trades he could start his own law firm and quit working with his obnoxious partners. Then he started setting aside little bits of cash to be the seed money for his account. Then he spent many hours trying to convince his wife that commodity trading really was philosophically distinct from gambling – investors have a reasonable way to predict an outcome based on supply and demand! Speculators serve a valid market purpose! They provide hard-working farmers with a way to avoid risk!

Finally, he woke up on his 50th birthday and decided he was going to go for it. He called his brother-in-law's broker and set up an account. He went to the library and checked out five different books on technical analysis. Those books convinced him he needed some fancy charting software, so he went online and purchased a rather obscenely expensive monthly subscription service. He signed up for newsletters and e-magazines. Every time he saw a new trading idea referenced, he'd build another chart and see how it performed (hypothetically) over the next few weeks. Finally, he was ready for some day trading.

He'd buy or sell a few coffee contracts each morning and try to skin a small profit when the five-minute chart reached a resistance level, or exit at a loss when it fell through support – all the while with his heart throbbing and adrenaline coursing through every cell of his body. Slowly, he developed some intuition for the idiosyncrasies of various markets: cotton, live cattle, wheat. He lost his shirt trading oats one week – who the heck knew what made oats move or when or why? Whether his net result at the end of the year was going to end up positive or negative, Bob had certainly discovered a good way to suck up a lot of time distracting him from his boring old lawyering work.

·········

At the most basic level, the tools one absolutely needs for futures trading are negligible. I suppose one *could* initiate trades with nothing more than a pencil, paper, and a postage stamp. ("Dear Broker, Please place a limit order to buy 10 corn contracts at $5.00 or better.") Certainly, it's not uncommon for someone to conduct all their futures trading business over the telephone with nothing better to track the markets' movements than the intermittent updates on AM farm radio channels. But there are other tools available:

Market Access – Especially for those who are particularly sensitive about the time it takes to get an order filled, or who expect to be making many orders each day, it could make sense to use trading software to directly enter your own electronic orders. Anyone using trading software to directly enter trades (rather than routing it through a human broker) will want to be really, really careful about the details of each trade he enters. There are no do-overs for fat-finger typos, like selling 55 contracts instead of 5 contracts or communicating a willingness to buy soybeans for $50 per bushel instead of $15 per bushel.

However, each brokerage's trading software will likely have its own style of double-checking orders or preventing outrageous mistakes from occurring. For instance, an FCM probably won't even allow somebody with $5,000 in their account to enter a 55-lot trade. In any case, the time it takes to go through the training or introductions to your trading software will probably pay for itself in prevented errors. It will also help you figure out the trading symbols for the markets you intend to trade, which may vary from one software package to the next, and the applications for all the different types of orders you may use.

The two most common types of orders are **market orders** and **limit orders**. A market order is filled as quickly as possible at the best price available, whatever price that may be. For instance, if you see corn trading at $5.00 and enter a market order to buy corn, it's theoretically possible that you end up owning a futures contract at $5.05 (or wherever) if that was the lowest offer available when the exchange matched up your 'buy' order with someone else's 'sell' order.

A limit order, on the other hand, is filled only at a specified price (or better). So if you had placed a limit order to buy corn at $5.000, you would own corn futures if and only if the market trades that low and the exchange can match you up with someone willing to sell that low. If other market participants were suddenly willing to sell at $4.99 ½, it's theoretically possible for your $5.00 limit order to get filled at that more advantageous price. But it's also possible for your limit order to never get filled at all because the market never moves that low, and therefore for you to lose out on the opportunity to be long corn.

The other type of order you really want to understand is a **stop order**. If and only if a market reaches a designated price, a stop order converts into a market order and executes a trade for you. It's called a stop order because it's typically used to exit losing positions, although you can use them to conditionally enter positions. Consider if you have that long corn position at $5.00 and you're only willing to risk a fifty-cent loss. It's impractical for you to sit and watch the market every second of every day and night, so you could place a stop order at $4.50 to sell your position (at a loss) if the market falls that low. The danger of a stop order is that the market could be falling in fast market conditions and your sell stop order, which turns into a market-order-to-sell once corn hits $4.50, could theoretically get filled at $4.49 or $4.45 … or wherever. So there is also such a thing as a **stop limit order**. A stop limit order at $4.50 would turn into a limit order if and only if the market hit that price. The danger there, of course, is that the market could trade right through the level of your limit order and it might never get filled.

Much less common order types include MOO (Market On Open) orders, which are market orders at the very start of a trading session; MOC (Market on Close) orders, which are market orders at the close of a trading session; SCO (Stop Close Orders); MIT (Market If Touched) orders; or DRT ('Disregard Tape' or Not Hold Orders), which give a floor broker discretion on when and at what level to fill an order.

A very important distinction about placing orders is to know how long you want that order to be sitting around at the exchange. If you're willing to buy corn at $5.00, however long it takes for the market to reach that level, you need to make sure your limit order gets marked as a **GTC (Good Till Cancelled)** order. The default may be for an order to just be entered as a **day order** (only good for that trading session; expiring at the session's close). Other duration designations include a GTD (Good Till Date) order that will stay at the exchange until a specified date; a FAK (Fill And Kill) order that will execute as many contracts as possible at a certain price and cancel the rest of the order if the full quantity of desired contracts can't be filled at the price; and a FOK (Fill Or Kill) order that will either get an entire order filled immediately or cancel the order if it can't be immediately filled.

Data – Executing the order is but a small part of a successful trade. The most important part is developing the original trading idea. How you choose to develop that idea will start to segregate you into one of the two schools of commodities traders: technical traders and fundamental traders.

Technical analysis of the commodity markets is the practice of evaluating past activity in a market to identify patterns that may predict future price movements. As a very basic example, a technical analyst could look at a series of daily prices over the past few weeks, notice the **trend** of those prices has been moving higher, and choose to buy assets in the market on the expectation that the trend will continue. Someone who wants to use technical analysis to develop trading ideas will greatly rely on charts, and if he doesn't want to spend hours of his life creating pen-and-paper charts by hand, he'll therefore need to find a source of good commodity charts.

The easiest way to find the price of commodity futures would be to go directly to the source: the futures exchange. So to find grain futures prices in the United States, a visit to the CME Group's website is good first step. In their Agriculture category, you'll see the entire list of futures contracts they clear, and clicking on 'Corn,' for instance, will get you a table like this:

Month	Last	Change	Prior	Open	High	Low	Volume	Updated
Dec'12	500'0	+2'0	498'0	498'2	503'4	497'6	11,500	9:31:02
Mar'13	515'2	+2'2	513'0	513'2	519'2	512'6	5,874	9:31:02
etc...								

This is all the basic data available, but it may also be displayed in charts. A basic **bar chart** will represent each time period on the chart (each day, week, month … or perhaps each five-minute or fifteen-minute segment of trade) as a vertical line with its top at the highest price level traded during that period, its bottom at the lowest price level traded during that period, a little horizontal dash to the left at the price level where the trade opened the time period, and a little horizontal dash to the right at the price level where the trade closed the time period. There are other types of charts (a simple **line chart** from one closing price to the next; a **Japanese**

candlestick chart), but a bar chart is the industry default, and that's what will automatically come up on the CME's free website.

Note, however, that the CME only releases this data for free with a ten-minute delay. Several trading websites or commercial grain companies also pull the free data from the exchange and offer it to you on the internet with a ten-minute delay. If your trading plan relies on more urgent information, or more advanced charting techniques, you'll have to either pay for real-time data from a website, or get yourself a subscription to more serious charting software.

The first place to ask for charting software would probably be through your brokerage, but a review of any trading industry magazine or online forum is going to quickly bring up some advertisements for trading software packages. The package you choose will depend on how much you want to spend and what you're trying to accomplish, so try a free demo of several packages to see which software works best with your own style.

Once you have that software, you'll be well on your way to doing technical analysis of the commodity markets. Entire books have been written about technical analysis techniques, so I won't retread a worn path here, but I'll list a few basic techniques to give you an idea of what this style of analysis is all about. For the record, all of these techniques *could* be done with a pencil and some graph paper, but to generate technical trading signals in a timely manner, today's traders typically let a computer do the charting.

The generation of a 'buy' or 'sell' signal is the end goal of any technical analysis technique. A **moving average**, for instance, charts the average of a number of past prices (a 50-day moving average would take the past 50 daily price points, repeating the averaging function each successive day) alongside the chart of prices themselves. This is done to make trends more clear, and technical analysts believe trading signals are generated when prices fall above or below a moving average, or when one moving average line crosses another. A **Relative Strength Index (RSI)** is similarly charted over time to show how a market's trend and momentum may be changing, but instead of being a simple average of prices, it's an index of up days compared to down days. A **Stochastic Oscillator** is another technical analysis measurement of momentum, done by comparing the current market price to its recent range of prices.

In addition to the movements of continuous lines on a chart, technical analysis trading signals could also come from the formation of certain patterns on the charts themselves. The most obvious of these is a **trend**, which represents the general direction of a market. You can draw a trend line by connecting a series of steadily higher period lows, or steadily lower period highs, and if you want to trade with the trend, there's your signal. However, technical analysts tend to be most concerned with identifying *changes* in trend, in order to sell when a trend hits its high point or buy when a trend hits its low point. They believe a changing trend indication is signaled by particular formations, like an **outside reversal** (when a market trades both higher than the previous period's high and lower than the previous period's low), or a **bull or bear flag** formation (a chart's trend pausing horizontally after a nearly vertical 'flagpole' was established), or a **head-and-shoulders** formation (a peak forming a 'left shoulder,' followed by a higher peak forming a 'head,' followed by a peak forming a 'right shoulder').

There are countless other technical analysis studies one could conduct on a chart, but I'm already oversimplifying these, so if this is an area of interest for you, I recommend you find a book or website source to give you more details about chart formations or even the equations that underlie various technical indicators. The right charting software package will do all of this for you automatically, and you'll just have to figure out how far you trust the signals to build your trading ideas.

Now on the other hand, **fundamental analysis** of the commodity markets involves evaluating anything that can affect a commodity's supply or demand, and then predicting how changes in that information may affect price. It's Econ 101: if supply decreases, price increases. If demand increases, price increases. And the obligatory vice versa. The philosophy of fundamental analysis is quite different than technical analysis. Whereas a technical analyst can develop a chart-based trading idea without even knowing the underlying asset being charted, a fundamental analyst is concerned with determining the inherent fair value of the asset, then deciding whether the current market level is underpriced or overpriced. It's essentially similar to "value investing" in the stock market, a la Warren Buffet or Benjamin Graham.

Fundamental analysis is no less reliant on numbers than chart-based analysis; in fact, it is deeply driven by *real* statistics. Whereas a technical analyst will draw lines on a chart dictated by past price data alone, a fundamental analyst will be more likely to run rigorous multi-variable regression analyses of historical production trends and the effect of one market's price on another market's demand.

The power of fundamental analysis comes from correctly analyzing reliable data about supply and demand (for simplicity, "S&D"). There are innumerable ways to measure and analyze the S&D data for any given commodity, and what's appropriate for one situation may not be appropriate elsewhere, but one benchmark metric that can show both supply and demand in relation to each other is a commodity's **stocks-to-use ratio** during a given time period. That measures the ending inventory of the commodity as a percentage of the overall demand for that commodity. Even the stocks-to-use ratio must be taken in context. A ratio that may be indicative of very bullish tight supply of one commodity (say a 10% stocks-to-use ratio) may be a pretty typical or comfortable inventory level for another commodity. Knowing which S&D factors are legitimately bullish or bearish indicators of potential price movement is what fundamental analysis is all about, and to a large extent, it just takes some experience in a particular market to examine those factors in their appropriate historical and seasonal context.

In any case, a fundamental analyst needs only a limited reliance on price charts. To get a general idea of trend, or to see historical prices in context, the free or low-cost chart sources may be good enough.

If you're taking the time to read the sections of this book about the underlying mechanics of producing and moving real, physical grain from supply points to demand points, presumably you're interested in fundamental analysis. Since I'm taking the time to write this book, it's also pretty safe to assume I fancy myself a fundamental analyst. There are reasons for this beyond the obvious romance of amber waves of grain – a lot of technical analysis is no more than hokum. I say this with the confidence of someone who has been trained in sophisticated statistical analysis – for a technical trader to pick an arbitrary series of numbers (the Fibonacci sequence, for instance) and expect market charts to behave according to those magic numbers or patterns can be (and has been) proven to be no better than random selection.[3] Heck, there are people who use moon phases as a basis for technical analysis. Tell me what about moon phases is a realistic influence on the price of corn? And no sooner will your tea leaves or tarot cards or technical reversal patterns tell you that wheat prices are going to fall, than a vicious frost will take out half the growing crop (i.e. something will happen that *really* affects the price of wheat) and all the technical analysis in the world will be instantly rendered useless. I believe a market can be deemed "**overbought**" or "**oversold**" according to technical indicators, yet simply be legitimately responding to true, fundamental changes in the market.

However, in the sense that 'supply and demand' can apply to futures contracts themselves, not just to the underlying commodity, I will concede that there is some value to paying attention to the most mainstream technical indicators. Stochastic indicators actually measure changes in a trend's momentum, so I sometimes use them to indicate when a futures market may be attracting undue volumes of behavioral buying or selling.

If enough people in a market *believe* that any given technical indicator dictates that the market *should* be bought or sold, then that belief itself may turn into a self-fulfilling prophecy, so it's important to keep track of what those traders are doing and anticipate an onslaught of buying or selling interest. Possibly that's why there are so few books about fundamental analysis and so many books about technical analysis – a technical trader's magic number system only works if he can convince a lot of other people to use the same system.

I consider the intersection of technical analysis, as it measures the volume and direction of market behavior, and fundamental analysis to be a separate, third school of trading, one I call "**structural analysis**." A trader could, for instance, develop a rigorous backtest to determine whether a certain technical analysis signal (e.g. a 'buy' trigger when the market falls below its 50-day moving average) actually results in heavy buying activity, by statistically analyzing the significance of changes in market volume on the days when such signals occur. Using data about which sector of the market (commercial hedgers, hedge funds, swap dealers, etc.) is doing the most trading at a certain point in time would be another way to drill the data about a market's structure. With that kind of analysis, a trader would really be analyzing the supply and demand of the derivative market – the futures contracts themselves, rather than the underlying commodity – so it would be similar to fundamental analysis, but it would also be similar to confirming the goals of technical analysis.

For example, fundamental analysis of the copper market might tell you if there was a real, actual shortage of copper in the world. Any company that was contractually committed to supply physical copper to its customers would face a "**short squeeze**" as it scrambled to pay increasingly exorbitant rates just to gain some ownership of any copper it could find, anywhere. Structural analysis of a futures market (or an options market, stock market, or bond market) could tip you off that the same kind of short squeeze might occur in those derivative assets, whether or not there really is a shortage of the underlying asset. If the front-month Minneapolis wheat contract, for instance, has only 100 open contracts in its last few days of trading before expiration, and most of those open positions are short positions (traders previously sold futures with the bearish idea that prices would eventually fall), the traders with long positions can "squeeze" the shorts by making higher and higher-priced offers which the short traders, desperate to close out their positions before they're obligated to deliver physical wheat to Minnesota, would have to accept.

<u>Advisors</u> – So if you get somebody telling you to short soybean oil because the 5-day disparity ratio has crossed the accumulated swing index (or something), well … maybe you'll want to use some caution. But to each their own, and there is definitely a population of people willing to seek out such advice and a subsequent population of people willing to give it.

Advice, along with market access and data, is another item you can use to develop and execute trading ideas. Again, the simplest form of getting trading advice is to just take advantage of what's out there for free on the internet. There are online forums for futures traders and farmers, and there are a number of people willing to publicize their trading ideas on social media outlets. You won't have to try too hard to get on somebody's free e-newsletter or e-magazine distribution list. The trading ideas you'll glean from these sources will run the gamut from technical signals to rumors of fundamental S&D changes; and from outrageously unwise to verifiably reasonable.

But, as with most things, you get what you pay for. Therefore, there are a number of folks – some rather useless, some very insightful indeed – who charge a subscription fee to send you their opinions on the commodity markets and advice about what sorts of trades you should be making. Remember that anyone who's charging money for making specific trading advice has to be registered with the NFA as a Commodity Trading Advisor (CTA), so you have at least one avenue for doing due diligence on a newsletter peddler before sending them a check.

The advisory service you choose will depend primarily on who you are. A farmer will want to seek out someone with knowledge and experience trading cash grains, because such an advisor will also be able to offer insight about timing the farmer's cash sales of grain, in addition to offering analysis of the market prices. A merchandiser working at an elevator or grain processing facility may not have to seek out any special advisor because his company probably already has a great deal of proprietary, in-house knowledge of the local supply and demand situation. Very large grain companies keep their own staff of market analysts, and they may be some of the best in the business because they get private access to accumulated data about real grain inventories all over the country (and all over the world) that not even the USDA can provide. Smaller cash grain companies, however, if they want some outside opinion about the grain markets, have to seek out the same advisors as everybody else.

But by far the easiest type of commodity advisor to find is one who will just offer a bullish or bearish opinion for speculators. These can still be newsletter writers, but of course, as you put increasing amounts of money into the commodity markets, you may need to seek out increasingly sophisticated advice. Somewhere between paying for a $50 newsletter to pick up a new short-term trading strategy once in a while, and paying somebody a $20 million bonus for managing your $1 billion proprietary fund, there is a way to get high quality advice and direction for your commodities account – by opening a **managed futures** account.

Such an account would be much like any other futures trading account – run through the same brokerage structure, but your capital would be directly controlled by a professional money manager (a CTA). Managed futures are considered to be their own asset class nestled within the **alternative investment** universe, which means they are often used specifically to diversify a sophisticated investor's overall portfolio. Rather than risking 100% of his trading capital in the stock market, such an investor may choose to limit his risk of a total blowout by assigning a portion of his portfolio to stocks, a portion to bonds, a portion to real estate, and a portion to commodities (via managed futures).

But recall that futures traders profit by going *either* long or short, so whether or not the commodity sector's prices are moving in the same direction as the stock market, a good CTA should be able to achieve returns in a managed futures account. The principle of diversification may be especially valuable when you distribute all your commodity trading capital among a selection of CTAs who each focus on different asset sectors (e.g. agriculture, energy, metals) or on different strategies (e.g. statistical arbitrage, spread trading, option writing, etc.). Confidently selecting a managed futures program becomes very difficult when you start to realize the number of choices you have – should you go with a CTA who has years of stable but lackluster returns? Or should you pick one that is just starting because she will be relatively more able to devote time to your account? There is an observed tendency for managed futures programs to post their best performances (expressed as annual rate of return) in their first few years because they have relatively fewer assets under management, and it becomes increasingly difficult as accounts get larger to make nimble trades that deliver the same returns. The other questions an investor should be asking when seeking out a CTA include:

- <u>What is the principal trader's background?</u> Look for someone who is well educated with a deep background in either trading, the industry being traded (agriculture, mining, etc.), or preferably both. Ask yourself if this is someone with a reputation of conducting business reliably and professionally. Know how many employees are involved in the operation, and keep in mind the increasing costs and difficulties of managing large operations.
- <u>What are the fees?</u> Typically, a CTA will charge a management fee (a proportion of the assets being traded – probably 1 or 2%) and a performance fee (a cut of the profits – probably between 10 and 20%). If these fees are wildly off from the prevailing industry standards, figure out why.
- <u>What is the minimum investment?</u> Typically, the higher this number is, the better a sign it is of good risk management because of this next question: What percentage of my capital will be risked on a single trade? Is there a maximum percentage at risk on any given trade? This can be a struggle for CTAs who accept small investments. Consider one who has a $20,000 minimum investment (there aren't many). The margin requirement for a single long or short trade in corn futures, for instance, will eat up more than 10% of a single investor's capital.
- <u>What is the program's strategy?</u> Pay attention to which asset classes are being traded, especially if the CTA has a very large capitalization. It's one thing for somebody to get $50,000 of trading capital in and out of the illiquid oat futures market without disaster, but a CTA who tries to move millions of dollars will have an awfully hard time getting trades filled unless he sticks with deep, highly liquid markets. Very large funds can amass **reportable positions** or even run up against **position limits** set by the CFTC.

    A CTA's strategy can be discretionary or systematic. A discretionary trader will use human judgment to enter or exit trades, so you really have to trust that human. A systematic strategy will develop computerized algorithms to trigger trades, so you really have to trust that computer programmer. Although the underlying parameters of any trading strategy will of course be proprietary, get as many details as you can about how those systems are developed – who is doing the math? What kind of math are they doing (statistics, simulation, etc.)? Always ask what the failsafe will be in a worst case scenario.

- <u>Ask about ongoing metrics</u>, like the frequency of trading in an average month. This would be expressed as "round turns per million." A **round turn** is an entry and an exit of a trade. Commission costs start to eat up an account's performance as high frequencies of trading occur.

- <u>Ask for performance records</u>. You not only want the average annual or monthly return data and risk-adjusted performance ratios, but also the worst monthly drawdown and the longest total equity drawdown to get a sense of how strictly the CTA will protect your capital from a risk of loss. This is at least as important, if not more important, than dreaming about the impressive returns you can get from a managed futures account.

- <u>Who are the service providers</u>? Find out who the CTA uses for clearing and prime brokerage, who does their back office and legal work, etc.

- <u>Are there limits to the trading program</u>? A CTA may choose not to accept further clients once it gets a certain value of assets under management; it may close a trading program after a certain period of time; it may set guidelines for how much of its own manager's money can be accepted.

- <u>What are the program's goals</u>? That's a very open-ended question, but it will give you a good sense of the CTA's philosophy. Is she focused entirely on return? How will she measure success? Most importantly, is that philosophy in line with how you want your own capital to be put to work?

Whether you choose to put large sums of capital under someone else's direction or not, I think it's valuable to assess your own trading choices in similar terms. What's *your* strategy? You may not end up building a supercomputer full of trading algorithms, but knowing how much you're willing to risk on any given trade, and knowing whether you want to engage in long-term commodity investment or quick little day trades will help you focus your research and plan for your trading costs. It will help you crystallize your trading goals.

Who Is Doing What

At any given point in time, one group of market participants may be more active or more influential to futures prices than another group. For instance, after a headline about greater-than-expected growth in the Chinese economy, speculators may be driven to buy up commodity futures contracts, but it may or may not alter the futures trading patterns of farmers and elevators on that particular day. Alternatively, if China actually purchased several cargoes of physical soybeans to be shipped out of the U.S. over the next few months, the futures market in Chicago would quickly experience a flurry of futures trading activity as the international merchandisers who made those sales hedged their soybean transactions.

The CFTC keeps track of who is doing what in the futures market on at least a weekly basis, although traders with large enough ("reportable") position sizes must also report their holdings daily. Their breakdown of futures market participants into categories is a good framework for you to think about how you fit into the population and how fundamental market events may affect other groups' intentions.

The first group is the "Producer / Merchant / Processor / User" category, which can be more easily referred to as **commercial** traders. These traders are bona fide hedgers in the commodity markets. Every futures contract they buy or sell is effectively a substitute purchase or sale of the physical commodity that they will need later in their commercial undertaking (a farm, an elevator, an ethanol plant, etc.). Although there is a lot of popular angst about the oversized influence of speculators on commodity prices, it's this commercial category of traders who actually make up the vast bulk of grain futures trade. Between 2006 and 2011, commercial entities traded 63% of all corn futures contracts and 76% of all wheat futures contracts cleared by the Chicago Board of Trade.

The next group is "Managed Money" – the investors with capital in managed futures accounts and all the hedge funds who are trading commodity futures. Between 2006 and 2011, the Managed Money category traded only 16% of the corn contracts and 24% of the wheat contracts in the Chicago futures markets. These traders will buy futures when they feel the price will be higher later or sell futures when they feel the price will be lower later. They experience pure profit or loss on that outcome; i.e. they're not hedged by an underlying physical commodity position.

So while there is certainly risk in running a commercial grain company, a commercial grain trader's price risk can usually be hedged, but a speculative grain trader is actually going out of his way to seek out and take on risk. People drive hundreds of miles to seek out risk at slot machines and card tables in casinos, and they do it because they hope the returns from their gambles will increase their available capital; they think the rewards will be worth the risk. Similarly, commodity speculators want to take what capital they already have and see that capital grow into a larger amount of capital, and they're willing to accept a risk of loss in order to have that chance. Therein lies the great, beautiful, underlying mechanism and existential purpose of the futures markets: to allow commodity businesses (ostensibly farmers) to remove risk from their operations by transferring that risk into the hands of those willing speculators. Remember that 99% of all futures contracts will never result in the delivery of physical grain to any warehouse; when a futures contract passes from a farmer (or livestock feeder) to a speculator, in effect, it is not so much grain that is being traded, but rather *risk* that is being traded – the risk that the price of the grain will change.

In that way, speculators serve a valuable purpose in the futures markets, even beyond the increase in liquidity the markets experience when each additional trader (of any category) participates. When commodity prices reach uncomfortably high levels for consumers, it's common to hear politicians go after speculators as some kind of threat to our society. They can drive up prices by purchasing futures at "too-high" prices, and therefore make the underlying substance cost more than it otherwise would (so the story goes). Incidentally, politicians never seem to worry when the price of fuel or food, or whatever, is uneconomically *low*.

But while I believe this theoretically *could* happen if speculators were the only ones trading futures, fortunately there is that built-in mechanism (delivery) to force futures and their underlying markets to converge. As long as futures prices have to eventually match the prices of the underlying cash market, futures speculators can't do much to make the physical commodity worth more than its true value.[4]

It is sometimes observable that speculators may add to the volatility of futures prices from one day to the next as the volume of their participation waxes and wanes. But while the proportion of speculative participation certainly changes over time – and theoretically *can* reach disruptive levels – as a general rule, at least in the grain markets, these speculators are far outweighed by commercial traders who must actually buy or sell something of economic value near the prices they're trading on the futures market. Because most market participants who need to hedge their needs on the futures markets will balk when prices get "too high," it's difficult for the futures markets to disassociate themselves from economic reality. A failure of **convergence** did happen for one notable period in the Chicago wheat market in 2008. As the December 2008 wheat futures contract was nearing expiration and was in delivery, it traded between $5.00 and $5.50 per bushel. Meanwhile, the average of cash prices across the country was no higher than $3.93 per bushel. This was partially the result of an unusually large amount of futures participation from speculative funds with no interest in the cash price, but such an occurrence is quite rare.

The speculative traders who swamped the Chicago wheat futures market in late 2008 weren't just CTA's and hedge funds; a sizeable portion of them were also index funds and swap dealers, two other categories of market participants tracked by the CFTC. **Index funds** tend to buy and hold commodity futures contracts essentially forever, only selling when they need to roll to the next contract month or re-weight their holdings. They can be huge, but they are rarely a source of unpredictable volatility in the supply and demand of commodity futures. **Swap dealers** are typically large banks who are writing private hedge contracts for their commercial clients and using the futures markets to offset their own subsequent risk. In essence, futures market participation by swap dealers, which is sizeable, can be a proxy for other commercial (Producer / Merchant / Processor / User) hedging activity, but because some *investment* activity can also be "hedged" by banks registered as swap dealers, it's a somewhat opaque category.

In any case, knowing who is doing what in the grain futures markets can help your structural analysis of supply and demand. To some extent, knowing who is doing the buying or selling affects my opinion of the market's inherent bullish or bearish sentiment. Large amounts of farmer selling at certain times of the year could just be related to their need for cash to pay off bills, rather than an expression of great bearishness. It's also helpful, when you see heavy trading activity one day, to know whether speculators previously held a large net-long or net-short futures position. For instance, frantic buying could be the result of **short covering** (buying futures to offset previously short positions) rather than fresh bullish sentiment. Conversely, a high volume of selling one day could be speculative **profit-taking** (selling futures to offset previously long positions) unrelated to the market itself, instead of an expression of fresh bearish sentiment.

Farmers' Use of Futures

Remember when Joe Smith went long five contracts of corn and five contracts of soybeans? And how apoplectic his broker got? The specific phrase was: "It's never a legitimate hedge for a farmer to go long." When Joe Smith, whose business it is to produce and own grain – i.e. to be inherently long in the grain market – *bought* grain futures contracts, he was not in any way offsetting his business's inherent market position. He wasn't making a substitute sale for some physical sale he would make at a later date. He was just doing some plain, old speculation.

And that's fine. The markets are as open to farmers who want to speculate as they are to anyone else. In fact, farmers make some of the best speculators, because they know so much about the fundamental mechanics of supply-side grain economics. Being physically located out among the nation's grain fields, they also can sometimes pick up on production concerns more quickly than the rest of the market, which is an advantage when you want to make a speculative trade before the knowledge gets "priced into the market."

But by and large, for a grain producer to use the futures market as a legitimate hedging tool, they will be selling futures contracts to offset their inherently long physical grain market exposure. The mechanics of doing this are quite different than any of the other previous types of farmer grain sales we've discussed so far.

First think about an actual futures contract for corn, for example, which represents 5,000 bushels of corn to be delivered to a warehouse along the Illinois River by a certain date. If Gary Green sells a March corn futures contract at $5.00 per bushel, on the face of it, that transaction commits him to deliver five truckloads of corn to the Illinois waterway by March 15th. Since he lives in the middle of Iowa, let's say it would cost him 60 cents per bushel to transport that corn to Peoria, so of the $25,000 he would receive for delivering on the futures contract, he would effectively only pocket $22,000 (the equivalent of $4.40 per bushel).

Anyway, for a number of reasons, Gary Green from the middle of Iowa is never going to choose to deliver his corn to some CME warehouse. It would take too much time, it costs a lot of money, there are perfectly good corn customers right in his own county, like the local ethanol plant, and above all, the paperwork and process of delivering on a futures contract is just a giant headache.

So when Gary Green sold that futures contract, he was representing physical corn he *could* deliver to a warehouse, but he was really only making that representation as a financial substitute for the real physical sale he was intending to make in March. What would actually happen, then, is that Gary Green would load up five truckloads of corn whenever was convenient for him after harvest and take them into his local elevator. The market for corn may have collapsed from the time when Gary made the $5.00 futures sale, and the elevator might only pay him $4.00 per bushel for the grain ($20,000). However, since the futures market would have also collapsed during the same period of time, perhaps from $5.00 to $4.20, Gary would receive a $4,000 cash profit from his brokerage account when he closed out his short futures position on the same day as the physical grain sale. His net cash income from the two transactions would be $24,000, or equivalent to $4.80 per bushel.

Therefore, the *net* profit or loss from selling grain via a futures hedge is financially identical to selling grain via forward cash contracts. That's why, no matter where or when the grain actually goes to an end user, whether or not the grain itself really could be physically delivered according the futures contract specifications, a futures hedge is a financial *substitute* for a real physical transaction.

In fact, corn futures contracts can be used to hedge products that aren't even corn! For instance, milo (a.k.a. sorghum) is a grain that's grown mostly in the drier regions of the U.S. but which can be used as animal feed or ethanol feedstock just like corn. Therefore the prices of milo, itself an economic substitute for corn, move up or down at the same times and at pretty much the same rates as corn futures prices. Farmers who need to hedge their milo production can do so by selling corn futures contracts, and end users who need to hedge their milo requirements can do so by buying corn futures contracts. Their potential losses in the cash market will be closely offset by their gains in the futures markets, or vice versa.

That illustrates the only condition necessary for one market to be used as a hedge for another market – the two markets must be strongly correlated. There are two sides to any hedge. One side will be long in one market (e.g. owning physical grain) and the other side will be short in another, closely related, market (e.g. selling grain futures). And for the financial consequences of one side to reliably, adequately offset the other side, both markets must move in the same direction, at the same time, to the same degree. Statistically, that's the definition of **correlation** – a positive correlation exists when two variables move together reliably, and a negative correlation exists when one variable moves up while the other goes down.

So if two markets were uncorrelated (cotton futures and McDonald's stock, for instance), holding a long position in one market and a short position in the other market wouldn't necessarily prevent a risk of loss. Both positions could be losing at the same time. Incidentally, if two markets were strongly and reliably *negatively* correlated (the U.S. dollar and corn futures, for instance), being either long or short in both markets would be an effective hedge against net losses.

Fortunately, the practice of hedging a farmer's cash grain position with futures is very straightforward because the futures markets and the underlying cash grain markets are so tightly related. The principle of arbitrage will always keep this true – if a grain futures market doesn't gain enough or fall enough to match the movement of the underlying cash market, when the futures contract goes into delivery, a mass of buying and selling in the underpriced and overpriced markets will bring them back in line.

But while a farmer can be confident his futures hedges will mathematically work out to lock in an equivalent financial outcome for his grain, the experience of locking in grain prices through the futures market is quite different than the less demanding experience of selling forward grain contracts. If Gary Green had sold his 5,000 bushels of corn at $4.80 per bushel with a forward cash contract, and then the corn market rose to $5.80 per bushel, he would have lost an opportunity to sell more valuable grain, and the **marked-to-market** value of his grain position would have reflected that loss. But he never would have had to write a check and watch $5,000 of actual cash leave his possession, which would be the case if he had sold a futures contract and watched the market rise $1.00 per bushel. In that sense, it's easier for a farmer to ignore opportunity costs when they're not staring at him as a negative number in a brokerage account, but that's not always a good thing. To a truly disciplined marketer, the current value of the grain should always be in mind anyway.

The other slightly awkward part of using futures contracts to hedge a cash grain position is the unlikelihood that the grain a farmer owns will be precisely divisible by 5,000 bushels. If Joe Smith will produce exactly 117,300 bushels of corn one year and will hedge it all using conventional, standardized futures contracts, he'll have to leave 2,300 bushels unhedged. And unhedged grain is susceptible to all the price risk of the volatile markets. This isn't actually a huge problem, because for one thing, the CME offers **mini-contracts** in standardized 1,000 bushel increments. For another thing, in practice no farmer ever hedges 100% of his production before harvest because he can never be fully sure what his crop will yield. His best guess will always just be an estimate. But if, theoretically, a farmer had exactly 117,300 accurately measured bushels of corn in a bin and he wanted to completely hedge all price risk from that cash grain position, he could use corn futures to do most of the hedging (23 full-size contracts and 2 mini-contracts), but would then have to use a cash forward contract to hedge the remaining 300 bushels.

Recall the reasons why futures were developed as preferable tools to forward contracts: the reduction in counter-party risk, the greater fungibility of the contract, and the greater liquidity of the market. When it comes to hedging their grain production, farmers having a tool that is financially flexible is especially important. By hedging his 5,000 bushels of corn with a futures contract rather than a forward contract, Gary Green gave himself the opportunity to change his mind about the price he locked in. At any time, if he chooses, he can exit that futures contract without having to renegotiate a bunch of terms or pay any fees (other than commission). He could also change his mind about the delivery timeframe. If he had hedged the corn against the March futures contract and then it turns out the road out to his bins gets buried in eight feet of snow, or the local ethanol plant presents a particularly compelling bid for May corn, it's no big trouble for Gary to call his broker and roll his futures hedge from the March to the May contract (and he'd get to keep all the additional carry spread between the two contracts).

Most importantly of all, when a farmer locks in a price with a futures hedge rather than a forward contract, he's not committing to any specific transfer of ownership. Once he writes a forward contract with an elevator, that buyer can start to account for those bushels in its total grain position, and the farmer has lost negotiating power. The bushels contractually must go to that buyer, and if the ethanol plant down the road suddenly becomes frantic for corn and pays 20 cents over the prevailing market rate, the farmer no longer has an opportunity to sell those bushels to the ethanol plant for the higher price. With a futures hedge, however, the farmer locks in a mathematical price for his grain, but the actual negotiation and transaction of selling the physical grain to a buyer can be delayed until the circumstances are in the farmer's best interest.

This can limit the number of days when local marketing opportunities seem really compelling to just a few times per year, if a farmer is willing to hedge all his production with futures and just strike the cash market when buyers are most eager to pay for grain. The big decision, however, is what price level to select for the futures hedge. It's never wrong to lock in a profit, so once the futures market reaches a level above the per-bushel cost of production, you can expect to see some farmers selling futures. Depending on their bullish or bearish opinion of the market's direction, however, they may rush or delay those hedging sales above or below their breakeven price level.

A farmer may only directly interact with the futures market on a few days of each year. He could theoretically sell a whole year's production in one fell swoop in just one day at just one price. But it's more common to make sales in increments and gradually achieve an average price for the year. Either way, most farmers will take a few minutes out of each day to track the market prices. If your salary, or your bank account, was likely to go up or down by 2% each day, you too would probably make an effort to keep up to date. The standard deviation of daily corn futures returns in the 2010/11 marketing year really was 2%.

Farmers not only need to track what the futures markets have been up to, but also to see how the local cash grain markets have been moving. Although the correlation between the grain futures markets and the cash grain markets is close enough to perfect to allow for hedging, it's not actually a 1.0000 correlation during all periods of time. It's entirely possible for the futures price to increase 50 cents over a month, let's say, and for the local cash bid from a particular ethanol plant to increase 55 cents during that same time period. This slippage between the futures and cash market can also occur in the other direction (the cash market can grow weaker faster than the futures fall), and that's why it's very important for farmers to track both markets. The value of a farmer's cash grain position *can*, in practice, fall faster than the profits of a short futures hedge can offset the loss. In fact, this phenomenon of cash grain prices and futures moving at slightly different rates is so crucially important to grain marketers, it has its own name: **basis**. And basis is the basis for all the greatest trading fortunes that have ever been made in the grain markets!

Basis!

To define it, **basis** is the mathematical difference between the price of a futures contract (the consolidated, standardized, and universally-accepted benchmark of a grain market) and the actual price of a local cash grain market at any given location at any given point in time. Virtually no one receives exactly the nominal value of grain futures for their grain. Meanwhile, there are a million separate values for grain out in the country, depending on where it is, what its quality is like, how badly buyers need the stuff that day, etc. To be able to compare all those millions of localized grain bids to one another and to the market in general, there's the basis equation:

$$(\text{Local cash price}) - (\text{Futures price}) = \textbf{(Basis)}$$
$$\text{or}$$
$$(\text{Futures price}) + \textbf{(Basis)} = (\text{Local cash price})$$

Basis gets its name from phrasing like, "We're bidding fifteen under, *basis* March futures." From that information, and from knowing the current value of the March futures contract, you could determine the actual "**flat price**," or local cash bid. Using this example, if March wheat futures were priced at $6.00, a farmer selling 1,000 bushels of wheat to this bidder would receive a check for $5,850, because the flat price would be $5.85 per bushel:

$$(\$6.00) + (-\$0.15) = (\$5.85)$$

When calculating basis or flat price, you have to be very, very careful about whether the basis is a negative or positive number. Typically, country bids for grain will be negative, but they certainly can be positive. So you will not only irritate pedants if you say mysterious things like "basis 15 the March" or "basis increased today," but you could also end up totally misunderstanding a trade. Maybe you mean basis is fifteen *under* the March (H) contract, but a basis bid certainly could be fifteen cents *over* the March, in which case those thousand bushels would have been worth $6,150:

$$(\$6.00) + (+\$0.15) = \$6.15$$

In the first example, an increasing basis *number* could be a change from -15H to -20H. That widening of basis would mean the cash market at that location was becoming relatively weaker than the futures market. Here is how the basis could weaken:

Date	Futures price	Flat price	Basis
Feb 1st	$6.00	$5.85	-15H
Feb 8th	$6.03	$5.83	-20H

Notice in that example that the futures market itself was rising over time, but the basis bid grew weaker and the flat price bids showed a relatively weaker cash market. But we have to say it was "weaker" not "wider" or "bigger" or "increased" because watch what happens in the second example when basis starts out as a positive number:

Date	Futures price	Flat price	Basis
Feb 1st	$6.00	$6.15	+15H
Feb 8th	$6.03	$6.23	+20H

In that instance, the basis *number* again grew larger, but because it was already positive, that was a reflection of the cash market growing relatively stronger than the futures market. "Wider / narrower" or "increasing / decreasing" terminology is therefore meaningless in basis arithmetic. To be truly accurate, we must always only say "basis strengthened" when we mean cash prices gained relatively more or lost relatively less than the futures prices, and we must always say "basis weakened" when we mean cash prices lost relatively more or gained relatively less than the futures prices. With that syntax firmly in mind, we can start to examine what actually makes basis grow stronger or weaker from one day to the next.

I said basis values in the country are typically negative, and that's historically true because in theory, basis is a reflection of transportation costs and supply & demand. If we work from an overly simplified assumption that the cash value of corn at a CME-registered warehouse on March 15th must, because of arbitrage, be equal to the value of March (H) corn futures at expiration, we can set a theoretical 'Ground Zero' for basis right along the Illinois River. Under these assumptions, basis should be exactly zero at that location at the time of futures expiration.

From there, basis values will radiate outward at weaker and weaker levels as the grain gets farther and farther away from a delivery point. If truck freight costs $1 per mile and there are no backhaul opportunities, it would take 30 cents per bushel to transport grain into the zero-basis zone from 150 miles away on a 1,000-bushel truck. So let's say everywhere at a 150-mile radius from the zero-basis zone has a basis bid of -30H. Everywhere at a 300-mile radius would have a basis bid of -60H. And everywhere at a 450-mile radius would have a basis bid of -90H. Et cetera.

That's a gross oversimplification because of all the variable supply and demand factors in different geographies, which have nothing to do with futures delivery points, but it explains historically why basis bids out in the middle of the country are usually negative numbers.

Even in that simple theoretical world, grain must not only be purchased out in the country where it is produced; it must also be sold to the entities who will ultimately consume it. Those entities could be a cattle feedyard in Texas, perhaps, or a country with a grain deficit to which we will export the grain out of a facility at the Gulf of Mexico. Transportation costs also play a role in determining what basis those consumers will have to pay. For instance, pretend it takes $0.70 per bushel to ship grain from Peoria, IL to New Orleans, LA on a barge. In our perfect theoretical world of arbitrage, basis at New Orleans, LA (NOLA) would be +70H. In the real world, **"CIF"** grain (the shorthand term for grain that's traded on waterway vessels with Cost, Insurance, and Freight included in the price) really does tend to have positive basis values. Now pretend it would take $1.00 per bushel to ship that same grain on a train to Texas. The cattle feeder's basis would then be +100H. And in reality, "rail" grain also usually has positive basis values.

So you see basis can be positive in some areas, and it usually is positive at those demand points. It gets a little more interesting when you start to consider that all the thousands of little elevators and farms around the country are *both* some distance from a futures delivery point and some smaller distance from a demand point. For instance, Buffalo, KS is about the halfway point between Peoria, IL and Amarillo, TX. It would cost about $0.98 per bushel to ship grain from Buffalo to either Peoria or Amarillo (again using $1 per mile for a truck and no backhauls ... which are not very realistic assumptions but they keep the math fair for this hypothetical). So you might expect basis in Buffalo, KS to be both 98 cents weaker than it is in Peoria and also 98 cents weaker than it is in Amarillo.

But in that perfect theoretical world we had, 0H minus 98 cents of transportation would equal -98H. But +100H minus 98 cents of transportation would equal +2H. There is clearly a lot of wiggle room between -98H and +2H basis!

So now we get to step away from that bizarro world of theoretically easy basis math and talk about basis in reality. As I'm writing this, basis in Amarillo is really only about 25 cents stronger than the basis in Peoria (which is *not* zero), and the Amarillo bid is about 50 cents stronger than the bid near Buffalo, KS. In practice, the pure math will almost never work out exactly between one far flung location and another location several hundred miles away. You can calculate the basis difference from a farm to an ethanol plant 50 miles away with confidence, but once you start shipping grain across several regions, which each have their own competing demand points (cattle feeders, poultry feeders, ethanol plants, export terminals, food manufacturers ...), there is never going to be any magic "Ground Zero" from which all other bids could be calculated.

Cash grain prices are different in each different location, and you can calculate arbitrage opportunities from those differences, as I've already shown in previous chapters. In reality, using basis values rather than flat prices is a far superior method to communicate local grain price differences. That's because a flat price calculated from a basis bid is accurate no matter what gyrations the futures markets go through that day; whereas a flat price bid with unknown basis could have a lot of slippage in understanding.

If Joe Smith calls up Jason at the Mungus Elevator and asks for their current grain bid, Jason might say, "We're 20 under the March, so $4.80 at the moment." That's good information, because in the amount of time it took me to write this paragraph, the March futures contract could very easily have fallen from $5.00 to $4.95 or $4.90 or anywhere. If Joe takes a few minutes or a few hours to think about whether or not he wants to sell that grain today, by the time he makes that decision, the $4.80 cash bid may no longer be available. However, he can look at the March futures price (let's say it's $4.90 a few hours later) and know that the flat price bid he would be likely to receive from Jason at that point in time would now be $4.70 ($4.90 - $0.20). Of course the basis bid itself could change the second after they hang up the phone, but basis is much less likely to experience a volatile change than the futures market is.

If a merchandiser only gives out his bid as a flat price, "$4.80," or if a farmer only pays attention to the flat price bid without listening for or keeping track of basis, a lot of confusion can result. Wherever there is confusion, there is also the potential for somebody on one side of a trade to take advantage of somebody on the other side of the trade. Trying to calculate price differences from flat price alone also makes life difficult for anyone trying to identify arbitrage opportunities.

Cash grain traders need to keep a multivariate matrix of hundreds of different grain sources and dozens of different grain consumers in play at all times, so they can always find the best home for grain or identify arbitrage opportunities. Knowing the grain's value expressed *as basis* is pretty much the only way to keep that matrix straight from one day to the next.

For instance, corn from Joe Smith's Iowa geography could end up getting exported out of the Gulf (via barge transportation down the Mississippi River), could end up in the grind at a local ethanol plant, could end up getting mixed and blended and loaded on a train (at the local elevator) to be sent to some other domestic market, or could be sold directly a local livestock feeder. There is a unique value for each of those propositions, and a grain trader's job (including Joe Smith's job) is to figure out which of those values presents the greatest profit opportunity between the origin and the final destination.

	Basis bid	Transportation cost from farm	Equivalent bid FOB Smith
Mungus elevator	+5H	5 cents	+5H-5 = **+0H**
Beefeaters' feedlot	+0H	6 cents	-6H
Springfield ethanol	+2H	6 cents	-4H
Peoria barge terminal	+23H	25 cents	-2H

From the table above, it's clear that even though Peoria has a nominally stronger basis bid, shipping grain from Joe Smith's farm to the Mungus elevator is the best opportunity for him to capture basis. Because all these basis bids are being calculated from the identical March futures contract as a benchmark, it's an arithmetic certainty that the strongest basis opportunity is also the highest flat price opportunity. That will be true no matter what the futures market does (drop 20 cents one day, gain 15 cents the next, or both in the same day), as long as the basis bids remain the same.

As the basis bids change from one day to the next, it will be easier to keep track of them and their reasons for doing so if all you have to do is know: "Mungus is five over, Beefeaters is zero over, etc." rather than "Mungus was bidding $5.10 on Wednesday, Beefeaters' was bidding $4.76 the day before that, so … which one is better now?" In reality, a grain trader might keep track of a market by thinking, "CIF corn is at +23H by +25H." That would mean willing buyers were *bidding* at +23H, and willing sellers were *offering* corn in that region for +25H. In that instance, the **bid-ask spread** would be two cents.

Basis is not only a function of transportation costs, but also a matter of supply and demand at each location, so that will affect each bid and offer. Beefeaters' feedlot and the Springfield ethanol plant are equidistant from Joe Smith's farm (they both have identical transportation costs), so if transportation were the only variable in basis values, arbitrage would suggest they must both post identical bids. However, that's not the case. Joe Smith could make his corn worth an extra two cents (-4H instead of -6H) by taking it to the ethanol plant rather than the feedlot. Why would that be? Maybe the ethanol plant is frantic to buy corn this week because it's about to run out and it can't just shut down all its equipment. Maybe the feedlot got a great deal on some cheap, lower quality corn six months ago and is still blending that off into its feed rations. That kind of knowledge is valuable to a grain trader. It could make you quicker to react when the ethanol plant suddenly has a breakdown, for instance.

But at this point in time, Joe Smith's corn is most likely to end up at the elevator. What is the elevator up to that it can outbid the local end users and the barge market? Possibly it could be loading trainloads of corn that are destined for an entirely different geography than the barge market. The train market not only has access to export terminals at the Gulf of Mexico, but also to export terminals in the Pacific Northwest ("the **PNW**"), to poultry feeders in the Southeast, cattle feeders in the Southwest and Mexico, and dairies in California. Those are just some examples of end users, and you could do this same basis matrix exercise for a trainload of grain that could be routed to any of those demand points, rather than for a truckload of grain off of Joe Smith's farm. Presumably Jason and his colleagues at Mungus have actually done that exercise and discovered they could make the corn worth +5H at their elevator, which results in an equivalent bid of 0H at Joe Smith's farm. Incidentally, in the lingo of the grain markets, rather than saying "zero over" or "zero under" we typically say "**option**," or ideally, "option the March."

And that's the other vital thing to keep straight when tracking the basis movement in a grain market – know which futures contract is being used. -5H is *NOT equivalent* to -5K because it is exceedingly rare for any two futures contract months to have equal prices. Due to the typical positive spread structure (a.k.a. carry), the May contract could be 10 cents higher than the March contract on any given day. To communicate the same flat price on that day, a basis bid could either be expressed as -5H or -15K. Especially as the front-month futures contract gets close to expiration, grain bidders will start to roll their basis bids over to the next contract month, and you could find yourself in a situation where Beefeaters' feedlot is bidding -10K, Springfield ethanol is bidding -8K, and Mungus elevator is still bidding +5H. In the near term, it's just going to make your comparisons a little more complex, but if you're comparing whether to sell grain in one timeframe or another, keeping track of the spreads between futures contracts and the basis bids for deferred months will also help you decide which timeframe presents the best flat price opportunity.

The timing of your cash grain trades may also be influenced by the seasonal weakness or strength of supply & demand in a local market. You might expect basis to reach its weakest point of the year at the **gut slot** of harvest, when the heaviest flow of grain is coming on the market and local elevators' capacity to handle grain has reached a bottleneck. There are also sometimes weaker dips in basis bids at the start of January or in March, because those are timeframes when it's convenient for farmers to haul grain. If there was a relatively poor harvest one year, the strongest peak of local basis levels may occur late in the following summer as end users struggle to find high-quality grain remaining on the local market.

But in order to discover the seasonal basis patterns specific to your own local market, there really is no way to do it other than to amass the data (either keep a record yourself for a year or several years, or ask your favorite merchandiser if they could send you their records) and see if patterns emerge. Your own geography will have a normal range and special considerations (like the specific harvest timeframe), so knowing how the national average basis seasonally tends to behave may not be especially helpful, but you can track that knowledge, also.

The Minneapolis Grain Exchange publishes cash price indexes for several grain markets and offers futures contracts on those indices. Each index is a calculation of thousands of cash bids collected across the country each day by DTN, a market information company, which then get averaged together to create one national average cash price for corn, soybeans, hard red spring wheat, hard red winter wheat, and soft red winter wheat each day. Comparing those index values to the daily futures settlement will give you a national average basis bid, and from that you can determine when an overall grain market is in a period of strong basis (relatively eager physical demand and/or shortage of supply) or in a period of weak basis (relatively ample supply and/or disinterested demand).

As it turns out, there is indeed a seasonal pattern to grain basis, just like you would expect. For the benchmark corn market, national average basis levels tend to weaken through the months of September, October, and December, then bottom out sometime in

January (the weakest value for a five-year national average between 2006 and 2011 occurs on January 10th at -54H), then fluctuate through spring and early summer. The strongest level seen in the five-year national average for 2006 through 2011 was in early August at about -20U, to give you an idea of the range of basis values that are typical for the corn market. When you start to see large portions of the cash grain market start bidding significantly weaker than -50 basis or significantly stronger than -20 basis, it's a signal of something unusually bearish or bullish happening in the physical grain market.

At the end of the day, end users will be buying grain and farmers will be selling grain at a flat price. They'll write or receive a check based on that flat price, so there can be some insulation from either basis movements or futures movements if one offsets the other. To someone who cares about flat price, it doesn't really matter whether $6.00 is the mathematical result of $5.80 futures and +20 basis ... or $6.20 futures and -20 basis. Merchandisers can sometimes use that to their advantage and shade their basis bids when futures prices rise. On the other hand, if their bid of -15 doesn't quite make a $6.00 target price for a farmer, sometimes they can push the basis a little to reach a flat price trigger.

That phenomenon has led to an enduring piece of conventional wisdom in the grain markets – that basis tends to get stronger when futures prices fall, and vice versa. A statistical examination of the data shows that relationship doesn't really exist, however, at least not on a large or long-term scale. Taking the daily percentage changes in a grain market's futures price over the past five years, and comparing that to the daily percentage changes in the market's national average basis level, there is no statistically significant correlation.

In fact, during periods of supply shortage when basis bids start to get especially hot, the strength of those bids tends to get stronger and stronger at the same time as futures prices rise higher and higher. If we isolate just those periods of time when national average corn basis bids are positive (late 2011, for example), the correlation between daily basis changes and daily futures returns is very nearly +1.0. When grain becomes scarce, eager buyers express their eagerness in every way available to them.

So beware any too-trite rules of thumb about how basis "should" move. It will be helpful to know what the seasonal basis patterns are in your own locality, and even more helpful to know what supply & demand factors affect your local end users, but each marketing year can behave differently than the ones before it. This means there are a lot of chances for farmers to leave money on the table by not properly timing basis sales ... which in turn means there are a lot of opportunities for somebody to make money by accurately trading basis movement ...

Merchandisers' Use of Futures

....

When Rosie received the first phone call of the day, the eastern sun was just creeping high enough to stop streaming through the elevator's one grimy window and cease illuminating the ever-present army of dancing dust motes. For the rest of this day, like every day of the past forty years, Rosie would sit perched on her office chair in the darkest, dustiest corner of the Grover Elevator feed store / merchandising office, not unlike a patient barn spider with a large, squat body and active, nimble fingers.

Her desk had always been her desk, even for those brief years in the 70's when Roy had still been alive and Rosie was just the secretary. Then Roy had died, and to the eternal consternation of her in-laws, Rosie had become the sole owner, manager, chief executive, and merchandiser of the Grover Elevator. Staying in business through the 80's, when nearly half her farmer customers had gone bankrupt and many of them had left her in the lurch for various feed bills, had been no picnic, but at the end of it all, Rosie had emerged solvent and shrewd and dedicated to the principles of disciplined hedging for all her grain trades.

Both the corn and soybean markets had been soft lately, and that was all anybody grew around Grover anymore, so Rosie hadn't been receiving many phone calls from farmers lately and she wasn't expecting any that morning. In fact, she was only halfway through the newspaper's crossword puzzle and didn't really enjoy being interrupted. So she growled, "Grover," into the phone's mouthpiece.

"Uh, hey, is this Rosie?"

"Yep."

"Hey, this is Jason over at the Mungus Elevator in Springfield. Uh, how are you doing today?"

"Well, I'm fine, Jason. How are things in Springfield?" Rosie cradled the phone against her shoulder as she scribbled the letters "S-N-E-E-R-S" into 17-across.

"Oh, fine. So, uh, we're gonna have some trucks over in your direction next month and I was wondering if maybe you had any heat-damaged corn or anything like that you're trying to get rid of."

"Hmmm. Nope, I don't think so. You know, we've got a feed mill here, so any heat-damaged corn we would have, we'd just get rid of on our own."

"Oh. Oh, well ... um, what kind of a value would you put on 30-day corn right now anyway?"

"Corn that you'd pick up here?"

"Yep. FOB Grover."

Rosie put down her pencil and swiveled her chair over to the wall where she could see the inventory diagram of all her bins. "Eh ... it doesn't really bother me to hang on to my corn for a few more months. Probably don't need to get rid of any right now."

"Oh."

Rosie rolled her eyes in the few seconds of silence, waiting for the kid to make the next move. "But just to help me out with my position, Jason, why don't you tell me what you'd value nearby corn FOB Grover at?"

"Oh, uh, I was thinking of bidding you -15H."

The more experienced merchandiser made little noises with her tongue against her teeth as she pretended to hesitate. She looked at the market spreads and her eyes gleamed. "I don't know. Like I said, we really don't have to get rid of any corn just now."

"Well, fifteen is the best I can make it worth for you."

"You don't have any push in that?"

"No, and think about it – how far away are you from Cedar Rapids? There can't be much of a way you can make it worth more than that trucking it all the way there yourself. I'm buying in for a previous sale, otherwise I probably couldn't make it worth that, either."

"Yeah, but Jason we grind up most of our corn and sell it out as feed, so the Cedar value doesn't really matter to me so much."

"Oh. OK, well if you change your mind ..."

Fearing he was really going to hang up the phone, Rosie finally went for it: "Hey, I tell you what. I've got my futures position all funny at the moment. If you can do that 30-day ship corn but write it up as -15K, I think I could spare you 20,000 bushels."

"Yeah! Ok, yeah, let's do that."

"You can write this up right now?"

"Yep, it'll be my contract number 8175 for 20,000 March bushels FOB Grover at -15K."

"Got it. 8175. Thanks, now just make sure those trucks show up."

"Yep, thanks, bye!"

Rosie hung up the phone and let a slow grin creep across her face. Kids.

But fifty miles away, when Jason wrote up the contract and showed it triumphantly to Dale, the Mungus elevator manager, there were no smiles. "You idiot! You just lost twelve cents on that trade!"

·········

The first golden rule of successful cash grain trading (a.k.a. merchandising) is that profit or loss should always be accounted as a function of basis. That is to say, Jason lost 12 cents on that trade because he bought March corn for -15K when it was only worth -27K ... not because he bought March corn for $4.85 when it was only worth $4.73. The second statement may also be true, but it's not the proper way to track performance in your head if you're a merchandiser.

There is no second, third, or fourth golden rule of merchandising. Each trade is unique and will require a unique combination of opportunity, relationship building, and negotiation. But there are some exceptions to that first rule. Some merchandisers in the grain industry will find themselves trading unusual commodities: wheat gluten, ethanol byproducts, organic barley, beet pulp, etc. Because there are no standardized futures markets for those commodities, there is no perfect way to hedge long or short positions in those markets. There may be some imperfect ways to hedge – for instance, soybean meal may be a rough substitute for cottonseed meal and the two markets should have some positive correlation, so a long position in one could sort of hedge a short position in the other. But in practice, there is no perfect benchmark futures-minus-cash-equals-basis for beet pulp. Those merchandisers have little choice but to buy and sell those specialized commodities using flat prices only.

Another exception to the basis trading regime is the independent elevators and grain dealers who actually choose to do cash speculation in the grain markets. However, the number of traders who do that is vanishingly small because they all tend to get wiped out by bankruptcy sooner or later. I can only think of one tiny elevator manager in a five-state area who I know doesn't use futures hedges, but instead just buys grain when he thinks prices are cheap and sells when he thinks prices are high (assuming he hasn't bankrupted already, also).

Think about why that's a terrible idea. You might believe there is a reliable pattern of grain being "cheap" at harvest and higher priced the following March, and if you owned a 100,000-bushel elevator, you might plan to fill it up in October with flat priced purchases and empty it out in March with a flat priced sale, and live off the profit. Here's how your plan's profit and loss (P/L) would have performed in the real historical corn market:

Year	October price	Price next March	Trade P/L
2000	$2.06	$2.03	-$3,000
2001	$2.05	$2.02	-$3,000
2002	$2.48	$2.36	-$12,000
2003	$2.47	$3.20	$73,000
2004	$2.02	$2.13	$11,000
2005	$1.96	$2.36	$40,000
2006	$3.20	$3.74	$54,000
2007	$3.75	$5.67	$192,000
2008	$4.01	$4.05	$4,000
2009	$3.66	$3.45	-$21,000
2010	$5.82	$6.93	$111,000
2011	$6.01	$6.44	$43,000
2012	$7.39	$6.95	-$44,000

So usually, it would work and sometimes it would like a charm. There really is reliable seasonality in the grain markets. However, that "reality" ignored the operating costs, shrink, taxes, depreciation, and interest cost of paying for 100,000 bushels of grain for four months. In most years, that income stream from that kind of upfront investment wouldn't impress any rational investor. More importantly, it would only take one bad year to get your creditors breathing down your neck. Whether a $21,000 loss in 2009 would be bad enough to trigger bankruptcy, who knows, but it's the unpredictable possibility that *some year* you could lose a spectacular amount which makes it a truly bad idea. No one has ever built a company the size of Cargill or ADM or Bunge by trying to outguess the direction of futures markets.

Rather than cash speculation, most merchandisers use two other types of cash grain trades: **back-to-back transactions** or basis trades. I've used some examples of back-to-back trades in the previous sections of this book, like when a merchandiser would buy soybeans from a farmer then sell those soybeans to a processing plant for ten cents per bushel more. In reality, he does this as two basis trades (e.g. buying from the farmer at -60H and selling to the processor for -50H), but however the accounting is done, it's a very clear arbitrage. The two transactions are done as close to simultaneously as possible – as soon as the merchandiser has hung up the phone with the farmer, he immediately gets back on the phone to offset the long soybean position with an equivalent sale. If he hesitates, he runs the risk of the basis market changing. Yet he's able to make a profit on this trade because of his mix & blend opportunities at the elevator or simply because he has better knowledge of the market or a better negotiating position than the farmer does. As soon as the trade is made, he knows what his profit will be and it will never be more than that, although it could be *less* if something about the physical grain goes awry.

Back-to-back transactions are a very low-risk method of trading grain. You'd never do a back-to-back trade unless there was some profit in it, so you'll never lose money on the math from those transactions. On the other hand, you might not make *enough* money to pay for your operating costs and salaries and taxes and depreciation, either. So an elevator could still theoretically go bankrupt if all it ever does is make back-to-back trades.

Besides, what's the fun in that? The real joy of being a trader is to actually *trade* something – to master a market and know when it's appropriate to take some risk and reap some reward. There is plenty of risk in handling physical grain, and speculating on flat prices may be an elevator's path toward financial ruin, but there is a variable in the market that can be reliably traded: basis itself!

I've heard frustrated farmers exclaim that basis is meaningless and totally random anyway, so why should anybody pay attention to it, anyhow. Nothing could be further from the truth. Basis is a predictable, tradeable expression of seasonal or regional supply and demand. Because basis is variable, that means it can be traded.

And that's exactly what cash grain merchandisers (a.k.a. "basis traders") do. All a merchandiser's tasks – originating grain, selling grain, transporting grain – are done as a function of basis and as a means to arbitrage one basis value against another. All grain accounting can be represented as basis values, with the futures markets a hidden layer underneath that and the flat price implied from both. An elevator's corn position might be represented like this:

Springfield Co-op	Inventory	Jun / Jul	Aug / Sep	Oct / Nov	Dec / Jan	Feb / Mar
Corn Bushels	2,000	5,000	-15,000	24,000	-100,000	-300,000
Price	-15K	-12N	-10U	-27Z	-20H	-17H
Current Value	-14K	-10N	-10U	-15Z	-15H	-15H
Premium Gain / Loss	$20	$100	0	$2,880	-$5,000	-$6,000

To get the current financial value of that position marked-to-market at any point in time, all you would have to do is input the present values of the May (K), July (N), September (U), December (Z), and March (H) corn futures contracts. For instance, if the May contract was currently trading at $5.00, the current value of the 2,000 bushels in inventory would be $9,720 (($5.00 - $0.14) x 2,000). However, the elevator bought in those bushels at an average price of -15K ($9,700), so there is a penny of profit ($20) in the inventory. As long as the long physical grain position is perfectly hedged with an equivalent short futures position, it won't matter what the futures market does. It can go to $4.00 or $6.00 and there will still always be a penny of profit between -15K and -14K.

Profit is made or lost according to how the current basis value of the market (in a given region for a given time period) compares to the basis value where the merchandiser bought or sold the grain in her position. The Springfield Co-op can expect to book some profit at harvest because it is able to buy grain from farmers at a -27Z basis value, when in fact it can make that grain worth -15Z during that same timeframe. It is also currently facing a marked-to-market loss in the Dec-Jan and Feb-Mar timeframes because it previously sold hundreds of thousands of bushels of corn (at -20H and -17H) but the basis market has strengthened since then (now -15H). When you sell a commodity and then the price of that commodity increases, you will lose money as you 'buy in' to offset your position.

Now you can begin to see why it's critically important for merchandisers to hedge their cash grain positions with futures and to only be traders of the basis itself. It gives them the freedom to master the actual supply and demand of the grain markets without living in fear of the futures markets diving in one direction or the other. There are enough ways to lose money buying or selling grain at the wrong basis level, or by mishandling the physical grain, without adding a futures market gamble into the mix.

That indifference to the futures price creates a nice symbiosis for merchandisers and farmers, or merchandisers and end users. Consideration of the actual flat price of the grain becomes divorced from the typical buy-low / sell-high trader mentality. A merchandiser is just as happy to buy your corn at $5.85 per bushel (if that's $6.00 futures and -15 basis) as she is to buy your corn at $4.85 per bushel (if that's $5.00 futures and identical basis). Similarly, she's as pleased to sell a train full of corn at $5.00 per bushel (at option the futures) as she would be to sell it at $6.00 per bushel (at identical basis). This is great, because it never puts the merchandiser in a position to haggle her customers – neither buyers nor sellers – out of making a profit. At their best, merchandisers truly can be supportive advisors to their customers' business.

There are really only two ways that the underlying value of the futures market affects a cash grain merchandiser's position. And the merchandiser herself only has control over one of those: the threat of an imperfect hedge. The example cash grain position above has a couple values that aren't perfectly divisible by 5,000: the 2,000 bushels in inventory and the 24,000 bushels at harvest. In order to perfectly hedge those positions, the merchandiser couldn't use just full-size futures contracts (5,000 bushels), but would also have to sell mini futures (1,000 bushels). In reality, a grain inventory in a bin or a spot sale off a truck could be much weirder numbers: a perfect 60,000-lb truck load, for instance, would actually be 1,071.43 bushels of 56-lb corn. To keep track of how long or how short a grain position gets over time isn't hard, but it requires a lot of discipline. Each merchandiser just has to keep the concept of hedging firmly in mind:

Buy Grain -> Sell Futures

Sell Grain -> Buy Futures

Especially if there is a team of merchandisers all trading a grain position together at the same time, the best way to keep track of those hedges is to use a **"T" account**, which could look like this:

CASH	FUTURES
Buy 1071.43 bushels (Joe Smith)	**Sell 1 mini corn ($5.00)**
Buy 20,000 bushels (Gary Green)	*Sell 4 corn ($5.01)*
Sell 25,000 bushels (Ethanol plant)	**Buy 5 corn ($5.04)**
Buy 2,546.25 bushels (Grover Elevator)	*Sell 2 mini corn ($5.04)*

Net: +617.68 bushels

For the nice, even values (the 20,000 bushel purchase and the 25,000 bushel sale), the merchandisers were able to perfectly hedge those cash transactions with exactly equivalent amounts of exposure, in exactly opposite directions, on the futures market. For the cash transactions with more awkward values, they still made offsetting futures transactions, but they just weren't a perfect match. At the end of the day, the merchandisers bought 617.68 bushels more than they were able to perfectly offset with futures positions. A lot of elevators or grain companies won't even hassle with mini futures because they make enough cash transactions to eventually end up near a 5,000 bushel number anyway. But regardless of whether they round to the nearest 1,000 bushels or nearest 5,000 bushels, they will invariably end up with some amount of unhedged exposure. In this instance, that's equivalent to cash speculating on 617.68 long bushels. If the corn futures market drops from $5.04 to $4.64 overnight, it would result in a $247 loss (617.68 x $0.40). That may not sound like a lot of money, but this is a deliberately small example. One does not want to have that happen to a significantly larger unhedged sum, so it's important for merchandisers to be accurate and immediate with their offsetting hedges.

The example was not only deliberately small; it was also grossly oversimplified. In reality, the merchandisers would be simultaneously trading commodities and making hedges with a variety of different markets in a variety of different timeframes. The hedging also might not be recorded in one single log like this, but rather as a collection of individual "T" sheets. As long as the actual hedging is done consistently and correctly, there can be some latitude in the record-keeping, and merchandisers can still minimize their exposure to futures price movement.

So the last remaining reason why a grain trading company would even care about how high or low the grain futures prices get is a more esoteric, financial one. If you put up margin money for futures hedges, or borrow money to buy cash grain, or defer income on grain you own, or worry about the counterparty risk of someone not paying you for grain, all of those things make you care deeply about the **time-value of money**, and they make your lending partners care about the underlying value of your goods. It's relatively easier to explain to your banker that you lost 10,000 bushels of $3.00 corn (because of quality losses or a counterparty's failure to perform) than that you lost 10,000 bushels of $6.00 corn. And obviously, the conversation gets increasingly difficult as the scales of volume or price increase.

It's not just an awkward conversation. The real overhead costs of trading increase when commodity companies must pay interest on higher-valued commodities. In general, commercial lending to commodity trading firms is considered a highly favorable banking activity – *because* the firms are trading basis rather than futures and have hedged most of their price risk – and grain companies get relatively cheap interest rates as a result. But in periods of the greatest market volatility or especially high prices, interest costs do rise. Merchandisers may be indifferent to futures prices, but merchandising *companies* aren't entirely apathetic about the markets.

To the individual merchandiser who doesn't have to engage with the company's finance department very frequently, there is still another way that the time-value of money affects their trading. A merchandiser might buy grain in October and sell that grain in March because the seasonal trend is for basis to appreciate during that timeframe, but even if futures fell during that timeframe and basis stayed exactly flat, the merchandiser could still make money by owning grain those four months ... because of **carry.**

Carry is the real magic of the grain industry. Recall that futures spreads tend to be positive (deferred contracts are typically worth a higher value than nearby contracts) because the market reimburses owners of grain for storing that grain from one timeframe to the next. Well, who do you think pockets that reimbursement? Anyone who owns a grain storage facility, that's who.

Farmers can take advantage of the carry structure of the market by keeping their grain off the market for a few months, but the real beneficiaries are the commercial grain companies who buy and store giant quantities of grain, then ship out that grain and turn around and store a new collection of grain in the same space. The market "pays" for space, so the degree to which a merchandiser can keep her elevator full of grain and earning money is the degree to which she will capture value from the market's typical carry structure.

Of course, the reason the market must pay for space is that space actually costs something. The trick is not only to capture the futures market's carry structure, but for that value to be more than it actually costs to store the grain for that time period. Think of what it really takes to store grain after harvest between December and March. You've got to own some physical structure (depreciation cost and taxes) and insure it and employ some people to maintain the structure itself and the grain contained within. On top of all that, the grain itself will **shrink** once you put it in a bin and let the moisture escape. If the rule of thumb at your facility is that grain shrinks 1%, then the loss of 1% of the grain's original value is part of the cost of storing that grain. Shrink losses vary by the type of grain being stored and how wet it is when put into storage. Those losses will be higher right after harvest than they will be once the grain has already dried down, so in reality, storage rates are variable. For a benchmark, the KCBOT uses a standard storage rate for wheat of $0.00296 per bushel per day between July 1 and November 30, then $0.00197 from December 1 to June 30. Basically, figure $0.06 per bushel per month, although different varieties of grain will respond differently to storage.

In addition to the actual costs of shrink and physically storing the grain, there is also the interest cost of deferring the income. For example, with 100,000 bushels of wheat worth $5.00 per bushel in three months' time, if the risk-free interest rate was presently 5%, by waiting that long to receive the income you'd be giving up the opportunity to earn over $6,000 of interest on that capital.

The full **cost of carry** is therefore the sum of the real storage costs and the interest costs of keeping grain off the market for a specified period of time. With the examples we just used, we could say the full cost of carry was $0.08 per bushel per month. Now the question becomes whether the futures market's carry structure reimburses that value or not.

For example, it's not uncommon for the May Kansas City wheat futures contract to be priced about 10 cents higher than the March futures contract. Two months of time pass between the March contract's expiration and the May contract's expiration, so that March-May spread is equivalent to 5 cents per month of carry. Five cents per month is 62.5% of 8 cents per month, so we could say the market is offering 62.5% of the full cost of carry to keep wheat off the market during that timeframe. If that's an adequate reimbursement for their costs, commercial grain companies would opt to earn those 10 cents per bushel on as many bushels as they could get their hands on. It won't matter whether the entire futures market rises or falls during that time period; as long as their physical grain position is hedged and as long as the spread between the March and May futures contracts remains that wide, they will be able to book those profits.

For a grain company, whose business it is to store grain and make a marginal profit on each bushel, the carry structure is a critical factor in the decision of when to finally release those bushels onto the market. Obviously, if the futures spread structures become inverted (deferred futures contracts are worth less than nearby futures, which would be unusual), it's a signal that there is no additional value to storing the grain until a later date and that the market urgently requires the grain. But carry calculations are not only an important factor in the buy/sell decision for a specific commodity, they also guide a merchandiser's decisions about which commodities deserve the most space. Should an elevator store more corn or soybeans or wheat for the next three months? Which will pay the best return on the space?

The difference between futures contract prices – the spread – is therefore far more important to a merchandiser than the actual contract prices themselves. If March and May futures contracts were exactly 11 cents apart, that would be more meaningful to a merchandiser than knowing the nearby futures price was exactly $5.01 ½ per bushel.

That's what the merchandiser, Jason, failed to consider in the story above. Although grain bids and offers for different timeframes are expressed as basis according to the closest futures contract month (corn for February delivery is bid off the March contract; corn for November delivery is bid off the December contract, etc.), the same basis value off different contract months won't result in an equivalent cash bid. If the carry between March and May futures happened to be 12 cents wide, then a bid of -15K would be 12 cents stronger than a bid of -15H. You can always express a nearby bid in terms of a deferred contract, and in fact, calculating that equivalency is an important part of understanding the true carry spreads being offered on the *cash* market – i.e. the true return to space for storing a cash commodity and selling it in a later timeframe. For the table below, assume the March-to-May futures spread is 8 cents wide and the May-to-July futures spread is 6 cents wide:

Month	Offer	Equivalent nearby offer	Cash market carry (1 month)	Cash market carry (accumulative)
Jan	-9H	-9H	--	--
Feb	-5H	-5H	9-5 = 4 cents	4 c
Mar	-2H	-2H	5-2 = 3 cents	7 c
Apr	-6K	-6 + 8 = +2H	2+2 = 4 cents	11 c
May	-4K	-4 + 8 = +4H	4 -2 = 2 cents	13 c
Jun	-8N	-8 + 8 + 6 = +6H	6 -4 = 2 cents	15 c
Jul	-5N	-5 + 8 + 6 = +9H	9 -6 = 3 cents	18 c

So by choosing to store corn six months and bringing it to market in July rather than January, the owner of that corn who is hedged with short futures not only gets a better basis *number* (-5N rather than -9H) but actually earns 18 cents more for the cash corn. That works out to 3 cents per month, which is actually a little less generous than the carry on the futures market (3.5 cents per month), but those cash bids are the real prices available. If the owner can store the corn more cheaply than 3 cents per month for the next six months, he should do so and wait until July to move the corn. On the other hand, if his real costs of carrying grain are higher than 3 cents per month, he won't want to wait past February.

The key here of course is for the owner of the grain to be hedged with short futures so that if the entire direction of the corn market turns bearish, any losses on the cash market will be reimbursed by gains in his futures account, and he will still receive the difference in futures contract prices each time he rolls his futures hedge from one contract timeframe to the next. A merchandiser may hedge grain against the contract month when he intends to move the grain, but he can always change his mind or just always keep his present inventory hedged against the nearby month.

Recall that when speculative index funds roll their long futures exposure from one nearby contract month to the next, they typically lose money because of the positive carry structure of grain futures markets (July contracts are typically higher priced than May contracts, which are typically higher priced than March contracts, etc.). Well, their loss is a commercial hedger's gain: when a farmer or grain merchandising company rolls its short hedges, it buys out of the cheaper market (nearby) and simultaneously sells back into the higher priced contract (deferred) and therefore "captures the carry." That's real cash money they get to book from their futures account, not offset by anything other than the actual physical costs of storing grain.

It's not my intention to turn this chapter into a primer on high-pressure sales techniques or old-fashioned horse trading tricks, although such wisdom probably has a place in the merchandising world. Rather, I'll just end by relaying some basic principles of merchandising which, in conjunction with earning carry from the market, show how grain companies really make their money.

Unless a merchandiser has the luxury of working somewhere simple that never ships its own grain, then without a doubt the biggest use of merchandisers' time is wrangling trucks or trains or barges or containers or whatever freight provider they happen to use. That's because in addition to identifying whatever market arbitrage opportunities are available, the merchandiser can also arbitrage the freight costs themselves as he gets the grain where it needs to go.

He can only do this by "buying FOB" and "selling delivered." That is to say, he needs to buy the grain Free On Board at its origin, take ownership of it there, be responsible for transporting it wherever it needs to go, and once it gets there, to transfer ownership at its destination. It's possible to buy delivered (he would only receive ownership of the grain once it was transported to its destination) or to sell FOB (to transfer ownership at its origin and let somebody else do the freight). But if a merchandiser does either of those things, he gives up the opportunity to arbitrage the freight. That's because the math for buying FOB and selling delivered looks like this:

Buy 1,000 bushels corn FOB Gary Green's farm @ -25H
...
Trucking between Gary Green's farm & Springfield Ethanol = 15 cents
...
Sell 1,000 bushels corn Delivered Springfield Ethanol @ -10H

With that back-to-back math, there is zero profit in the trade for the merchandiser. His opportunity now is to somehow get the freight costs cheaper than 15 cents per bushel. If he can hire a truck to move that corn for only 10 cents per bushel, he will have made 5 cents per bushel of pure profit. The same arithmetic is at work for rail freight, barge freight, ocean freight, containerized freight ... anything, and for any commodity (not just grain).

There are various methods of acquiring freight more cheaply than the going market rate. Commodity trading companies may simply negotiate with a freight provider (railroad, trucking company, etc.) and get discounts for large volumes of business. They may also speculate in the freight markets themselves and book "cheap" freight in advance when prices seem undervalued. But the most elegant way to reduce the freight costs between a commodity load's origin and its destination is to use **backhauls** to make the full round trip more valuable for each mile.

The market's freight spread between Gary Green's farm and Springfield Ethanol might be 15 cents because the two points are 75 miles apart and a truck would have to make a 150-mile round trip, at $1.00 per mile, to drive empty out to Gary's farm, pick up the corn, and then haul it back to Springfield. But if that truck were able to earn something for hauling a different commodity on the way out to Gary's farm (e.g. ethanol byproducts to a nearby feedlot, or rock to a nearby highway project), then of the total $150 cost of the round trip, maybe the corn leg would only account for half of that cost. The price spread for grain between any two locations is generally defined by the transportation cost between those two locations, and a cross-country arbitrageur can only capture a profit from that spread if he can transport the grain for a price lower than that. Freight negotiation may be one strategy for getting relatively cheaper grain transportation, but identifying backhaul opportunities is the more effective, profitable strategy.

Incidentally, if the cost of fuel goes up or down, or the supply & demand of trucking labor changes, those per-mile calculations will also change. So add freight market prices to the list of things merchandisers have to keep up-to-date on at all times. They need to be building relationships with all their customers (buyers and sellers); managing their freight providers; always conscious of the futures spread values; and always aware of the current basis values in all their markets. By the time some old merchandisers retire, they will have forgotten more about a particular region's trucking routes and a particular ethanol plant's idiosyncrasies than you or I will ever know.

Blessedly, the one thing they don't have to worry about (much) is the futures price. They can leave that particular headache to the producers, end users, and speculators.

Not a Zero Sum Game

Merchandisers may be neutral about what futures price they use to hedge their cash grain positions, but the people and businesses who must actually produce or consume that grain certainly feel strongly about prices. A farmer's profit – the very salary from which he must support his family – is determined by the price he receives for his grain. Similarly, the input costs for every flour mill, feedlot, and ethanol plant are determined by how cheaply they can source grain.

So to some extent, if one commercial business makes money from a futures hedge, another commercial business on the other side of that hedge is losing that exact same quantity of money. Here's an example how futures trading plays into real economic profit or loss:

- Gary Green sells a cash forward contract for 5,000 bushels of soybeans at harvest for $9.00 per bushel to the Springfield Co-op.
- To offset the purchase of 5,000 bushels in the October timeframe, the Springfield Co-op immediately sells one November soybean futures contract at $9.50.
- Eventually, the Springfield Co-op sells those beans as part of a larger, 50,000-bushel package to a soybean processor, profiting from the basis trade. Let's say the sale is made at -30K when the May futures are trading at $8.30 per bushel, so the flat price on the trade is $8.00 per bushel. When the Co-op makes the sale, they must offset it by buying futures contracts. To prevent any slippage between where the contract is written and where the futures trade really gets filled, the Co-op and the processor trade futures contracts with an **Exchange of Futures for Cash, a.k.a. Exchange for Physicals (EFP)**. The 10 soybean futures contracts, in this example, will be processed by the futures

exchange for the two trading parties' accounts, but at a pre-agreed price (the market price at the time of the basis trade) that won't affect the rest of the futures market's bids and asks. During that futures exchange, the processor sold 10 soybean futures contracts to offset 10 previously-established long positions. Let's say those long positions had been bought when the soybean futures market was trading at $9.00 per bushel, as a hedge against potentially even higher input costs. So the processor just bought 50,000 bushels of soybeans at a cash price of $8.00 per bushel (they will write a check for $400,000), and it fully booked a hedge loss of $1.00 per bushel in its futures account (another $50,000). Those beans effectively cost the processor $9.00 per bushel once all the trading was done.

Most end users are also able to hedge their products, not just their inputs. In this example, the soybean processor probably also sold soybean meal and soybean oil futures contracts at the same time it was buying those $9.00 soybean futures. It would have hedged not just its input costs, but its entire soybean **crush margin**.

Regardless, the example demonstrates how the decisions of real economic participants in the grain markets affect futures activity. Any time a farmer chooses to lock in a price for grain, whether he does it via his own independent futures hedge or via a forward contract, there will be some downward **pressure** on the futures market (some volume of selling activity). One way or another, somebody is going to sell equivalent futures exposure at that time, even if it's not the farmer himself but rather the merchandiser who's hedging his purchase.

Equally, any time an end user chooses to lock in a price for grain, there will be some upward **support** for the futures market (some volume of buying activity). Selling and buying activity from market-neutral merchandisers may not be price sensitive, but overall, futures prices really reflect the grain market's economic reality in this way. When prices get high enough to compel producers to sell grain at a profit, selling volume will exert pressure against a further rise in prices. When prices get low enough to compel end users to buy grain at a projected profit, their buying volume will exert upward support against a further drop in prices.

Of course, we know participation in the futures markets isn't limited to commercial producers and end users; speculators are also welcome to buy and sell contracts. **Support / pressure** from speculators' volume of buying or selling is also important to price behavior, but it's relatively harder to pin down.

$8 beans may be bad (unprofitable) for farmers and good (cheap) for poultry feeders, while $14 beans may be good (profitable) for farmers and bad (expensive) for poultry feeders. Between those two sections of the futures market, you can directly pencil out who is "winning" and who is "losing" at any point in time (and they may both be profitable at the same time). But there's no equivalent way to do that for speculators. $8 beans are good for bullish speculators *if* the market moves higher later. $14 beans could also be good for bullish speculators *if* the market moved even higher than that. Those traders have no underlying profit calculation - just the estimation of what direction the market will take in the future.

Therefore, the net result of all grain futures trade doesn't necessarily result in an equal number of winners and losers. A farmer may have a hedge loss of $1 per bushel in his futures trading account, and somewhere else in the market, there *may* be an end user with a $1 hedge gain in its futures account. On the other hand, the buyer on the other side of that farmer's sale *could* have been a bearish speculator who was closing out a losing position. It *could* have been a bullish speculator who benefits penny-for-penny as the farmer's position loses penny-by-penny. There is no way to know in the anonymous amalgamation of the futures markets.

Just remember that philosophically, even if the bullish speculator benefits penny-for-penny as the farmer accumulates a hedge loss, both parties are gaining something from that transaction. The speculator gained an opportunity to take on risk and potentially receive financial reward. The farmer got the benefit of removing risk from his operation and knowing what stable price he will receive for his production, no matter what the crazy futures market does in the meantime.

CHAPTER 5
Futures Strategies and Derivatives

At its simplest, a successful futures trading strategy doesn't need to be any more complicated than correctly anticipating the bullish or bearish movement of a market and making a corresponding purchase or sale. To keep the math simple, let's say I had just sold 2 soybean futures contracts (representative of 10,000 bushels of soybeans). In the time it has taken me to write this paragraph, the soybean market has just dropped two cents. I would have just made $200 ... and all for doing nothing but sitting around for two minutes. I didn't create any economic value for the world; all I really did was guess an outcome correctly.

Ideally, I would have had a good reason for shorting the soybean market and would have been *trading* rather than *guessing*. Either way, experienced traders will tell you the exit of a futures trade is just as important as the entry. Should I take the money and run, or wait and see what happens next? At what level of profit will my disciplined sense of trading spur me to offset the trade? More importantly, at what level of loss would I abandon the trade, to prevent continued losses and live to fight another day? Doubling down on each loss may work (eventually) at a blackjack table, but it's a surefire recipe for bankruptcy in a leveraged futures market.

How you choose to select your entry points and target profit levels or loss-limit levels, along with your selection of tools to keep that discipline, will be the hallmarks of your own personal trading system. Whether you choose to use technical analysis, fundamental market news, phases of the moon, or rolls of the dice to guide your system is beyond the purview of this chapter. Rather, it's meant to be a guide to the trading tools available.

The strategy involved in executing a simple long or short trade in grain futures isn't very complex:

- <u>Define your goals and limits</u> – Perhaps you've analyzed that November soybeans, currently trading at $14.00 per bushel are overvalued in relation to corn and theoretically could drop $2.00 per bushel to re-establish a historical norm. But you're not willing to risk more than $500 on this trading idea. You could short the soybean market with a target of taking profits when the price reaches $12.00, and an intention to limit your losses if the price rises to $14.10.
- <u>Enter the position</u> – Sell a November soybean futures contract at $14.00. You can set up your goals and limits to be automatically executed, using a limit buy order at $12.00 (the order to buy at that lower level won't be executed until the market reaches that level) and a buy stop order at $14.10.
- <u>Exit the position</u> – Once the market hits either $12.00 or $14.10, your short position will be offset by one or the other of your good-til-cancelled buy orders. You'll either be $10,000 richer or $500 poorer, although there's no telling how long it will take for either outcome to materialize. Remember to cancel the unfilled limit order or stop order.

There's no law requiring you to bracket your position with automatic exit points, but it's often easier for a trader to stay disciplined about his goals and limits with those orders in place. He could, of course, just sell the $14 beans and tell himself, "Well, I'll just see how this goes." He could wake up a few days later and discover the market rallied 70 cents overnight while he was sleeping. Alternatively, weeks could go by with increasing levels of profit in his trading account, and he could keep thinking "Hmm ... maybe I should just take this profit," only to watch it all vanish after a few moments of indecision. Stop orders are particularly important, in my opinion, for limiting losses, but they can also be useful to lock in profits. **Trailing stops** can be placed just over or under a market's current level to prevent a profitable position from backsliding. There are no commission costs associated with stop orders until they are filled, so feel free to move them around as the market changes.

Without using any instruments more sophisticated than long and short futures positions, there's another trading strategy that allows you to profit from your analysis of the grain markets. A **spread trade** is a form of pure arbitrage: it involves one short position that is simultaneously offset by a long position in the same market. However, what is meant by 'in the same market' can vary. Buying March corn while simultaneously selling May corn is a spread trade. So is buying Minneapolis wheat futures while simultaneously selling Kansas City wheat futures. So is buying palm oil traded on the Chicago futures exchange while simultaneously selling palm oil futures in Malaysia. It can get more abstract than that: buying corn and selling soybeans is a spread trade because even though those two trades may not seem like they're in the same market, in fact they are closely related by some of the same customers (animal feeders) and the same producers (farmers).

The beauty of a spread trade is its theoretically lower risk of loss. As one price level rises or falls, the price level of any other asset *in that same market* should also theoretically rise or fall to roughly the same degree. If the whole market goes up, for instance, you will lose money on the short position half of your spread trade, but you will simultaneously make money on the long position half of the trade.

The trick, of course, is to make relatively more money than you lose. To do that, you don't really need to know what direction the entire market will take (you can be **market neutral**), but you need to accurately predict how the **spread** between the two assets will change. March and May corn futures could go from being 5 cents apart to being 10 cents apart as the predicted supply of spring corn increases, for instance. Demand for high protein spring wheat could become much stronger than the demand for hard red winter wheat, and the spread between Minneapolis and Kansas City wheat futures could correspondingly widen. Maybe you identified an inefficient price difference between U.S. and Malaysian palm oil futures that can't be entirely explained away by currency differences. A spread trade arbitrage would take advantage of any of those observations.

Trading **crush margins** is a very specific type of spread trading. These are the hedges that actual ag processors use to lock in the gross processing margins between buying raw materials and selling processed materials, but because they can use the spreads between futures contracts as a proxy for their margins, speculators are also free to use those spreads to anticipate how the industry may grow more or less profitable over time. The classic example is the soybean crush: 1 bushel of soybeans (60 lbs) yields about 44 pounds of soybean meal, 11 pounds of soybean oil, 4 pounds of hulls and 1 pound of waste. These numbers are subject to the protein level of the beans and meal as well as the processing plant's idiosyncrasies. That means a soybean processor can lock in upcoming profit margins by buying 10 soybean futures contracts and simultaneously selling 11 soybean meal futures contracts and 9 soybean oil futures contracts. A speculative trader could either do that, if he felt the crush margin was likely to narrow, or do the opposite – sell soybeans futures and buy byproduct futures – if he felt the crush margin was likely to grow wider (more profitable) over time. The necessary ratios of meal and oil contracts to soybean contracts can change as the actual results of soybean **extrusion** changes.

Other crush margins in the ag industry include the ethanol crush: 1 bushel of corn yields about 2.8 gallons of ethanol and 18 pounds of dried distillers grain (also subject to change). The futures spread trade would be 10 corn futures contracts on one side (long or short) and 1 ethanol futures contract on the other side (short or long). Similarly, 1 bushel of soybeans produces about 1.5 gallons of biodiesel, but trading that crush margin with heating oil futures, for instance, isn't very common because it's not a perfect hedge for biodiesel. Another spread trade is the "cattle crush," which is a reflection of the profitability of feeding young animals for market. It would involve buying 1 feeder cattle futures contract and simultaneously buying 1 corn contract a few months further out and selling 2 live cattle futures contracts about six months out. Or vice versa. And the ratios of inputs (feeder cattle and feed) and product (live cattle) can change as your estimate for how much feed it takes to produce a pound of beef changes. It's also sometimes done as 3 corn and 4 feeder contracts against 8 live cattle contracts.[1]

Outside of the grain and agriculture world, there are other crush spreads like the "crack spread" that hedges 2 crude oil futures contracts against 1 gasoline and 1 heating oil contract. These are all examples of **intermarket** spread trades – spreads that have one side in one market and the other side in one or more slightly different markets. As spread trades go, these offer both considerable risk and considerable potential reward because two or more different futures markets can't always be expected to move in the same direction at the same time, thereby removing some of the assurance that as one side of the spread position loses value, the other side will gain an equivalent amount. The other great charm of spread trading – margin credits – is correspondingly more variable for intermarket spreads than for intramarket spreads.

Intramarket spread trades have both their sides all within one market: for instance, spreading July corn futures against December corn futures. These trades can also be called **calendar spreads**, and here's where the margin benefit really starts to add up. Because the futures exchanges are aware that some markets tend to move up or down together, especially the markets for any two months of the same commodity, they believe there is relatively less risk of loss in trading those spreads, and subsequently require relatively less upfront margin deposit for spread trades. For instance, if the exchange would require $5,000 initial margin to trade two corn futures contracts in the same direction ($2,500 each), it may only require $200 initial margin to buy one corn contract and simultaneously sell a different corn contract. They will require slightly more if the two contracts don't represent corn in the same marketing year, but it is still quite a benefit.

Don't let it lure you into false sense of security about spread trading, however. It's certainly possible for two contracts to move in different directions, even within the same commodity market. In 2011, 2012, and 2013, when the supplies of old crop corn started to become scarce in the spring and summer, it wasn't uncommon to see the nearby futures contracts (like July) trade higher by 10 or 20 cents on the same days as the new crop contracts (like December) were moving lower because the market anticipated bearish production in the upcoming year. If someone had entered a **bull spread** trade (buying a nearby month and selling a deferred month), he would have received a nice profit as that unusual situation developed. But if someone had entered a **bear spread** trade (selling a nearby month and buying a deferring month), it wouldn't have taken very long to blow through the tiny initial margin requirement and start losing serious money. *There is no* *guarantee that spread trading is less risky than outright long or short positions.*

Between grain contracts within the same marketing year, however, spreads are theoretically limited by a fundamental relationship – the **cost of carry**. Remember that the full cost of commercial carry is how much someone would have to spend to store grain for a certain period of time, inclusive of physical costs (leases, labor, grain shrink loss, etc.) and the interest cost of deferred income. The true cost changes over time and depends on the underlying value of the grain, and therefore needs to be calculated anew any time you use it as the justification for a spread trade. But for simplicity's sake, let's say we made those calculations and today the cost to carry one bushel of corn for one month is $0.07.

The market may offer to reimburse owners of corn any proportion of that cost, anywhere from 0% to 100%. If the March corn contract is priced higher or equal to the May contract (which would be unusual), there would be no economic benefit to "carrying" that corn forward for two months. More typically, if the March contract was 10 cents cheaper than the May contract, then there would be some motivation to store the grain, and we could say the extra ten cents of deferred income represents 71% of the full cost of commercial carry ($0.10 ÷ (2 months x $0.07)). The crucial thing to understand is that the market should *never offer more than 100% of full commercial carry*. Commercial grain companies could rack up giant risk-free profits if they could deliver grain two months out for more than it would cost them to store it. Arbitrage would keep that from happening because market participants would exert selling pressure against any irrationally-wide carry spread. If you ever calculate the carry spread between two grain futures contracts in the same marketing year to be more than 100% of the full cost of commercial carry ... something is funky. It's probably that your calculation of commercial carry costs are off from what the big grain companies are actually assuming their costs to be, otherwise they'd be arbitraging the heck out of that spread.

That's why, in a market with carry structure, a bull spread trade has theoretically limited risk. If you buy a nearby contract and sell a deferred contract in the same marketing year, your best case scenario would be for the two contracts' prices to move closer together, i.e. for the spread between those two contracts to narrow, i.e. for the carry to weaken. You would want the price of the nearby contract to rise relatively more or fall relatively less than the price of the deferred contract, because that is how you would see the one winning half of your spread trade earn more profit than the losing half of the spread trade. It doesn't matter if the whole grain market goes up or down, just as long as the two contracts move in the same direction, but with one earning slightly more profit than the other.

Of course, you're not likely to earn very big profits in these calendar spread trades, which tend not to move more than few cents per week, unless you trade very large volumes. But a small potential reward can still be attractive when you consider that there is limited risk in a bull spread trade in a grain market. The worst thing that could happen to your position would be the spread widening, i.e. carry strengthening, and remember: a carry spread can only grow so wide: 100% of full commercial carrying costs. Then, arbitrage will rein it in. Consequently, if you enter the bull spread trade between March and May corn when there was 10 cents of carry between the two contracts, and full commercial carry is estimated at 14 cents, you might feel confident you won't lose more than 4 cents per bushel on that trade.

On the other hand, there is unlimited theoretical risk of loss in a bear spread trade in the grain markets. Consider selling March corn futures and buying May corn futures when there is a +10 cent spread between them. The best you could hope on that trade would be for the spread to widen to 14 cents (a 4 cent profit), but if the opposite occurred – if May corn prices started to fall relatively faster than March corn prices, or if March corn prices started to rise relatively faster than May corn prices – you could lose more than just the 10 cents it would take to make the two contracts equivalent in price. If nearby supplies are very scarce, the market could adopt an inverted structure, and there is no theoretical limit to how much higher March corn could be priced than May corn. At the time of this writing, the largest inverted spread between the nearby corn contract than the second-month contract was -166 ½ cents between the May and July contracts on July 11, 2013. To anyone who went long on that spread at +10 cents, that would have been a loss of $1.76 ½ per bushel.

The people who have the best instincts for calendar spread trading in the grain markets are also the people who have access to the best information on commercial grain inventories and costs of carry: merchandisers themselves. Because they earn profit by storing grain and capturing carry from one month to the next, and because they must choose which months to buy or sell millions of bushels of grain or to enter or exit millions of bushels of futures hedges, you can imagine how miniscule changes to those calendar spreads can alter their profits. Carry in the futures markets gets a lot of attention on cash grain trading floors, and commercial grain merchandisers are the best spread traders there are. However, spreads aren't the only way that futures and their derivatives affect merchandisers' strategies.

Merchandiser Strategies

First, I would just like to reiterate that futures speculation is wildly inappropriate for merchandisers (basis traders). Merchandisers obviously have access to the futures markets to make hedges against their physical grain purchases and sales, and if nobody was watching a bored merchandiser's computer screen on a quiet afternoon, he theoretically *could* spend his time making little $200 day trades. But that would be the surest way for that merchandiser to get fired. Tick off a customer or make a bad basis trade, and he could probably be rehabilitated. Start using the company's money to speculate in futures? He would be out the door faster than you could say "stop order." Commercial grain companies base their entire operations on the known and manageable risks of basis trading – that's just what they do. But allowing exposure to the futures movement or flat price movement of grain would put their trading capital at vastly increased risk. There's a reason why hedge funds often blow out within a few years, but the ADMs and Bunges of the world have over a century of successful trading under their belts. And if some hotshot kid who got hired as a merchandiser thinks he can outguess the futures markets and wants to play spec trader with somebody else's money, well then why not relieve him of his position and let him go apply for that career?

As far as I know, this logic successfully permeates the minds of virtually all new merchandisers. I don't know any merchandiser who ever engaged in futures speculation outright, but even so, there can be unintentional exposure to the volatile futures markets. Let's say Jason wrote a forward cash contract with Gary Green to buy November corn at $5.00, or -30Z, because that was the Mungus elevator's posted basis bid, and at the time Gary asked for a flat price quote, December (Z) futures were trading at exactly $5.30. When Jason and Gary hang up the phone, Jason has committed the Mungus Grain Company to buy 10,000 bushels of physical corn at $5.00 per bushel. To lay off that long price risk, Jason will need to sell 2 December corn futures contracts. But let's say Jason is hungry, and the futures market has been quiet all morning. So he gets up from his desk, stretches a little, then goes to the elevator's break room to snack on some rhubarb coffee cake that one of the scale operators had brought in that day. He saunters back to his desk and figures he better make that futures hedge ... only to discover corn futures have nosedived 10 cents in the few minutes he postponed the hedge sale. The market had gotten wind of relatively increased estimates for Argentinean corn production, or something.

So now Jason has to sell $5.20 futures against a $5.00 cash purchase, which has effectively ruined his otherwise perfectly routine -30Z trade. Now it's a -20Z trade, a 10-cent per bushel loss in the accounting of his forward grain position. He may have some flexibility on his position statement regarding whether he wants to show that loss as a bad basis purchase (-20Z in a -30Z market) or whether he wants to show it as a futures loss, but either way, Jason's trip to the rhubarb coffee cake just cost the Mungus Grain Company $1,000 ($0.10 times 10,000 bushels). This is what is called futures slippage, and it emphasizes the importance of timely discipline for anyone in the futures market, even if the futures movement itself isn't what you are intending to trade.

So the only futures "strategy" a merchandiser will need is just to get his hedges made in a timely manner - instantaneously, if at all possible. On the other hand, there are a few different types of merchandising contracts, which allow some flexibility for the farmer and the merchandiser to select futures and flat prices:

Flat price contracts – These are the contracts we've been discussing all throughout this book so far. A buyer and a seller simultaneously agree on the present futures level and a basis level, and wrap all that information together in the flat price level of the grain being traded. The buyer knows exactly how much money he will pay per bushel of grain, and the seller knows exactly how much he will receive, plus or minus quality premiums or discounts.

Basis-only contracts – A cash grain contract may also be written with only the basis level negotiated between the buyer and seller. Because merchandisers make their profits exclusively by trading basis, and are mostly indifferent to the flat prices or underlying futures prices of their trades, this is a perfectly agreeable type of contract for them. Particularly if two fully-hedged commercial grain companies are trading between themselves (e.g. a co-op selling some spring grain to a terminal elevator), all their accounting of the market value of the trade will be done according to the basis level itself, and there is no particular reason to attach a futures level to the trade, until the time comes to actually transfer ownership of the grain. These can also be called "unpriced contracts." The NGFA has rules about giving the buyer the option of when to set the underlying futures price (and thus, the overall flat price) of any basis-only contract, but they are required to do so before anybody actually ships the grain.

Hedge-to-Arrive (**HTA**) contracts – Because basis levels have a seasonal pattern, a farmer may feel conflicted about selling grain too far in advance. In March, for instance, his elevator may be bidding a $5.00 flat price for grain in the upcoming harvest timeframe (October / November), but the $5.00 could be a reflection of $5.70 December futures and -70Z basis. If a farmer is concerned about the futures market tumbling lower than $5.70, he may be motivated to sell. But if he feels the basis bid is likely to be stronger than -70Z someday, what should he do? Fortunately, most elevators and commercial grain companies allow farmers to forward sell grain by setting a futures price on a contract and leaving the basis un-set.

They do this because they know they can make a profit margin handling as many bushels of grain as they can originate and paying their posted basis whenever, even if it's not at the weakest level of the year. Once one of these Hedge-to-Arrive contracts is made between a farmer and a buyer, that farmer has committed his bushels to the buyer and can't put those same bushels out on the open market to a competitor. So grain buyers use HTAs as an origination tool to lock in some captive bushels. They also tend to charge a fee for the service (I've seen anything from 3 cents to 10 cents), ostensibly to cover their margin costs and the risks of holding a futures hedge on behalf of the farmer. At the more punitive levels, HTA fees may discourage the use of these contracts. The farmer has to believe the basis level itself will strengthen 10 cents or more before he gives up 10 cents of fees on an HTA contract.

The grain buyer and the farmer may also agree to roll the futures hedge forward (for instance, from the December contract to the March contract) if the farmer would like to delay delivery past the original timeframe of the contract, but this, too, usually triggers some fee, and it can start to increase the risk of the contract. In the mid 1990's, when use of HTA contracts was relatively new, many elevators and farmers agreed to roll their HTA contracts from one crop year (1995) to the next (1996). However, that was one of those years when the nearby old crop market (e.g. July futures) was wildly inverted over the deferred new crop market (1996 December futures). So in rolling those HTA contracts to a new delivery timeframe, farmers got hit with a loss on the inverted futures spread as wide as $1.88 (the spread's widest level on July 9, 1996). This, as you can imagine, left a very sour taste in the mouth of many farmers who to this day greatly distrust HTA contracts. Investigations were made; studies were run; the topic has been well covered.[2] And the takeaway for anyone who intends to trade grain with HTAs is this: there will always be basis risk in an HTA contract – leaving basis unsettled its very purpose. As long as the delivery period is never rolled over to a different futures contract, basis risk and counterparty risk are the only risks. But once you start allowing the futures hedge to be rolled forward, there is new price risk: the risk of the spread itself between any two futures contracts. Within any one crop year, the carry structure will typically limit that to a fairly small, manageable risk. *Between* any two crop years, however, there's nothing inherently stopping the futures spreads from getting wild; therefore, many HTA contracts written today will have explicit terms preventing them from being rolled out of one crop year and into the next.

Deferred Pricing (**DP**) contracts – Also called "delayed price" or "price later" contracts, these allow a farmer to deliver grain to a buyer – and transfer title of that grain to the buyer – without actually setting a price on the grain, presumably because the farmer believes the price will be higher later. Grain can also just be delivered and kept "on storage" at the buyer's facility without transferring title, but then the buyer will typically start charging rather severe storage charges. One way or another, the grain buyer will get reimbursed for storing the grain: either by capturing the carry in the markets (which requires it to own and account for the ownership of those bushels on its grain position), or by collecting equivalent storage fees from the grain's owner. So, rather than charging their farmer clients 5 or 6 cents per month of storage costs while they wait for the futures prices to (theoretically) move up, some elevators offer "free" DP programs. This allows the elevator to record ownership of the bushels on their basis position, and to legally do whatever they want with the grain (sell it on a train, process it through an ethanol plant, etc.) without actually writing a check for the grain until the farmer decides he likes the prevailing price. It's a gamble for the farmer – remember prices could also move lower after he delivers the grain – and it's not always free, but it's a quite popular way to market grain, especially if a farmer doesn't have enough storage capacity to handle all his own bushels.

In addition to setting the basis level or the futures level at independent times, there are other strategies merchandisers can use to develop contracts that attract farmer bushels. Let's lump them all together as "**designer contracts**," taken to mean any grain contract used to originate bushels by offering more flexible pricing terms than simply giving a flat price or basis bid. Some of these may include accumulator contracts, premium offer contracts, or pro-pricing contracts, but different marketing phrases from different grain companies and continual innovation in these designer contracts prevent me from being able to write an accurate, all-inclusive list at any one point in time.

The publicity scheme goes something like this. A grain originator might say to a farmer, "Joe, my price today for new crop corn is $5.00, but if you'd like to do a special contract with me, I can get you $5.20 per bushel on up to 10,000 bushels. We'll just price 100 bushels per day for 100 days as long as the market stays above a certain level and then average it all together. So if you like the price today but don't want to miss out on some higher moves, this will average out your sales over the next six months at an even better price." To the extent that the description really might tie in with Joe's grain marketing goals, it probably sounds pretty good. But don't think the grain companies are just doing this for the delight and benefit of their farmer customers – the real reason for these contracts' existence is to attract as many bushels as possible. It's partly a neat service to farmers that attracts some bushels away from a grain company's competitors, but it can also be a strategy to source higher and higher volumes of grain. Particularly in the case of those accumulator contracts, sometimes these tools can commit farmers to selling more grain than they fully understand they're selling, or more than they would otherwise be willing to sell as the market conditions change.

And how do the grain companies manage to offer futures prices 20 cents above the market price, anyway? What black magic is going on behind the scenes for those designer contracts? In a word: options.

Options Strategies

There are two types of option contracts, **puts** and **calls**, and here's the standard description of options: A put option gives its owner the right but not the obligation to sell an asset at a certain **strike price** if, at a certain time, the market's price is lower than that strike price. A call option gives its owner the right but not the obligation to buy an asset at a certain strike price if, at a certain time, the market's price is higher than that strike price. That sounds awfully nice – you get to sell stuff for more than it's currently worth! You get to buy stuff for less than its market price! Neat!

America's founding fathers wrote of certain unalienable rights, inherent rights that are automatically ours simply because of our status as human beings. The "rights" attached to owning options aren't unalienable … and they most definitely are *not* free. They must be paid for, and how.

An option contract is just like any other traded contract – there is a buyer and there is a seller. In order to have those "rights" of buying or selling at a strike price, you must purchase them. Now the question becomes: how much should that privilege be worth to you?

Let's say you see the December corn futures contract is worth $5.50 per bushel now, but you think its price will fall and it will only be worth $5.00 per bushel on November 23rd (the day that December corn options expire). You could buy a December put option with any strike price, but let's say you pick a $5.50 strike. If your prediction comes true, and the underlying futures contract really is valued at $5.00 on the put's expiration date, the **intrinsic value** of that put option would be worth $0.50 per bushel to you (or $2,500, since options trade in 5,000 bushel increments, like futures).

That scenario alone starts to illustrate why options are notoriously hard to understand and tricky to trade. Just as futures contracts are **derivatives** of the underlying cash grain market (they *represent* grain, and their price is derived from the price of the underlying grain, but they're really just financial contracts; they're *not* grain.), a similar relationship exists between options contracts and futures contracts. Options are derivatives of an underlying futures market, so they're actually derivatives of derivatives. They are exchange-traded and regulated and brokered just like futures contracts, but an option contract is a separate beast from a futures contract. Its performance will ultimately be determined by the price of the underlying futures contract, which is influenced by the price of the underlying grain market, but the market of buyers and sellers for any particular option contract is separate from the market for the underlying futures contract or the market for the underlying grain.

With that philosophical and mechanical distinction in mind, now we can begin to think about all the reasons why the math will never be as easy as the $5.50 December put example above. The buyer of that put option should only be willing to spend exactly $0.50 on the contract if she is 100% certain the underlying futures price at expiration will be exactly $5.00. And how can anyone ever be *certain* of any such thing? In reality, she might feel there's a 33% chance the futures price will be above $5.50 (her put would be worthless), a 33% chance the futures price will be $5.25 (her put would have $0.25 of intrinsic value), and a 33% chance the futures price will be $5.00 (the $0.50 value scenario). Given those potential outcomes, the predicted value of owning a $5.50 put option would only be $0.25. But it's never that simple – there's actually an infinite number of outcomes and no way to attach simple probabilities to any of them. The whole structure of pricing options is based on the potential values of the entire range of uncertain outcomes.

It's helpful to think of options like insurance policies. You know one outcome may never happen: your house may never burn down or December corn may never fall below $5.50 before expiration. You also know there are several things that could happen which would negatively affect your finances: a house fire could result in a little smoke damage, the loss of your garage, or the total loss of your house and all your belongings. A falling corn market could result in reduced revenue for a farmer: just a few cents less than she could receive now ($5.50 per bushel), 10% less than the current price, 50% less than the current price, or anywhere above or below the current price, all the way down to $0 per bushel. In order to get a home insurance policy, which is a contract that will pay out some financial reimbursement in those unpleasant scenarios, the buyer must pay a price upfront, known as a **premium**. With option contracts, the language is the same. A buyer pays premium upfront and will receive a payout under certain conditions. The seller receives that premium upfront and either gets to keep all of it if those conditions never occur, or must financially reimburse the buyer if they do.

To communicate which scenario an option contract is actually in, we say it is "**in-the-money**" if the underlying market price is lower than the strike price of a put option or higher than the strike price of a call option. The owner of that option would get to buy cheaper or sell higher than the current market would otherwise allow. Options are "**at-the-money**" for those rare, fleeting moments when the market is trading at exactly the same level as the strike price. And options are "**out-of-the-money**" if the underlying market price is higher than the strike price of a put option or lower than the strike price of a call option. No financial benefit would come to the option's owner by selling at a strike price which is lower than the prevailing market or buying at a strike price that is higher than the prevailing market. Owners of out-of-the-money options aren't obligated to exercise those options, so they're not forced to sell or buy at unprofitable levels, and instead they just forfeit the premium they paid for the options and may let them expire worthless.

From that description and all that metaphorical insurance premium talk, you may see that these contracts are great for hedging risks. Grain producers who really need to cover their financial risks if grain prices fall, or end users who really need to cover their risks if grain prices rise, are the ideal purchasers of puts and calls, respectively. They are, in fact, the very people for whom these instruments were invented and built up into a liquid, exchange-traded market.

But here's the thing about options – each contract isn't a static agreement between two parties (the insured and the insurer). Rather, it's just one piece of an actively traded market, so the value of its premium is always changing from one moment to the next as all the uncertain factors that went into its calculation keep changing. You probably can't call up your car insurance company and sell back the entire insurance policy you bought from them, although maybe they will pro-rate the remaining days on the policy for you. With options on the futures markets, however, it's totally possible to get into and out of contracts easily in a liquid market, and as you do so, the premium value of the options themselves may change. Options are eminently tradeable.

It's entirely possible to buy or sell an option and make a profit from changes to that option's premium, even if the option itself remains out-of-the-money. For instance, let's say the December corn futures contract is currently trading at $5.25. You could buy an out-of-the-money 500 put option for 30 cents. The only way you would ever exercise that put option and receive intrinsic value for it would be if the December corn contract traded below $5.00 sometime between now and the end of November (when the December options expire). However, let's say five days from now, the December futures contract has fallen to $5.05. Your put would still be out-of-the-money, but because the underlying asset price fell, other people are going to be relatively more eager to buy puts with a 500 strike price. The premium price of your put could have risen to 40 cents. If you wanted to, you could turn around and exit the put option for a 10-cent profit on the premium appreciation.

Of course, that premium movement means that it is also possible to buy an option and lose money on the premium, even if the option contract itself is in-the-money. If the December corn contract is trading at $5.25, you could buy at call option with a 500 strike price, and even though there is only 25 cents of intrinsic value between $5.25 and $5.00, the going price for Dec 500 calls might be as high as 60 cents of premium. In five days' time, the premium value could fall to 50 cents, perhaps if the rest of the market feels corn prices are growing less volatile. If you exited by selling your long call then, you would book a 10-cent loss, even though your call option was in-the-money the whole time. And if you simply held your long call all the way until expiration, even if the call expired in-the-money, you might never recover the full 60 cents of premium you paid at the outset of the trade. The December futures contract would have to be at $5.60 or higher when the options expire for the intrinsic value of your long 500 call to be higher than the premium you paid.

All that upfront premium can get chewed through in four main ways. The first influence on premium is the underlying asset's price. Consider that there are just 5 distinct corn futures contracts (March, May, July, September, and December) traded each marketing year to represent the entire continuum of the cash corn market's price at every second of every day of that year. Similarly, options on futures get broken down into a chain of discrete strike prices, all of which are somewhere above or below the ever-changing futures market price. A segment of the options chain for all the corn options that are derivative of the September futures contract, if it was trading at $5.25, might look like this (below), but the full chain of "far-out-of-the-money" and "deep-in-the-money" options would actually stretch several dollars above and below the current market level:

AUGUST options on the CU contract, expiring July 27th				SEPTEMBER options on the CU contract, expiring August 24th			
Calls		Puts		Calls		Puts	
Strike	Price	Strike	Price	Strike	Price	Strike	Price
500	44¢	500	18¢	500	49¢	500	23¢
510	38¢	510	23¢	510	43¢	510	28¢
520	32¢	520	27¢	520	37¢	520	32¢
530	28¢	530	33¢	530	33¢	530	38¢
540	24¢	540	39¢	540	29¢	540	44¢

If you choose to trade a September call option that is 20 cents out of the money today, at the 540 strike price, for instance, the market for that contract will only include the buyers and sellers for that particular option at that particular strike price for that particular expiration and that particular underlying futures contract. The buyers and sellers of September 540 calls make up one discrete bunch of trading interest, different than the trading interest for September 500 calls, or August 540 calls or August 500 puts. In a few months' time, if September futures fall 20 cents, your position will still be in a September 540 call specifically, and that contract will just be 40 cents out of the money rather than 20 cents.

But its price will be different than it is on today's options chain. If the underlying asset price fell 20 cents, the premium on that call might fall 10 cents. If for every cent the underlying asset changes, the premium on the call changes half as much in the same direction, we would say that call has a **delta** of +0.5. Delta is one "the **Greeks**," symbols used in options mathematics to represent how option values change with regard to certain factors. A less cutesy name for them would be "risk sensitivities," and delta is formally the mathematical derivative of the value of the option itself (V) with respect to the underlying instrument's price (P):

$$\Delta = \frac{\partial V}{\partial P}$$

Don't get too hung up on the calculus. Delta is just a way to express how much premium will change as the underlying market changes. If you see one day that September 540 calls have a delta of +0.47, don't assume that delta will remain constant as the market progresses. As options get farther out-of-the-money, the delta itself starts to wane. So the farther away an option is from developing intrinsic value, the less value its premium will gain even as the underlying market moves in the "right" direction for the option.

Other factors that affect how options values behave are volatility (measured by **vega**), time (measured by **theta**), and the risk-free interest rate (measured by **rho**). The more volatile a market is, the higher the option premiums will be. Think of volatility as something that increases the likelihoods of all the potential in-the-money payout scenarios. Also, the more time there is between today and an option's expiration, the more chances that option will have to eventually move in-the-money or deeper in-the-money, which is why time sensitivity, theta, is such a big part of option trading. Even if nothing else changes about an underlying market, even if the price stays the same, the premium of any option will experience time value decay every moment of every day as that option gets closer to expiration. Anyone who buys an option and later exits that option may receive back some of the premium he initially paid, and he may even make a profit if the value of the option has increased, but the time value portion of that premium will never be fully recoverable. Sensitivity to the interest rate is generally negligible (especially in low-interest-rate environments), but in a full mathematical model of options value, it should be included because it represents the opportunity cost of not using that money in some other, safer investment.

Options traders who model how values change according to all these various factors can use even more complex greeks – measures of mathematical derivatives of mathematical derivatives. And mastering all those greeks can be the path to some excellent arbitrage strategies. If the present market price of an option is above or below what an option trader's model calculates it "should" be, he can sell or buy that option to bring it back in line with rational expectations. Options trading is extremely well-suited for algorithmic trading, because there can be direct benefits to building better and better algorithms that do a better and better job of predicting options values. The most well-known mathematical model for options valuation is the **Black-Scholes** equation, but if everyone in the market is using that equation to price options, and meanwhile you can develop a slightly better algorithm to predict how prices will behave, arbitrage trades from your algorithm will win profits.

Bear in mind that options arbitrageurs are as willing to sell options as they are to buy them. Options selling, a.k.a. "options writing," can be a great strategy to bring income into your trading account. Back to the insurance metaphor, options writers are the insurance companies who receive monthly premium checks, not the poor schmucks writing those checks and driving around trying not to run into anything. If you can confidently identify an outcome you feel sure *won't* happen – let's say you don't think December corn futures will ever rise above $7.00 per bushel – then you can sell options against that outcome and earn all the premium. Even if December 700 corn calls are only worth 2 cents, you could sell as many calls as the market is willing to buy, and as long as the underlying price of December corn futures really never does rise above $7.00 before the calls expire, you would get to keep all that money.

Of course, you can lose massive amounts of money writing options. If the outcome you're predicting against does come true, you will be on the hook to pay out the eventual value of the option at expiration. You can exit the position before expiration, but it might still be at a loss compared to where you sold the premium. Because selling a put or a call effectively makes you liable for an eventual long futures position or short futures position, the exchange requires upfront margin for short option positions. Traders who only buy options only need to pay the premium upfront and will never lose more than that premium – they will never experience a margin call. Traders who write options can find themselves on margin call. The following table details how long puts, long calls, short puts, and short calls can be used to express market opinion. A trader can do any one of these things or a combination of these things to profit from her opinion:

	Bullish	Bearish
Futures	Buy futures and profit as the market rises or lose as the market falls.	Sell futures and profit as the market falls or lose as the market rises.
Puts	Sell puts and profit as the underlying market rises, or potentially suffer losses equivalent to a long futures position if the market falls below the strike price.	Buy puts and profit as the underlying market falls. Potentially lose the premium if the market never falls below the strike price.
Calls	Buy calls and profit as the underlying market rises. Potentially lose the premium if the market never rises above the strike price.	Sell calls and profit as the underlying market falls, or potentially suffer losses equivalent to a short futures position if the market rises above the strike price.

In my opinion, the two ways a trader can get into trouble with options are 1) Oversimplifying them in your mind. This can result in alarmingly sudden losses in your trading account without a ready explanation. And 2) Overcomplicating them in your mind. This tends to result in completely dismissing options trading as a rip-off. And that's a shame, because there are some very nice strategies for options, but they should only be used with a full understanding of all those underlying causes for premium movement.

Like trading futures, trading options doesn't need to be any more complicated than buying an instrument if you think its premium value is likely to increase or selling an instrument if you think its value is likely to decrease. You even use all the same trading software and order types when making trades – market orders, limit orders, stop orders, etc. But one of the real advantages of options trading is all the spread trading opportunities that are opened by instruments that trade not only for different timeframes, but also at different strike prices, or with different functions (a put versus a call).

Options can be spread against each other or against futures contracts or against a position in the physical market, but a spread trade is still a spread trade. You want the underlying value of the two sides of the spread to move in roughly the same direction at the same time, and your goal is to have one side of the trade profit relatively more than the other side of the trade simultaneously loses. Most options strategies are just spread trades which time and tradition have happened to assign fancy, vaguely sexual-sounding names:

Naked Puts or Calls – These are options trades that stand alone with nothing spread against them. Someone who simply buys a put will therefore own a "**naked put**," and only risk the upfront premium it took to buy the position. Someone who simply sells a call is said to have sold a "**naked call**" and has unlimited theoretical risk if the underlying asset price moves above the strike price toward infinity.

Protective Puts or Calls – These are the risk management strategies. If you own an asset (5,000 bushels of physical grain or 1 long futures contract) you could purchase a put option to effectively spread against that asset. If you are short an asset, you could buy a call to spread against that asset. If the price of the asset falls, the premium value of the put will increase, so these are very basic hedge spread trades.

Covered Puts or Calls – For the traders who sell ("write") put or call options, if they spread a long underlying asset against their short options position, that's considered "covering" their options. So if you write a call for November soybeans, you could make it into a spread trade by simultaneously going long November soybean futures. If your short call goes in-the-money and you start to rack up losses on that side of the trade, your profits from the long futures position will cover you.

Call Spreads or Put Spreads – These are perhaps easier to visualize. Just like a futures spread trade where you buy March corn and simultaneously sell May corn, an options spread trade doesn't need to be any more complicated than buying a March 500 corn put and selling a March 450 corn put. Calculating your expected payoff from such a trade can start to get complex. If March futures fall to $4.75, you'll be in-the-money on the March 500 put but accumulating losses on the short out-of-the-money put position. And you can design these spreads to cross any number of market boundaries. Obviously, you can spread different strike prices against each other, but calendar spreads are also possible: a September wheat put could be spread against a December wheat put. Meanwhile, a long Minneapolis wheat call against a short Kansas City wheat call would be an intermarket call spread. With options, your spreads can be diagonal across every possible parameter: e.g. a short March 500 corn call against a long May 1250 soybean call.

Put-Call Spread – You can also spread the two different option types against each other. A specific example of a put-call spread is a **collar** – let's say you buy a Dec 500 corn put option and sell a Dec 600 call option. Sometimes, these spread trades can be thought of as a way to "finance" a risk-management strategy, or at least make it more affordable. The Dec 500 put might cost 35 cents of premium, but selling the Dec 600 call might earn the seller 15 cents of premium. The net premium cost of the put-call spread would therefore only be 20 cents. The trader would still have all the profit potential (or risk management) if the underlying December corn futures fall below $5.00 per bushel. On the other hand, if corn futures rise above $6.00 per bushel, the trader would face unlimited risk in his trading account (although if he's a farmer hedger, those losses will be offset by receiving a higher cash price for his physical grain). That should illustrate the importance of evaluating all the possible scenarios for any options spread trade, and predicting how each side's delta and time value and total premium might change in each scenario.

Straddle – Some options strategies, like straddles, are market neutral. A trader may not even care about or have an opinion about what direction a market will take, but if he believes the volatility of the market is likely to increase, he can profit from that influence (volatility) alone by trading an options **straddle**. He would simultaneously buy a put and a call at the same strike price, in the same market, with the same expiration date. His profit will come as the volatility portion of the premiums increase, and one side of his spread trade will profit relatively more than the other side, although he's indifferent which side it is.

Strangle – A **strangle** also involves buying both a put option and a call option in the same market with the same expiration date, but the options would have two different strike prices, both of them out-of-the-money (the put's strike would be below the market's current value and the call's strike would be above the market's current value). Because the trader is long options, his maximum theoretical loss is the premium value spent on the trade (which could be significant). His profit would come if the market experiences a large jump in one direction, although again, the trader is neutral about which direction that might be.

Butterfly Spread – A **butterfly spread** incorporates several of the ideas of the more basic options spread trades into one, big, bi-winged trade. It involves selling two options (puts or calls) at one strike price, while simultaneously buying one of the same type of option at a lower strike price and buying another of the same type of option at a higher strike price. So it is both a long put or call spread and a short put or call spread, all at the same time, which means you finance a lot of the premium cost, but there is only a small sweet spot where the trade will be profitable. A trader can express his bullishness or bearishness for the market by designing a butterfly spread to have a sweet spot above or below the current market level.

Iron Condor – This strategy involves buying a put at one strike price and selling a put at a higher strike price while simultaneously selling a call at an even higher strike price and buying a call at a strike price yet higher than that. So think of it as a simultaneous put spread and call spread, or as two simultaneous strangles. Again, it's a strategy with four positions (and therefore, four different premium values to keep track of in any scenario), with the two short positions financing the premium cost of the two long positions, and which only has a certain sweet spot where it will be profitable.

Now you may have a feel for how complex and creative options strategies can be. Twists can be placed on any of these strategies by adjusting how far apart or how symmetrical the strike prices or expirations in the spread may be, and the many variations get their own fun names: fig leaves, skip strike butterflies, Christmas tree butterflies, double diagonals, etc. I would only caution that you not undertake any of these strategies without first fully understanding how they are likely to perform in any market scenario. How much do they cost up front? What is the best case scenario for this trade (and how likely do you think that will be to happen)? What is the worst case scenario for this trade and its likelihood? Ideally, you might even build a simulation spreadsheet to show the potential payoffs and costs, and do rigorous backtesting of the strategy given real historical market performances. All of which is just my way of saying please don't consider reading the past few pages as a full qualification for undertaking the more complex option strategies. They should, however, give you a starting point to understand what your broker is talking about or to start investigating these strategies more deeply.

Over-the-Counter Contracts

....

The racetrack in Del Mar, California deserves its reputation as one of the most beautiful in the world. A summer's afternoon can be spent watching graceful horses chase across dirt or turf, but the viewer only needs to turn her head a little to the left to be equally captivated by the wild, blue Pacific ocean crashing against the shoreline. While I lived north of San Diego, I was always so pleased when I could convince a group of friends to join me at the track for a day. Although I'm by no means a racing expert, I did grow up on a farm and even won some prizes for judging horse confirmation and once, a belt buckle for the Grand Champion trail ride at the South Dakota state 4-H horse show. So at least among my group of friends, I was willing enough to assume the mantle of resident horse expert.

I must not have been very convincing, though. Very few people were confident enough to take my lessons about picking a race entry and then actually risk money on that selection. So I developed a different strategy to get my friends' emotions truly invested in a race's outcome. "You pick the horse you think is going to win the race, and I'll pick the horse I think is going to win the race, and whoever's choice performs the worst will buy the next round of beer." That always worked – their indifference of 'not having a horse in the race' would quickly get washed away like a hoofprint on the beach.

....

If my friends and I had formally written out and signed those beer-for-race-performance contracts, that's all it would have taken for us to engage in **over-the-counter**, or "OTC," trading. Obviously, that particular OTC contract would have been an unregulated and illegal gamble, but I'm hopeful the California Horse Racing Board won't come after me for bypassing their pari-mutuel system.

OTC trading takes place in a number of different manifestations. An investment bank could use an OTC contract to trade shares of a company to an investor, even if those shares aren't available through a stock exchange. They can also create more exotic hedges and write them up as OTC contracts, like an interest rate hedge or a credit default swap that will reimburse an investor in the event of some unfortunate outcome. Some OTC contracts are cleared through a central counterparty (run by an exchange or large bank), similar to the process for clearing exchange-traded futures contracts, but other OTC contracts are just done between one buyer and one seller. It's impossible to put hard-and-fast parameters around the definition of an OTC contract, because an OTC contract can be anything – from my friend betting me a beer based on the outcome of a horse race, to a grain company "betting" its bank some money based on the outcome of the corn market in six months' time.

So there is a great deal of skepticism about over-the-counter contracts. There is no particularly good way for a government to demand to regulate every asset that is traded between two private parties, any more than they can demand to regulate every beer wager I make. Where would they draw the line? What if, rather than trading actual stock in a company, the bank was just promising a financial payout that would mimic the performance of a theoretical stock – how would that be different than my beer bet? OTC contracts' open-endedness makes them impossible to fully monitor, analyze, or regulate. For example, the extent to which credit default swaps (CDS), a specific variety of OTC contracts, played a part in the 2008 financial crisis is difficult to calculate because there is no official source of data about how much exposure the global financial sector had to those private, unpublicized financial instruments.

So that's one problem of OTC contracts, if we can call it a problem: the market for them isn't transparent. The problem isn't necessarily complexity; OTC contracts can be as simple or as mathematically complex as their creators can invent them to be. But whatever "bets" are made, they can be made in private.

The other problem with OTC contracts, compared to exchange-traded contracts, is the greatly increased chances for a counterparty to fail to perform. An OTC contract could match a March corn futures contract detail-for-detail, but it would be financially safer to make that trade on an exchange than to just have a piece of paper you could take to a judge if the trader on the other side of the contract fails to pay you what the contract stipulates. Futures and options are fungible assets in liquid markets, with an entire, anonymous population of other traders willing to take the other side of any trade and an exchange that will make good on its traders' commitments. OTC contracts can be similarly-structured financial assets, but one trader needs to seek out another, specific trader to be the counterparty to the trade. Having a specific counterparty and no exchange to back up the risk of default means OTC traders face as much counterparty risk as the traders of cash forward contracts ... and potentially more risk if the terms are complex.

But for some purposes, an over-the-counter contract may be the only thing available to a trader. Let's say you wanted to buy beet pulp futures. There is no exchange-traded market for beet pulp futures. If you wanted to lay off the risk of the beet pulp price changing next year, but don't necessarily want to write a forward contract for physical delivery, you could perhaps find someone (e.g. a bank) to write a purely financial OTC contract with you, benchmarked against the price of beet pulp at a particular location, and take the other side of your trade. That swap would really be no different than a formalized bet ("If the price of beet pulp next year is higher than today's price, I will pay you the difference. If the price of beet pulp moves lower, you will pay me the difference."), but it's also not much different than a cash-settled futures contract, either.

So that's one application for OTC trading in the grain markets – simple swaps that mimic futures or options contracts but which don't have an exchange-traded market. Beyond that, the sky is the limit. The options on U.S. grain futures that are exchange traded are a type of option called **American options**, which calculate their payoffs based on the difference between the underlying asset's price and the strike price when they're exercised. There is another type of option – **Asian options** – which calculate their payoffs based on the *average* price of an underlying asset over a specific period of time. But Asian options aren't exchange-traded, so if you want to trade them, you would need to find a counterparty willing to write up an OTC Asian option contract with you.

Asian options are one standard form of exotic options, but anything else you can invent and mathematically describe to an investment bank or re-insurance company, you can probably trade as an OTC contract. The writer of the option (the seller) will mathematically model the risk of that position, using its projected price sensitivity, time value sensitivity, volatility sensitivity, etc. From that calculation, they'll set a premium price for the option, and if everybody agrees to the trade and signs the contract, there you would have an OTC option trade.

OTCs become useful anytime a trader needs to trade something non-standard, or which isn't available on an exchange. Another example might be a farmer who would have to buy a lot of natural gas to run his irrigation engines if it turns out to be a dry summer. So he might like to purchase an option to hedge the cost of natural gas, but only if the price moves higher than it is today … and only if it rains less than a certain amount in his specific county over the next ten weeks. Then he will need financial reimbursement for a certain, small amount of natural gas each week. Natural gas futures and options contracts trade in blocks of 10,000 million British thermal units, which is way more than this farmer could use in a week.

He could design a multi-variable OTC contract to hedge that risk, one that would be triggered not only by the market price of natural gas but also by the local precipitation, and which would pay out in increments rather than one final settlement, and those increments themselves would be non-standard. He may or may not be able to find anyone to take the other side of that trade, but that's an example of the kind of possibilities that get opened up by OTC trading.

Weather Contracts

One thing might have jumped out at you, though. Benchmarking an OTC trade against the exchange-traded market price of a commodity, like natural gas or corn, is easy enough, but how does one design a contract that pays out according to a *weather* outcome? It's easy, actually – you just have to find a data stream you can trust and then you have all the same statistical modeling ability to calculate volatility and probabilities as you would have when using market data.

The National Weather Service has literally thousands of observing stations collecting meteorological data all over the United States, and the data from those observations has been collected for decades and decades. So weather risk can be modeled very easily and assigned a premium price (just like an insurance contract or an options contract) for a specific location's temperature or precipitation.

Many industries are affected by weather, but perhaps none so much as grain production. A farm's annual output and revenue can be limited if:

- The temperature gets so low the crop suffers frost damage.
- The temperatures during a growing season don't get warm enough; i.e. if there aren't enough heat units for the crop to develop.
- The temperatures during a growing season get too warm, especially when the crop is meant to be pollinating.
- There is too much precipitation, especially at planting when it prevents a farmer from working in his fields, but also once the crop is already growing if it drowns the crop's roots.
- There is too much precipitation on an open pile of stored grain and quality losses occur.
- There is too little precipitation and the crop withers.

As an example, let's say I was worried about my corn field in Edmunds County, South Dakota failing if it receives anything less than 5 inches of rain between June 1st and July 31st, and I estimate I could lose as much as $10,000 in revenue if the field receives 2 inches or less in that timeframe. Using historical observations from 1950 to 2011, the algorithms from eWeatherRisk.com, a purveyor of OTC weather contracts, calculate that they would be willing to sell me an 'Insufficient Cumulative Precipitation' contract for a $2,418 premium price. Essentially, it would be a precipitation put option with a strike level set at 5 inches. The average amount of precipitation during that timeframe for that location is 6.35 inches of rain, with a historical maximum of 15.6 inches (1993) and a minimum of 1.95 inches (1973). If this particular OTC contract would be set to reimburse me incrementally for each tenth of an inch less than five inches received during that timeframe, it would have paid out over $3,000 in 2010 and 2002 (4 inches of cumulative precipitation in June and July), and over $5000 in 2006 (slightly more than 3 inches).

As another example, remember how worried Joe Smith is about his corn not pollinating well when the summer weather was too hot? If he could calculate that he had as much as $100,000 at risk if poor pollination reduced his corn yields, eWeatherRisk.com might sell him an OTC call option contract for excessive heat units above 85 degrees, with the payout calculated per cumulative degree above the strike.

Crop insurance contracts serve a similar function, of course, to reimburse farmers some of the income they would lose in the event of a crop failure. It allows them to pay their creditors for the inputs used in attempting to grow the crop, and allows them to stay in business for another year and therefore keeps the nation's supply of foodstuffs relatively stable. However, crop insurance payouts are based on final yield performance, pretty much regardless of the specific reason for the yield failure. Over-the-counter weather contracts aren't dependent at all on the crop's actual performance, but rather on a specific weather scenario at a specific location. There are some yield losses which might never be fully captured by a weather contract – underperformance by a certain variety of seed, for instance. And there are some financial losses which might never be fully reimbursed by a crop insurance product – let's say an autumn frost doesn't specifically reduce a mature crop's yield, but it can affect that crop's quality and increase the costs of mechanically drying the grain.

The buyers of OTC contracts tend to be producers or end users who have serious price risks to protect, and the writers of OTC contracts are generally trying to generate income from the swap fees or premiums. They must be very confident in their own risk-modeling algorithms to believe they are being adequately reimbursed for the likelihood of the contracts expiring in-the-money.

These institutions typically won't engage in OTC trading unless they can offset their own price risks, which include counterparty risks. Before anyone engages in an OTC trade, it's likely they will want to vet the counterparty's credit and have everyone sign adequate documentation. The International Swaps and Derivatives Association (ISDA) maintains industry-standard documentation for OTC trades, including Master Agreements that spell out all the details of any particular OTC transaction.

Land Investments

"A man complained that on his way home to dinner he had every day to pass through that long field of his neighbor's. I advised him to buy it, and it would never seem long again."
- Ralph Waldo Emerson

All it takes to be a farmer is to join some grain seed with some soil, water, and sunshine. This may seem like the ultimate arbitrage – selling grain against the purchase of its simple inputs - especially if one considers that water and sunshine can generally be acquired for free. However, modern grain seed is designed at the very cutting edge of biotechnology, with genetic modifications that maximize yield potential while controlling against various pests, and it's nowhere near free. In the two decades since 1990, crop seed costs more than doubled relative to the prices farmers received for their grain.[3]

Soil is also far from being free. If a farmer doesn't own land, he must rent access to cropland. In 2011, USDA's Economic Research Service estimated the average cropland annual rent to be just above

3% of the land's market value,[4] and rent can add up to more than 40% of a farmer's total input costs. This proportion varies by region, but in the Corn Belt about 62% of farmland is owned by farmers themselves and 38% is owned by landlords.[5] If a farmer does own his land, he may be paying a mortgage on the property. And even if a farmer owns his land free and clear, there are still always property taxes. So cropland is an asset that can't be left idle; it must always be producing something to pay for itself.

Furthermore, water and sunshine may or may not be free in some areas, but they are not always easily acquired. Cropland without any artificial watering mechanism is called **dryland**, versus the **irrigated** fields of western Nebraska or California's Central Valley. Most of the fields in Iowa, Illinois, and Indiana are dryland, or "rain fed" fields. In the event of a drought, neither for love nor money could farmers acquire enough water for their nascent plants to allow them to mature into grain. On the other hand, farmers who do have access to an irrigation system thereby commit themselves to spending money to transport water to the thirsty plants. A gravity-fed irrigation system of ditches and channels may not require a lot of financial maintenance once it is built, but the costs of running a **center-pivot irrigation** system (the tall sprinkler frames that sweep around a field in circular patterns) can be significant. And that's all without addressing the cost of the water itself. Some regions may not have to pay for the water directly, but they may be limited to pumping out a certain amount within a 3-year timeframe, for instance. Once the water is pumped, some types of soils have better Available Water-Holding Capacity[6] than others and respond more efficiently to irrigation.

So ... seed's not free, soil isn't free, water isn't free ... but the sunshine is still free, I guess. It just may not be as ample in some regions as it is in others. Therefore, investors who are looking to buy cropland have a wide range of options available to them. A deforested region in Brazil? A chunk of prairie in Saskatchewan? For simplicity's sake, let's only consider the various regions within the United States.

I mentioned the three "I" states of Iowa, Illinois and Indiana – those states produce over 40% of the nation's corn each year (Iowa 19% at over 2 billion bushels in 2011, Illinois 16%, and Indiana 9%)

and nearly 40% of the nation's soybeans. As these are the most plentiful crops we raise in the U.S., the prevalence of their production in certain regions is a good benchmark for identifying fertile, profitable cropland. Because corn yields are so large compared the yields offered by other crops, typically if a region is able to produce corn, they are economically motivated to do so. Corn yields tend to be about 3 ½ times larger per acre than soybean yields, on average, although the market price for a bushel of soybeans tends to be more than two times higher than the price for a bushel of corn.

There's a lot of good cropland outside of the three "I" states, though. The **Corn Belt** is generally considered to include, from East to West: Ohio, Michigan, Indiana, Illinois, Wisconsin, Missouri, Iowa, Minnesota, Kansas, Nebraska, South Dakota, and North Dakota. Look farther west, and the average rainfall tends to be too low to sustain corn. Farther south, however, you will still find states that plant a lot of corn. The USDA reports that 18 states planted 92% of the 2011 corn acreage; in addition to the Corn Belt states, they include Colorado, Kentucky, North Carolina, Pennsylvania, Tennessee, and Texas.

But there are obviously other crops being planted in other regions, whether they are more or less profitable than the benchmark corn crop. As recently as twenty years ago, before corn seed technology was as advanced as it is today, the Dakotas were not big producers of corn and were more suited for small grains like spring wheat and barley. Today, Montana and the other Northwestern states, as well as most of the Canadian prairie, are still more suited to the production of specialized grains or forage than to corn and soybeans. California's Central Valley is *so* well suited to growing highly profitable crops like vegetables and nuts, with its ample sunshine and ideal soil, that its farmers typically forgo the more commoditized grains. The Southern Plains region of Texas, Oklahoma, and Kansas, with its long growing season and relatively mild winters, is well suited to growing winter wheat. Another relatively arid region that produces its share of wheat is the High Plains region of western Kansas, Colorado, and western Nebraska. Cotton and rice production in the United States is mostly limited to either the Delta region (Alabama, Mississippi, Louisiana, Arkansas, Tennessee) or to irrigated cropland in Texas, Arizona, or California.

Anywhere you look, you're likely to find a region that has developed its own unique approach to producing grain. Farming practices can vary wildly even from one county to the next, so it behooves a potential land investor to do his homework and understand what is or isn't possible to produce in a certain area. In any situation, once you've made your assumptions and projections, the financial wisdom of any land purchase can be modeled in much the same way as any other asset purchase. Treat the annual income from a crop, or from farmer rent, as a dividend and determine if the net present value of that income stream is higher or lower than the value you would have to pay at auction for that land.

Your valuation model may handle the expenses and income streams as gross values for an entire parcel of land, but it's more common to see prices broken out on a per-acre basis. An **acre** is a unit of area equal to 4,047 square meters – slightly smaller than the size of a football field. In a square mile, called a "**section**," there are 640 acres. So in a "**quarter**" of a section, there are 160 acres. This is why you've heard of the proverbial "back forty" (a quarter of a quarter section) or "section lines" (the right-of-way paths between sections). Most of the rest of the world measures land in **hectares** (10,000 square meters). About two and a half acres can fit inside a hectare.

However you set up your valuation model, there are some nice tools that may help you gather data for your buying decision. Iowa State University has developed an index procedure that puts a solid number on any field to quantitatively communicate how fertile that cropland is. Every soil type in Iowa has been assigned a **Corn Suitability Rating (CSR).** A Crescent loam may tend to produce higher corn yields than a Harps clay loam, for instance, and therefore receive a higher CSR rating. Land rents and land prices in Iowa are often expressed outright as a multiple of the field's CSR.

To get the CSR rating for an entire field, one simply surveys all the soil types in the field and calculates a weighted average accounting for how much of each type there is. The study of soil types can be an endlessly useful pursuit for a serious land investor, and corn suitability indexing can be done anywhere – just map out what proportion of a field is made up of any given soil type and do the arithmetic. For your convenience, the National Resources Conservation Service has already surveyed and created soil maps for more than 95% of the United States, and they're all available online.[7]

Math or no math, however, land investors tend to come up with all kinds of reasons to justify their purchases. Some of these reasons are better than others. In the years after the 2008 commodities boom, low interest rates and relatively high grain prices created a surge of interest in cropland investing. This also happened to coincide with a number of farmers retiring (the average age of a U.S. farmer is nearly 60 years old) and other farmers wildly expanding their operations to develop economies of scale. Anecdotally, the highest purchase prices I've heard from auctions in the heart of the Corn Belt were paid by farmers, rather than land investors. In one instance, the buyer bought the farm across the road from his house for a price that I would argue wasn't, strictly speaking, economically wise. But to him there was some value in controlling the neighborhood around him, emotionally-speaking, and also something to be said for averaging the book value of all the land he already owned against the value of that new purchase. As a farmer with his own (probably fully paid-for) equipment and local facilities, he could make more profit from that piece of ground than anyone else could.

A long-distance investor who would have had to pay a farm management company and a custom farmer to produce a crop out of that land would not have been able to pencil out the same profit. And yet, in an environment with a very low risk-free interest rate, the relative safety of real estate and the relative scarcity of cropland make it an appealing asset class to many. "They can't manufacture any more of it," is how one ag banker put it to me. I would simply urge caution against hearing one extreme land price from one auction and extrapolating that all land would be worth such an extreme price.

Aside from the differing potentials for production from one geographical region to another, there can be value-added differences between one field and the field right next to it. Soil types are just one example. Field A might have center pivot irrigation and Field B might not – you would not only have to account for the value of the equipment itself, but also for the increased yield potential on an irrigated field over the life of the investment. Yield histories might be available for review. Similarly, in hilly regions, one field may have **terracing** that prevents erosion and increases soil fertility and yield potential over the life of your investment, but another field may not. In regions with excessive moisture or very heavy soils, one field may have tiling that drains surplus moisture away from crops' roots, but a neighboring field may not. One field may simply have been cared for better – with less compaction or less erosion or better nutrient applications over the past several years – while another field's soil may have been a little used and abused. Perhaps a piece of ground would have some potential value above and beyond that of simple cropland, like as a property development or livestock production area. There are a lot of idiosyncrasies that are hard enough to account for in a rational calculation from afar in a spreadsheet, to say nothing of how hard they are to keep straight when an auctioneer is pitting you against several other adrenaline-fueled bidders.

Ag Equities

The variety of publicly-traded agriculture companies is wide; it ranges from grain processors to international traders, equipment manufacturers, fertilizer producers, and biotechnology seed and chemical companies. So there are many ways to gain exposure to agriculture and the grain markets without making any investment more adventurous than a straightforward stock purchase.

Far be it from me to try and re-state the sound investing principles of Benjamin Graham or Warren Buffet. You'll be better served to learn about stock valuation somewhere other than in these pages. However, to the extent that a company's earnings may be dependent on the grain markets, I can offer some notes on how to treat that exposure.

Grain Processors
Examples: Archer Daniels Midland Company (ADM); Corn Products International Inc. (CPO)

The first thing to know when considering the entire marketspace of commercial grain companies is that many – if not most – of them are privately owned. Cargill and Louis Dreyfus are among the largest processors of agricultural products, but they are closely held and there's no good way for an individual investor to gain exposure to their business. Even younger, smaller companies like POET, which operates 27 biorefineries in the U.S., don't have a public stock listing. So calculating market share for a grain processor or evaluating it against its competition can involve a certain amount of guesswork.

The second thing to keep in mind is that large multinational grain companies tend to have their fingers in a lot of pies. If the soybean crush margin is unfavorable one quarter, a processing company's ethanol margins or corn sweeteners business may still be doing quite well, or it may be earning carry on all the grain it has originated and stored away in elevators. Because of their vertical integration across the industry, they tend not to be as sensitive to grain prices as you might think. They may have to buy high priced grain to run through their processing plants, but they may also be able to pass on those higher costs to the consumers of their products. They are also likely to be hedged against changes in either their input costs or their product prices. Their profits are coming from basis trading, capturing carry in the grain markets, and most of all from capturing the crush margins in their processing plants.

For instance, ADM's stock price is positively correlated to the price of corn, but most of that correlation can be explained by the simultaneous growth in demand for corn itself and for corn byproducts (the correlation of front month corn futures' returns and ADM shares' returns between 2003 and 2012 is +0.21). Grain processing companies are suited to capturing the growth in the overall volume of grain production, grain handling, and byproduct demand worldwide, so their incremental profit margin on each additional bushel they process is what leads to their own growth, more than their sensitivity to grain prices.

Traders
Examples: Glencore International (GLEN.L) or Bunge Limited (BG)

Grain trading companies are similar to grain processing companies in many ways, and in some cases even overlap. Bunge, for instance, is also a processor of oilseeds and ADM, of course, is also a trader of many grains and other commodities. Glencore is the world's largest trader of several commodities, and these aren't limited to the agriculture sector. It also trades metals, minerals, and energy products.

In extreme cases, underlying commodity prices can have an effect on a trading company. For instance, when the global cotton market tripled in price from 2010 to 2011, some of the suppliers with whom Glencore held physical purchase contracts reneged on those contracts to take advantage of the vastly better opportunities out on the open market. That's a good example of counterparty risk in the physical commodity markets. So Glencore struggled to source enough physical cotton at higher prices than it originally had on the books to fulfill its sales contracts, and the futures market started to slip away from the cash market, too. Remember that the margin costs for holding futures hedges grow when the markets' values increase and become more volatile. So even a fully hedged, back-to-back commodity trader can experience extreme results when the underlying market prices behave in extreme ways.

But that's an unusual example. Again, with this category of company, the sensitivity to the actual market price of the goods they're trading generally isn't as strong as you might guess. They tend to be making arbitrage trades, with purchases hedged against sales, and are therefore typically price neutral. In fact, the relative stability of their profits allows them to usually borrow capital at favorable rates compared to other types of companies. Lenders who are aware of trading companies' fully-hedged, price-neutral model, and who believe they have a disciplined trading system with little risk of rogue trades, generally feel safe being in business with commodity trading companies, regardless of the behavior of the underlying commodity markets.

Equipment Manufacturers
Examples: Deere & Company (DE) or Kubota Corporation (KUB)
The makers of agriculture machinery – tractors, combines, tillage equipment, irrigation equipment, etc. – are another category of company that is suited to take advantage of the overall growth of global grain production and demand, but which is not entirely

sensitive to grain prices themselves. Their business models are well diversified into other industries beyond agriculture (forestry, construction, landscape equipment, public infrastructure, etc.). But for the agriculture section of their business alone, you can consider some ways grain prices affect retail demand. Farmers are obviously more able and willing to purchase several hundred thousand dollars' worth of brand new equipment, or several million dollars' worth of equipment depending on the size of the farm, when they are experiencing a profitable year. The useful lifetime of a tractor can stretch longer than a decade, however, so equipment companies must develop strategies to make new equipment more appealing than used equipment and to sustain demand from one year to the next. That could be by limiting the amount of equipment manufactured in any one year, or simply by innovating the next big thing that every farmer will want to use.

Fertilizer
Examples: Potash Corp (POT) or The Mosaic Company (MOS)
Fertilizer is a critical input for higher-yielding crops. The global challenge farmers face as the world demands more food is not necessarily to put more land into production, but to achieve higher production levels from existing plots of land. That requires more sophisticated inputs, like better seed and more nutrients, i.e. fertilizers. Plants require nitrogen and other nutrients in usable forms in order to thrive, so fertilizer companies may produce and sell urea, anhydrous ammonia, DAP (diammonium phosphate), MAP (monoammonium phosphate), potash, a 10-34-0 ammonium polyphosphate solution, or UAN (urea and ammonium nitrate in solution).

The agriculture industry experienced a sharp rise in the cost of chemical fertilizers in 2008 and 2009 because fertilizer pricing is not only dependent on farmer demand, which is directly related to grain market prices, but also very much by underlying energy costs. Natural gas is the main component used to manufacture nitrogen fertilizer, so fertilizer companies' profits are typically determined by the extent to which they can pass on natural gas costs to their customers. As it happens, the weekly returns of Mosaic's stock price since 2004 has a positive correlation of only +0.09 with the weekly returns of natural gas prices, but a positive correlation as high as +0.39 with the weekly returns of corn prices. So here, indeed, is an equity category with a strong relationship to the grain markets.

Biotechnology & Chemical
Examples: Monsanto Co. (MON) or Syngenta AG (SYT)

Here is another category that shares some of the outcomes of the grain markets themselves. As biotechnology companies can develop higher-yielding seed traits or more effective crop protection, like herbicides, insecticides, and fungicides, they increase the value of their products to their farmer customers, whose appetite and ability to pay for such technology is directly determined by their own profitability. American farmers have widely adopted the best technology available to them each year and have become accustomed to paying for that technology, so the real upcoming market opportunities for biotechnology and chemical companies is to expand the adoption of their product lines into other regions of the world (South America, Asia, Europe). This industry is also notable for its fierce competitiveness. In the past, it may have taken decades for a seed company to breed and develop a new biotechnology trait into crop seed, but as these companies compete to find faster paths to the market with ever-more-innovative traits, they are directly competing for market share.

They also tend to tie sales of their proprietary crop protection traits into the seed sales. The most famous example is probably the Roundup Ready line of products. Monsanto patented the glyphosate molecule in the 1970's and its rights in the U.S. didn't expire until 2000. Roundup is the brand name of glyphosate, which is a herbicide. The real game changer, though, was inventing and patenting genes within seeds that grow into crops that are tolerant to glyphosate. So even after the soybeans or corn plants have emerged above the ground, a farmer can apply Roundup herbicide onto those fields and kill off the pressure from weeds, without killing the crop itself. That has been a great marketing tool – selling not only the herbicide but the patented seed, as well, as part of a whole production system, and other systems are now on the market with other pest-controlling mechanisms. The race will always be on between biotechnology companies to research and develop the next big proprietary molecule or mechanism.

Agricultural Production
Examples: First Resources Ltd. or China Agri-Industries Holdings Limited

Within the United States, actual agriculture production is undertaken almost exclusively by small or mid-sized private companies, usually family owned. It would be pretty jarring for me to ever see "Joe Smith Farm, Inc." traded on the New York Stock Exchange. However, if an equity investor is willing to look at foreign companies, he may find a few opportunities to have direct exposure to agriculture production. Palm plantation owners, which produce edible palm oil, are sometimes large enough operations to be publicly listed. First Resources Ltd. is an example of a palm producer in Singapore and Indonesia. I hope it goes without my saying that careful due diligence is called for before investing in foreign agriculture production firms.

Throughout history, farms have tended to be small, family-operated enterprises. Although the production of mined minerals or other commodities required group labor, it actually was possible for one human alone to plant enough grain on which to live and have a little left over to sell to his non-farming neighbors. However, there has always been a limit to how much land any one family can physically manage, given the technology of the day, and it was a benefit to society to have large numbers of small stakeholders spread out across a country's arable land. Through ownership or through fealty to some political body, each farmer would only be responsible for a small chunk of the earth.

There also wasn't much motivation for the state or for large businessmen to become involved directly in farming. There's just so much risk – crops can be wiped out by drought, flood, hail, or pests. Historically, it's been better to let those risks wipe out one small stakeholder at a time rather than for a successful entity to willingly adopt those risks upon itself. Also, those in power typically find it more advantageous to pay as little as possible for grain, making it happily cheap for the urban masses but also relatively unprofitable for the small farmers. It's in a government's interest to offer farmers just enough support to keep the food supply stable, but not more than that.

So the tradition of relatively small enterprise farming has become ingrained within human society. Within America today, $500,000 in gross annual sales would put a farm in the top 5% of all "farms," but that demographic term includes every roadside watermelon stand and every retiree who crafts artisanal goat-milk soap as a hobby. To hear our relatively large, successful grain producers attacked as "corporate farmers" or "industrial farmers" seems pejorative and hurtful to those of us who understand the economies of scale necessary for profit, especially considering how in other industries, a company can average up to $7 million in annual receipts and still be deemed a "small" business by the Small Business Administration.[8]

As it is, only 2.3% of farms are owned by non-family entities. Only 9.8% of U.S. farms are family farms with more than $250,000 in annual sales. Even that number is deceptive – first of all, that's annual *sales*, to say nothing of *profit*, and even the profit numbers for farms are tricky because the accounting of production costs isn't always separate from the accounting of living expenses. Anyway, this leaves 88% of America's 2.2 million farms as "small" family farms, which own 63 percent of U.S. farmland, and most of these small farms rely on off-farm income for their household's livelihood. Of the 97.7% of farms which are family farms of any size, it is the "large" ones that produce more of our food. The farmers with more than $250,000 in annual sales, who I would argue might still be pretty modest businessmen, produce 71.6% of our total production.[9]

For whatever reason consumers are so intent on having their food grown by a "little guy," they have been for many decades. Even in Gary Comstock's 1987 book, "Is There a Moral Obligation to Save the Family Farm?," he asked readers to try and think of any other industry with so much still "in the hands of the little guy."[10] As long ago as 1937, when Robert Diller wrote a study on "Farm Ownership, Tenancy, and Land Use in a Nebraska Community," he predicted – wrongly – "the small farmer owning and working his land, the good old self-subsisting and independent family farm – these are probably on the way out."[11]

Tradition and feelings aside, however, I have to wonder what the future will hold for the typical legal formation of farming entities. Now that there are so many ways to manage farming risk with financial derivatives, the profit structure of modern farming may become more appealing to outside investors.

History would suggest that large-scale, soulless farming operations have pretty grim prospects. When the Soviet Union forced its peasants into laboring on state-owned farms, those "farmers" not only lost their ability to make individual decisions about crop production and input use; they also lost their motivation to innovate or to work the outrageous hours and tasks that farming requires.

However, in 1989, USDA's Economic Research Service conducted an empirical study that showed it wasn't the wage payment system, or the inefficient input use, or the irrational prices, or the misdirected decision-making that restricted Soviet agriculture; rather, it was their slow pace of technological innovation.[12] If that suggests large-scale corporate farms could be as productive and profitable as the current family-run operations, as long as they adopt all the latest innovations, then I could be led to believe we'll see a "Smith Farms, Inc." trading on the New York Stock Exchange within my lifetime.

However, the long hours and weird tasks associated with farming aren't trivial. It can already be difficult for American farmers to hire willing and able employees when the job involves working a 20-hour day operating heavy machinery in hot, dusty conditions. And why *would* an employee – who has no particular loyalty to the farm beyond that of an employee to his employer – embrace that kind of work? Logically, only someone who has the rights of tenure and disposition of the land itself would be willing to contribute the blood, sweat, and tears necessary for a successful farm. Don't get me wrong – America's agriculture industry is full of people with surreal dedication to their jobs, but generally, no one should work harder on a farm than the farm's owner/operator him- or herself.

The disposition rights of land owners (the liberty to control, direct, sell to another, or pass on to one's heirs) is the critical piece of the family farming puzzle. A farm manager who is trying to maximize the profit on a farm for just a few years will make different land management decisions than a farmer who intends to pass that land on to his children and grandchildren. Joe Smith could spend up to $20,000 terracing a hilly field in Iowa. It's questionable whether the marginal increase in profit he may see in his lifetime from having less soil erosion in that field would make the payback of that project positive. But wouldn't Joe do it to keep the fertility of that soil intact for his children? For his children's children? Because it's the right thing to do? There would be no good way to account for projects like that on a quarterly earnings report to public shareholders who demand fiscally responsible use of their capital above all other considerations.

I can think of a notable example of large-scale communal farming, with little-to-no individual decision-making, which is still very successful. The Hutterian Brethren are a non-resistant Anabaptist sect, similar to the Amish and Mennonites, who emigrated from persecution in Germany/Russia to the North American prairie in the late 19th century. They believe in sharing their possessions in commons, and therefore established communal farms across the region with about 15 families per farm, which have been as successful at agriculture production over the past century as their secular neighbors. But it's important to note they have always adopted the latest innovations in ag technology, the lack of which doomed those other famous communal farmers, the Soviets. Most importantly of all, today's Hutterites know they are passing down to the next generation of Hutterites not only their traditions and way of life, but also the land itself.

It's therefore possible for farming operations to be both big and sustainable. As a society, we may be wary if farming starts to configure itself as a collection of faceless companies with relatively apathetic employees who just show up for eight hours and collect a paycheck, rather than as a multitude of individual families who invest their whole lives in the long-term productivity of their land. I think such a development would have long-term implications for the economy, because I don't believe land could ever be as productive as it is in the hands of farmer who intends to pass it down to his children. But regardless of that prediction, I could envision large-scale corporate farming happening in America now – and only now – that the markets have developed ways to manage risk and now that the capital costs of farming have become so onerous.

CHAPTER 6
Making and Using the Grain

"With the introduction of agriculture mankind entered upon a long period of meanness, misery and madness from which they are only now being freed by the beneficent operation of the machine"
-Bertrand Russell

Modern Farming & Society

There are few people who have stronger feelings about farming than farmers themselves, whose hearts quicken at the scent of fresh-tilled soil and whose sleep is constantly disrupted by thoughts of threats against their growing plants. But recently in society, farming has attained a new romanticism. Food that has been produced with archaic practices and hard labor seems somehow more nutritious or perhaps just more righteous to wealthy urban consumers than food that has been produced with the full benefit of modern technology.

This is a vast departure from the majority of human historical experience. Almost every generation of farmers before this one has toiled not only in hard physical labor, but also generally in an imposed poverty (due to that political convenience of cheap food for the masses), and even in ignominy. As the daughter in National Lampoon's Vacation says to her country bumpkin cousin: "Uh, don't take this personally, Vicki; but being a farmer isn't too cool, you know." And I think it's a little unfair that some consumers would seem to rather have their nation's farmers remain bound to small-scale poverty, physical toil, and outdated practices than to become fairly educated about the processes of modern agriculture themselves.

Yet agriculture has probably had more of an influence on society than society has had on it. In 2011, researchers at Harvard and UCLA examined ethnographic data from over 1,200 civilizations around the world, dividing them into the groups whose traditional farming practices involved use of the hoe (a small instrument that can be adequately deployed by both men and women) or groups whose agriculture developed use of the plow (a heavy instrument that requires great upper body strength to operate). If a civilization's ancestors relied on plow-based agriculture to grow wheat, barley, etc. in their climates (basically all of Western civilization) rather than androgynous hoe-based agriculture (potatoes, rice), the theory goes, that civilization's ancestors experienced generation after generation of men working outside the home and taking the largest economic role in the family: the role of farmer. Statistically, the researchers were able to show that those same plow-based civilizations, even now, are less likely to have women working outside the home, less likely to have women elected to government, and less likely to have women running businesses. Descendants of plow-users are more likely to believe men deserve the first shot at jobs when unemployment is high.[1] Apparently, today's beliefs about "a woman's place" in society and gender inequality in general can largely be explained by the ancient advantage men had to operate plows with relatively greater upper-body strength.

So each time we subconsciously believe a male candidate is inherently more capable of serving in political office than a female candidate, or each time we imply mothers have intrinsically more household responsibilities than fathers, we are dancing in the puppet strings of thousands of years of societal evolution, hearkening back to the days when our species was no better than its ability to perform a physical task, like oxen.

Agriculture seems poised to continue to shape our society. For instance, long before we have any widespread deployment of self-driving cars, thousands of American farmers are using nearly-autonomous tractors to plant their crops with the most advanced GPS technology available to the public. Rather than wrangling beasts of burden and a single-blade plow through soil, today's farmers use a tractor with more than 400 horsepower in its engine. Rather than sowing individual seeds he jealously guarded through the winter, today's farmer uses an in-cab computer and dual-array satellite receivers to guide a 24-row planter in patterns that are precise to within an inch. Rather than hoeing or pulling weeds by hand, today's farmer again uses a precise GPS system to efficiently apply herbicides where they're needed and only where they're needed. The same system can apply just the right amount of fertilizers and nutrients, wasting nothing. Rather than picking, cutting, or threshing mature grain with his own hands and back, today's farmer again engages the finest machinery technology available. At the end of a growing season, he has every data point he could possibly need (seed population, seed depth, input rates, final yield, final moisture, etc.) to fine-tune his production practices on each GPS-mapped square foot of his farm. His grain storage, too, is more evolved than a stack of bushel baskets in the barn – it tracks the temperature, moisture and overall condition of the grain within its storage bin.

These developments have radically altered the physical labor aspect of farming. Don't get me wrong – anyone who's grown up on a farm will wax poetic about the virtues of hard work and character building, but there is no virtue in hanging on to physical tasks which hinder efficiency or limit the labor pool. It will always take a certain amount of strength to tighten bolts or hook up hydraulic linkages on farming equipment, but that level of strength isn't restrictive. We've entered the age when upper body strength is no longer a prerequisite to be a successful farmer. It's even possible for a paraplegic, once he's entered a tractor cab, to operate that tractor and farm as capably as any able-bodied person (and yes, this has been done).

Who knows for how many generations or for how many hundreds of years we may still carry the attitudes of our earliest farming ancestors. But today the ways farming practices affect our society are no longer regressive; in fact, agriculture is advancing our species to the very forefront of technology.

·········

Joe Smith had felt a pain in his gut for days. At first he thought it was just gas, but even that didn't make sense because his diet during harvest was actually simpler and more regular than usual. Each day he would pack a little cooler with a turkey sandwich, carrot sticks, a Snickers bar, and several bottles of water and Mountain Dew. One must stay hydrated and caffeinated while sitting in a combine all day every day, alternating one's stare between the hypnotic flow of corn ears into the machine and the rhythmic digital cartoon of the GPS map and yield monitor.

It wasn't until he got out of the combine one afternoon to clear a branch out of the header and bumped his bellybutton against a sharp metal point that the pain in his gut became so acute he knew something was truly wrong. Irritated to take the time out of his day, he reluctantly drove himself into the doctor's office and was told he had a hernia and would need an operation. Which was great, just great – he only had three fields left to harvest and here the doc was telling him he'd be stuck in the hospital for a day and laid up for a week afterward.

"Listen, all I do is sit in the combine all day. It's no different than sitting in a chair all day. Can't I still do that after the operation?"

The doctor was adamant: "No. No, you can't be bouncing around in a tractor afterward. Not for many days."

Joe wanted to roll his eyes. It wasn't like he'd be rolling over a boulder field on an old Farmall H with a metal seat – he'd be on a padded seat in a combine with hydraulic suspension rolling over smooth river bottom ground. Honestly. But between the doctor and Joe's wife, there was no way around the farming moratorium.

So now Joe was sitting in his grain truck watching other people harvest his corn. If he could drive himself to the hospital with a hernia, he figured he could at least drive his own corn to the elevator after a hernia repair operation. Fortunately, his parents hadn't yet left for their winter home in Arizona, so Joe could put his dad in charge of his Case IH combine ... albeit with severe qualms. Joe himself struggled sometimes to make the GPS receiver and computerized yield monitor work properly, but to explain the system to a stubborn 72-year-old man who refused to use even e-mail was frustrating, to say the least.

His neighbors had also heard about his trip to the hospital, so they were finishing up his other two fields. It wasn't a big deal – the medical problem wasn't life-threatening and harvest had been early that year so there was plenty of time and good weather left to finish up. But it was a very big deal to know that a guy's neighbors were willing to do that, to take the time out of their own harvests and use their own equipment on his behalf. Joe would have liked to throw them each a big barbecue and keg party to thank them, but in the one instance, old Leonard Stern wasn't a drinker and in the other instance, it probably wouldn't look good for Joe to be liquoring up young Mrs. Kearney while her husband was away in Afghanistan.

Stern was harvesting the bottom ground north of Joe's machine shop, so Joe would be nearby if he had any questions. The older farmer had planted every acre of his farm every year since he was 14 years old, and he was now 83. If there was something to know about farming in Grundy County, Iowa, Leonard Stern was the one who knew it. He could recall sixty-nine years of weather patterns and the ownership history of every quarter of land in several townships. He was as faithful about buying and using only John Deere farming equipment now as he had been in 1943, but even though John Deere offers GPS systems in its equipment, Stern had planted all those acres over all those years successfully by his own dead reckoning, and he didn't feel the need to learn some new trick now. Last spring, Joe had taken an entire afternoon and evening out of a very tight planting schedule to help Stern get his tractor un-stuck from axle-deep mud, and the Sterns and the Smiths had been lending each other equipment and time back and forth over many, many decades, so there was already an established pattern of favor-giving when Stern offered to harvest Joe's field.

Joe also had some good deeds built up with Lindsey Kearney. She had always been the technology and marketing whiz on the Kearney farm for the seven years she and Brett had been married, but Joe had helped her with some welding and disk sharpening while Brett was deployed. Joe's wife sometimes babysat for the Kearneys' kids. Mrs. Kearney was running a New Holland combine with the latest after-market AgLeader GPS system. Therefore, when she had called offering to help out for a day, Joe asked her to harvest the 80 Williams acres he had just started renting that year. He was very curious about the quirks of that field – how would the low spots perform? Should he apply some more nutrients on the hilltops next year? He'd be able to match up the digital yield data from Lindsey's combine against the data he'd collected from his planter last spring and identify trouble spots within the field.

He was paging through AgLeader's website on his smartphone when the CB in his grain truck crackled to life and his dad's voice poured into the cab: "Hey, Joe."

"Yeah."

"I been telling you for years you gotta do some deep tillage on this south end of the field here. And didn't I tile this exact spot about twenty years ago? This is terrible – you should come look at this. You gotta ... what hybrid did you use down here, anyway?"

"What does the yield monitor say?"

"That's what I'm saying – it says 15. You're never going to pay off all this fancy computer shit if you can't raise better corn than this, Joe."

Joe scratched his head. Fifteen bushels per acre? Something must be funny with the yield monitor. "Well, what does the corn look like? You got the header set right?"

"Huh."

"Huh what?"

"Looks great, actually. Looks just like the 175 stuff up on the top of the hill."

Joe rolled his eyes and went back to his smartphone without responding. There was a certain rhythm required to successfully divide one's attention between the computer screen and the corn itself, but Joe had expected his father would just ignore the former entirely and only watch the latter. Oh well, losing half a field's worth of yield data was going to be easier to deal with than fixing whatever was wrong (or probably wasn't wrong) with his combine while his dad was operating it.

"Joe, this is really weird. How come if the corn looks so good your goofy screen here is telling me 15?"

"It's probably the moisture reading."

"Oh." ... silence for a few beats ... "Huh. 180 yield, 15% moisture. Huh."

"Yep." Boy, was Joe going to be happy once this year's harvest was finally just done.

....

The Farming Calendar

I hope no one intends to use this chapter as a how-to guide for actually growing or processing grain. Nevertheless, for anyone who intends to trade grain, it can be useful to have an overview of what is happening in modern grain production and when. Then, if you hear a farmer from North Dakota worry about dry soil in February, you'll know that complaint has less market influence than hearing, "Missed the rain that was forecast for Saturday night, and now my corn furrow is starting to open up," from an Iowa farmer in mid-May. Crop production considerations that may influence the markets can be organized into a rough calendar:

January & February

In these months, most of North America's farmland is in the middle of a season that doesn't support much plant growth. Many farmers take advantage of this timeframe to perform maintenance and repairs on equipment or tackle any other tasks that may get neglected during busier times, including taking vacations. From a grain market standpoint, as long as the road conditions are favorable for grain trucks, we frequently see a lot of grain being taken out of storage on the farm and brought into the market via local elevators. Some farmers may prefer to receive income right after the start of a new fiscal year.

March

Now starts the busy season for farmers. While no farmer wants to place seed in the ground before the threat of frost has passed, and while the weather in March may still be prohibitive for fieldwork in many regions, in the heart of the Corn Belt March can be a month when a lot of field preparation occurs – tillage of the soil, application of nutrients, etc. In southern states like Texas, as many as half the state's corn acres may be planted by the end of March.

When the markets rally during the spring timeframe, it's often said that they're "buying acres," which means farmers can be motivated to plant more of one crop than another if the upcoming autumn futures prices suggest there will be relatively greater opportunities for profit. However, it's unusual for a farmer to really switch his planting plans based on price alone. It's considered good farm management to rotate crops on any given field from one year to the next. A "corn on corn" rotation would imply the farmer was planting corn on the same field where corn grew the previous year, and although the nutrition and disease pressures of having the same species in the same spot must be handled properly, it's an increasingly popular practice when corn production offers more exciting yields and the corn market offers better profitability. Farmers may be inclined to stick to a **crop rotation** plan (a 50/50 corn and soybeans rotation is common throughout the Corn Belt) and buy the necessary inputs for that plan, somewhat regardless of what prices the markets offer.

April

Farmers who plant faster-maturing small grains, like spring wheat, plant those crops first before planting row crops like corn and soybeans, so in April you will see the planting progress start first and move fastest for those small grain crops. But corn won't be far behind. By the end of April, Illinois and Iowa will tend to have about 45% of their intended corn acres already planted, and some of the seeds will have emerged above ground and started their lives as little green plants. Weather across the Corn Belt, therefore, is a major market factor in April and subsequent months. A killing frost can damage production prospects, as can excess precipitation (which can prevent farmers from accessing their fields and planting a crop). Weather that is too dry, on the other hand, may not bode well for the emergence of the seed and its ultimate production capabilities, but farmers – being the eternal optimists they are – will readily plant seed into dry ground. There is a saying in Kansas: "Plant in the dust and bins will bust."

May

Because of the threat of frost, the planting pace throughout the spring will naturally be more advanced in the southern portions of the Corn Belt than in the northern parts. North Dakota, for instance, doesn't usually hit the halfway point for planting its corn acres until mid-May. But these days, soil temperature and weather are about the only things that can slow down planting. Given the prevalence of large, efficient farming equipment, it's estimated that all the corn acres anywhere could theoretically be planted within a 7-day period. In other words, the physical task of getting the seed into the ground isn't the bottleneck it used to be a generation ago, when it took farmers a month of working to get a crop seeded into the ground.

Spring is a timeframe when the market closely watches if the planting pace is getting the seed into the ground earlier or later than usual. When a corn seed is inserted into the soil, it contains within its thin shell 100% of its production potential. From that point forward, its yield prospects can only be decreased by non-ideal conditions. So normal or early planting can't increase a crop's yield prospects, but it can remove one of the sources of production risk and therefore remove some risk premium from futures prices. On the other hand, late planting of a crop means that it could reach critical stages of its lifespan – pollination and grain fill – during non-ideal weather conditions, like the heat of late July or early August. In the heart of the Corn Belt, for each day after May 15 that a corn field gets planted, it's estimated that the final yield will be reduced by more than a bushel per acre, but it's actually best expressed as a percentage of expected yield (e.g. 1.2% of what would ordinarily be 150 bpa corn would be equivalent to 1.8 bushels per acre lost per day).

Soybeans require a shorter timeframe to mature and will reach their critical production stages later than corn, so they are typically planted after corn throughout the Corn Belt. By mid-May, the Iowa / Illinois / Indiana center of the Corn Belt will typically have about a third of its soybean acres planted. Because they are relatively more tolerant of late planting, whenever weather does prevent some farmers from getting their corn planted on schedule, those farmers may switch some of their planting intentions from corn to soybeans (bullish to corn prices because of fewer acres and simultaneously bearish to soybean prices because of relatively larger plantings). But other than that, planting progress should theoretically be a less important market consideration than the overall number of acres being planted and the longer-term weather projections for the summer ahead.

June

Farmers in the U.S. usually have all their soybean planting finished up within the first few weeks of June because again, the physical task of planting is rarely the bottleneck, unless spring rain prevents planting from getting done quite as quickly as farmers would like. Once all their crops are planted and growing, however, other tasks lie ahead. Farmers apply fertilizers and/or herbicides, pesticides, and fungicides to their growing crops. If they're not busy doing all that, grain farmers who also raise livestock are probably busy putting up hay. Except for needing to access their fields for those reasons, they would be happy to have June be one long, rainforest-like stretch of steady precipitation and relatively hot weather. Plant growth is fostered by good nutrition, adequate moisture, and the accumulation of **growing degree days** (a unit system to measure the cumulative heat needed to grow a crop).

As the crops bask in an ideal environment – or suffer in a non-ideal one – June is a timeframe when the crops' condition will start to be directly observable. A "windshield tour" of a region can be done simply by driving through the countryside and taking notes about whether or not the young plants seem to be thriving: Do they seem choked by weeds? Do they seem to not have enough soil moisture? Do they seem yellow and anemic for lack of certain nutrients? Do they seem smaller and later-developing than they should be for this time of year? Unfortunately, a windshield tour alone can't give a full picture of what may be happening within the middle of some fields (drowned-out areas, for instance), so some observers may use aerial images, including infrared images, taken from airplanes or even satellites to get a fuller analysis of crop condition during the summer growing months.

July

While the row crops were just getting started, the winter wheat crop was maturing and starting to be harvested. By the beginning of July, most southern states with winter wheat acres (Texas, California, Arkansas) will tend to have most of those acres harvested already. In Kansas, where about 15% of the nation's wheat is grown – more than in any other state – July is the hottest month of winter wheat harvest. This is the time of the infamous "gut slot" of harvest, when the entire crop must find space somewhere – in a farmer's bins or in a local elevator before it can be loaded out on trains and sent off to end users. Obviously, this can have an effect on the wheat markets, as owners who don't have enough space to store the grain become very eager to sell it to someone who does. Also, anecdotal reports from the fields give the market an idea of how much grain is being harvested – a normal amount? A smaller-than-expected, bullish amount? Or a larger-than-expected, bearish amount?

The timing of winter wheat harvest also makes it possible, in some areas, to grow two crops on the same field within one year, a practice called **double-cropping**. In southern states, where winter wheat could be harvested sometime in June, the farmer could turn around and plant soybeans directly where the wheat had just been harvested, with confidence that he has enough warm, frost-free days before those soybeans reach maturity in the fall.

For soybeans that were planted at the more traditional timeframe, July is the month when the plants will start blooming, if they are healthy. This pollination timeframe, wherein soybean plants produce flowers and then start setting pods, is the soybean plant's most moisture-sensitive phase. However, the flowering stage stretches across two months and isn't much affected by heat. Flowers that are set early have precedence in setting pods on the plant, but later flowers can compensate for some losses, so therefore soybeans are relatively less weather-sensitive than corn during this timeframe. It's still critical that the weather not be so dry that the pollen desiccates, and the plants must have access to enough moisture to support them as they fill the pods.

Corn plants, on the other hand, are quite sensitive to weather during the month of July. The corn plants will by now have reached their full height and started to produce silk (which is the equivalent of flowers). Pollen from the tassels at the tops of corn plants will fall down onto the silks and fertilize the cells that will grow into kernels of corn. Therefore, how well the corn plants fare during this timeframe will directly determine how many kernels of corn will be produced on each ear out in each field. Obviously, corn pollination can't tolerate drought conditions which cause the silks to desiccate, but the plants themselves are also sensitive to nights that are too hot and humid. They need to have a cooling-off period at the night-times to respirate and generate the energy to produce grain. By the end of July, it becomes possible to go out into a cornfield and pull small, immature ears off the plants to see how well pollinated they are and how well the grain is filling. The weather during all these critical periods of grain production is closely watched by the market to determine the bullishness or bearishness of the crop's yield prospects.

August

In August, corn kernels will still be "doughing" (filling with flesh) and, starting from the southern states moving northward, corn will start to "dent." That's the stage reached when the ear's kernels have filled with their maximum amount of flesh. The corn is considered physiologically mature soon after this point and all that's left to do is for it to dry down and get ready for harvest. It's therefore impossible for good weather to have an effect on improving corn's yield prospects from that point forward, but poor weather can still be a threat – hail could still wipe out fields, or an early frost could shut down the plant and prevent the grain kernels from drying properly. If the plants run out of soil moisture or nitrogen and shut down before their natural maturation and dry-down occurs, the leaves of the plant may start to roll and the plants themselves may start "firing." You can identify firing when the plants dry up and turn brown from the bottom up, rather than from the top tips of the leaves downward, and it's a sign that the ears wouldn't have been able to ideally fill their kernels.

Some corn fields may get harvested while still green, before the actual kernels of corn are fully mature. The end product of such harvesting is called **silage**, and it's typically harvested as a feed for livestock, but it could also be used to produce biofuel. To produce silage, a farmer would harvest and chop up entire moist green plants – leaves, stalks, ears, and all – then compress and store the roughage out of the elements (in a silo or tarped bunker, for instance) so the substance can ferment and preserve the nutrients in the feed.

So while corn is basically either made or not made by the time August rolls around, it's actually the most critical month for soybean production. Soybean plants across the nation are still setting pods during this timeframe, which means they crucially need adequate moisture. Without it, observers may notice droopy leaves or aborted flowers in soybean fields. But once the pods have fully developed beans inside them, the plants will naturally start dropping leaves. Even though it doesn't make the plants look particularly healthy (eventually, they'll be nothing more than sticks and pods), leaf-drop is actually the usual, healthy pattern of development. Again, benchmark stages of soybean production will first be noticed in southern states and move northward.

While the spring-planted row crops were pollinating and filling up kernels of grain, spring-planted wheat was also maturing: tillering, heading, filling each kernel with flesh, and finally drying down into maturity. August is the hot month for spring wheat harvest in the Northern Plains - Minnesota, South Dakota, and North Dakota - so the Minneapolis futures market will be the one to respond to harvest reports in this timeframe.

September

Once a corn field is mature, which most of them will tend to be by the end of September, farmers still must wait until the grain is dry before they'll be willing to harvest it. If grain has more than 15% moisture content, it may be susceptible to deterioration or even rotting in storage, so buyers will dock farmers if they bring in grain that's too wet. However, it is possible to harvest grain that's a little wet, then put it through a grain dryer to evaporate the moisture out. This involves some delicate math: grain that is too dry will weigh less and have the same volume as grain with 15% moisture, so it doesn't make much economic sense to pay for the natural gas (or whatever energy source) to run a grain dryer, only to be paid for fewer pounds of grain. There is almost always a discount for wet grain, but rarely any premium paid for especially-dry grain.

In any case, unless they're harvesting a few fields for silage, most of the Corn Belt's farmers spend the month of September getting their equipment ready and waiting for harvest. In the last few weeks of September, farmers in the southern tips of Illinois and Indiana may start harvesting, and the majority of Texas and North Carolina's corn may already be harvested. Of course, the actual timing of harvest in any given year depends on that year's weather –

late spring planting can lead to a relatively late fall harvest (or the opposite), or a rainy fall can delay harvest and lead to quality losses in the overall crop. But whenever large quantities of corn start coming to market, it will affect the price. Futures traders will of course respond bearishly to reports of larger-than-expected harvest prospects or bullishly to reports of smaller-than-expected harvest prospects. But an even clearer response to harvest pressure can be noted in the local basis levels wherever the harvest is hitting its gut slot. To the degree that southern states experience a relatively large or relatively early harvest that gets delivered against hedges in the September futures market, that September contract can be considered a "new crop" futures contract in some years or an "old crop" futures contract in other years.

October

Once the September futures contract expires, all the corn harvested in October onward has to be delivered against hedges made in the December futures contract, so that is usually the first futures contract market we can confidently say is fully a "new crop" market. October is the big month for row crop harvest. This varies in some regions and some years, but Corn Belt farmers typically harvest soybeans before harvesting corn. Also, because it's inconvenient to switch equipment and storage facilities around mid-harvest, they usually harvest all their soybeans first before starting on corn, even if the corn is possibly dry and ready for harvest before they're totally done with soybean harvest. In any case, a good portion of U.S. soybean acres may already be harvested before the start of October, but by mid-October, perhaps only a third of the Corn Belt's corn acres will have been harvested.

As with planting, it's usually not the physical pace of harvesting that's the bottleneck for getting the grain out of the fields and onto the market. Weather permitting, farmers can harvest fields about as fast as they can plant them, although it does require more labor. There can be local bottlenecks if the elevator can't dump trucks very quickly or if it fills up and can't create more space for grain. However, aside from affecting the local basis market, such considerations shouldn't figure into the actual bullishness or bearishness for the overall market's supply and demand. About the only way harvesting *pace* (separate from a harvest's yield results) should theoretically affect market prices would be if the harvest was significantly delayed by wet or stormy weather that could affect the quality of the grain, limiting the supply of good grain available to end users that year.

The other big activity in October is winter wheat planting. If a farmer intends to plant winter wheat after a crop of soybeans or small grains, it's entirely possible that the original crop would have been harvested by mid-September or early October, and the farmer could turn right around and put winter wheat seed into the same ground. In Kansas, for instance, three quarters of their winter wheat acres could be planted before the middle of October. So even though you might not think the weather matters on empty, harvested fields, in the regions where winter wheat is grown, it's already important to receive timely precipitation from October onward so the seeds can germinate and the plants can get a good start.

November

By the middle of November, all but the last few soybeans fields around the country should be harvested, and the nation's corn harvest should be reaching its ¾ mark, even in states like North Dakota and Michigan. Consider that the northern tiers of the Corn Belt not only had to wait a little longer to plant their crops to avoid spring frosts, but they also have more urgency to harvest their crops before heavy snows start to blanket the ground. Elsewhere, winter wheat plants should all have emerged before the end of November, if they are going to emerge at all.

December

Once the harvest is done and the equipment and the grain is all tucked away, winter approaches and fall-seeded crops, like winter wheat, enter a period of dormancy. Farmers, however, aren't entirely dormant in December. This is a good timeframe to plan ahead for next year – to evaluate which seed varieties or production techniques worked well that year and which didn't; to order next year's seed; to market grain; to perform repairs on existing equipment, or to make purchases of new equipment before the tax year comes to an end.

Having fully digested all the fundamental data about the new supply of harvested grain, the futures markets may be more responsive to outside market forces during this timeframe than to grain-specific considerations. There are basically no North American weather concerns to affect trade in December, but investment fund rebalancing or investors' general opinions about the economy and geopolitical risk can still create volatility in grain prices during this period.

Also, don't ever forget that while all these annual production patterns are going on in the U.S., similar or opposite production patterns are going on all over the world. Significant amounts of grain are also produced in Canada, Europe, Russia, the Ukraine, and China – all of which fall within the northern hemisphere and therefore produce grain on roughly the same schedule as America, although with different crop mixes and sometimes with different production practices. Meanwhile, about a third of the world's soybeans are produced in Brazil, and they usually export about 40% of their production, so things that affect production in the southern hemisphere (prices, input availability, weather, etc.) are very influential. The world soybean market has more of a six-month seasonal cadence, because of the production in both hemispheres, rather than an annual pattern.

The row crop growing regions in Brazil and Argentina stretch more than 1,000 miles, north to south, so just as a corn farmer in Texas is likely to plant his crops sooner than a farmer in North Dakota might, the seasonal production patterns in these countries have rather wide variations. But for a general idea, you can expect South American farmers to be planting their soybeans from October through December; watching their plants flower and fill with grain (stages that are particularly sensitive to weather) during late January, February, and March; then harvesting the soybeans in April and May. Because the infrastructure of roads, railways, and grain storage facilities hasn't been developing for as many years as the same systems in the U.S. have been around, it can take relatively longer for the harvested South American crops to get from the fields to the world export market. Also, some Brazilian farmland with a long growing season can be double-cropped within a year, so there can be two row crop harvest seasons in that region. Australia is another production region in the southern hemisphere that can move world markets – it plants wheat from May to July and harvests it from October through December. Other agricultural crops like coffee, sugar, orange juice and palm oil have significant production areas in the southern hemisphere, but these have a less direct influence on grain trading.

Condition Reports

Back in the U.S., however, data about how quickly or how well crops like corn, soybeans, and wheat are progressing through their annual production schedule is closely watched by market participants. For farmers who see their own small region of the Corn Belt – and one small region only – throughout a growing season, there can be a tendency to concentrate only on what is happening in their backyards, or out their truck windshields. If southeast Missouri is very dry one summer, for instance, farmers there may experience some consternation if the grain futures markets don't react to their drought with higher prices. However, if the rest of the Corn Belt receives adequate moisture even while Missouri's crops are burning up, the average yield and aggregate production throughout the U.S. can insulate the overall markets from any major effect (though it would be a different matter for the local basis market, of course).

The same is true for any independent analyst who takes a windshield tour through any particular crop region – he can't possibly see the entire crop or even enough of the crop to make a fully accurate estimation of the entire nation's production. To counteract this "backyarditis" phenomenon, the USDA releases weekly **Crop Progress** reports. Government observers take note each Sunday evening how much of the crop has been planted in their area, or what growth stage the crop is in, or what condition it is in. When these thousands of observations get aggregated together on the state and national levels, the market can start to understand whether the full production prospects for the upcoming year are bullish or bearish.

It's not so important for the market to know how quickly farmers are completing certain tasks, except in extreme circumstances when a slow pace might lead to a loss of planted acreage or a loss of quality. But it is very critical to have estimates for how well crops will yield, which depends strongly on how well the crops fare throughout their growing season. Knowing that 81% of Iowa's corn has emerged by May 20th is therefore a less useful data point (for traders) than knowing 16% of Iowa's corn was rated no better than in "fair" condition on July 15th.

Crop Progress surveyors make visual observations of the growing crop and give their own subjective evaluations about how well that crop is looking – they can respond with what proportions of the crop they consider to be "very poor," "poor," "fair," "good," or "excellent." This means there's not just one number to compare each week against the previous week's situation, but market analysts will sometimes use the sum of the "good" and the "excellent" proportions together as a benchmark from week to week, or index the ratings. Even though the surveys are subjective, the Crop Progress report is a valuable tool for market analysts. The survey responses are reviewed for "reasonableness and consistency" by comparing them against previous weeks' or surrounding counties' responses, and in any case, approximately 4,000 surveys are compiled into the weekly national report, so there is statistical confidence in the average response.

Some traders may want an edge on the weekly Crop Progress report that every other trader on earth is also poring over. And it's possible to point out the weaknesses of the government's official report without even suggesting the USDA is negligent in any way. It's simply not always possible to determine a crop's production prospects with just a drive-by visual observation. Corn, for instance, can look very green and tall and healthy and yet experience yield losses if hot temperatures restrict the plants' pollination. Infrared aerial imagery, which is perhaps the best way to show the true national planted acreage,[2] accounting for the drowned-out low spots within certain fields, can be great for showing the overall health of the nationwide crop, but even this method could miss the effects of poor pollination. So traders and analysts who develop a broad network of observers throughout the Corn Belt can sometimes get a tip on some market concern which *may* just be a localized production problem … or it *may* signal a fresh, serious problem the rest of the market hasn't fully incorporated into their production estimates yet.

Weather

It's clear why weather is so influential to grain market price: if a crop is likely to have a poor yield, that's bullish because there will be relatively less supply over which end users can compete. If a crop is likely to have an ample yield, that's bearish because the supply of grain will flood the market and sellers will be relatively keen. So throughout a growing season, prices may include gradually less **risk premium** as time goes on. At the start, there is the full season's worth of weather stressors to get through and a great deal of uncertainty about final yields. That uncertainty itself is somewhat bullish – the market is reluctant to sell before it's confident about production. On each subsequent day of the growing season, however, there are gradually fewer and fewer ways for weather to damage the crop, and therefore gradually more confidence about how much grain will really be produced.

The timing of weather-related yield estimates not only affects speculators' opinions on the market; it also has a profound effect on the timing of farmers' pre-harvest **grain marketing**, the process of deciding how much grain to sell at which time, at which price level, and with which financial instrument. If a farmer always plants some corn and some soybeans every year, then he knows he'll have some of each to sell to the market every year. If he likes the price of the December corn futures contract posted three years out in the future, he could hedge *some* of his corn crop with those futures. He should not, however, hedge his *entire* projected corn crop too far in the future because he can't be entirely confident there won't be flooding or drought or some other natural disaster that limits how much grain he will produce in that year.

This is true even for grain that is planted and growing in the field – farmers tend to be hesitant to commit to forward selling physical grain they can't be confident will even grow into existence. For instance, in March a farmer may think he's going to plant enough acres to produce 100,000 bushels of corn. He might sell 50,000 bushels (or 50% of intended production) to his local elevator. However, by the time July rolls around and his crop is withering and dying out in the field, those 50,000 bushels might represent 100% of what he now expects his production to be. No matter how the market price changes, that farmer can't commit to selling any more corn. In this kind of scenario, financial hedges (options contracts or short futures positions) allow a farmer's grain marketing plan to be a lot more flexible. He can get out of a short futures position instantaneously by just calling his broker, but an elevator or end user may never let him out of a cash forward grain contract; if he can't produce the grain one year, they may just ask him to bring in the next year's bushels to honor the contract. If he does have a crop failure and has to buy out of his cash contracts, a crop insurance payout may help him financially.

In any case, that's one reason why the futures markets respond directly to weather. If farmers' fields have experienced adequate weather, they may be relatively willing to sell grain before harvest. Remember that even if they only sell cash contracts and never participate in the futures markets themselves, the grain buyers will be hedging their purchases with short futures positions, so no matter how a farmer chooses to sell grain, it will pretty much always result in some equivalent selling pressure in the futures market. On the other hand, if farmers' fields are suffering from poor weather conditions, that selling may dry up entirely and end users might become eager to hedge future purchases with long futures positions.

Those considerations can be backward-looking and very much influenced by "backyarditis," and rightly so. Those are independent decisions being made about independent fields that have experienced real, observed weather. Merchandisers will experience a strengthening or weakening of their local basis levels based on their local weather alone, with the secondary effects of a drought 500 miles away being less pronounced. For speculators trading grain futures, however, the real trick is not only to see crop weather as a big, nationwide picture, but also to *anticipate* upcoming weather rather than *react* to observed weather.

I'm not just talking about the 7-day weather forecasts you might watch on your local news channel, although those can be interesting, too. Long-time market analyst Gary Wilhelmi once told me how he could directly see the futures prices react to rain in northern Illinois when Chicago traders watched Tom Skilling's daily weather report on WGN's Midday News, although I think now that worldwide electronic traders have surpassed the Chicago pit's volume, the "Skilling Effect" may be less pronounced.

The real weather forecasts grain traders should be watching are long-term and very scientific in nature. Money is made in futures trading by intuiting or predicting a market movement before the rest of the market has already had a chance to incorporate that information into the price. An efficient market will always reflect all the known information about that market into its price ... eventually ... but traders who can access the information faster than others, or make more accurate predictions about the information than others, have an advantage to buy sooner at cheaper prices or sell sooner at higher prices.

So a fundamental grain trader who wants to identify a new trading opportunity, or just be protective of positions he has on, should acquire detailed weather forecasts and maps. The National Weather Service provides free access to their short range forecasts and climatic outlooks (6-10 days, 8-14 days, one month out, and three months out), but for more detailed, grain-market specific comments and for international weather commentary, traders may subscribe to any of a number of weather research services. Those should provide frequent updates with any changes to the forecast, as well as the context in which the weather will occur. Heavy snow in North Dakota in January or a dry pattern in Australia in March may not mean very much to the grain market prices when there are no developing crops in those places at those times.

Traders will also discover a wealth of weather information and harvest information freely proffered on social media websites. If it's dry in Kansas and the wheat crop is suffering, no one will be more likely to make that news public than a Kansas wheat farmer. Farmers' backyarditis everywhere is especially pronounced when their local weather is seen as bullish to the grain markets. Of course, observers on the ground in grain producing regions really do have the best view to determine how weather is affecting crop development, and the aggregation of their news can be very valuable to a trader, but you should also be a little wary about anyone who is "talking their position."

Farmers' Many Tasks

Farmers, obviously, worry about the weather forecasts not just when their developing crops are affected but also with respect to the many tasks they have to carry out throughout a growing season. A 30 mph wind out of the south in early June may or may not affect how much a corn field will ultimately yield, but it might prevent the farmer from applying herbicide that day because he wouldn't want the spray to drift onto a neighbor's field or tree strip. I've gone through the calendar of how crops develop throughout a year, but it may be useful for you to know the specific tasks that farmers perform to facilitate that crop growth. These tasks don't have much relevance to the underlying market price for grains, but nonetheless, it might be helpful for you to know what your farmer colleagues and neighbors are up to:

Field Preparation – Think back to the story of my ancestors picking rocks out of South Dakota fields. Field preparation tasks can vary depending on the environment and the soil type of any particular field, and there can be a lot of physical work required to initially prepare a field, or to maintain it from one year to the next. In the northern plains, the initial task may be rock removal. For river bottom ground farther east, it may be clearing brush and grinding tree stumps. For very hilly ground, farmers may build **terraces** – leveled "steps" tracing a field's topography, built wide enough to get farming equipment across and which prevent soil from eroding and washing down the hill.

For heavy soils that retain a lot of moisture, farmers may install a **tiling** system beneath the surface, which historically involved digging a pattern of clay or concrete pipes under the soil by hand to draw water away from crops' roots and let gravity direct it away to a nearby body of water. Today, tiling is usually done with power equipment and porous plastic pipe. On the other hand, if a field is too sandy or located in either a dry climate or above a cheap source of water, farmers may install an **irrigation** system. Historically and still today, some irrigation has been accomplished by a system of permanent gravity-fed canals and ditches, with temporary gated pipes placed in a field by hand each year. Center-pivot irrigation, with sprinklers on tall rolling metal frames that sweep around fields in circular or "windshield wiper" patterns, is also an efficient way to deliver water and nutrients to growing plants. Even more efficient is the practice of subsurface drip irrigation. Thin plastic "drip tape" tubes are buried more than a foot below the soil in parallel lines every few feet across a field, with fluid emitters every 2 feet along the tubes. With drip tape irrigation, fluids can be delivered directly to crops' roots without risk of evaporation, and fields can be programmed into zones, with computerized control of how nutrients get delivered to each zone.[3] Computerized control of nutrient delivery based on GPS data can also be accomplished with center pivot irrigation, and none of this is cheap. Even to do nothing more complicated than get water from below the ground (e.g. from a well) onto a crop requires some kind of pump and some kind of energy to power that pump, like diesel or natural gas.

Even in fields that require no major infrastructure projects, there can still be seedbed preparation tasks that pop up in any given year. Erosion or compaction in certain areas of a field might require some time-consuming soil preparation one year. The bridges, roads, and approaches a farmer requires to get his equipment into a field may require maintenance the next year. Altogether, field preparation activities can be some of the most time-consuming and expensive tasks in a farmer's annual repertoire.

Tillage – A more routine farming task is tilling the soil. Contrary to the image of oxen pulling heavy equipment in a historical drama, today's farmers don't do much plowing anymore. The moldboard **plow** was the device that skewed society toward assigning relatively more value to the gender with the most upper body strength: it's basically a wedge-shaped piece of metal which must be forced into the ground with significant down-pressure, then dragged through the soil and roots with a great deal of power. Multiple plows can be attached side by side in "gangs" to till a wider swath of soil with each pass, and that of course requires even more horsepower.

Today's farmers may still need to use a moldboard plow to turn very heavy soil types or soil with a lot of deep roots in it. However, a far more common tillage tool is a chisel plow, which has much thinner blades than a moldboard plow, digs a shallower path into the soil, and therefore requires less horsepower per shank to pull. This means one tractor can pull a much wider implement – chisel plows *can* be more than 60 feet wide, although most farmers don't have powerful enough pulling equipment, large enough fields, or urgent enough efficiency needs to make a 60' chisel a necessity. Farmers may also use a **disk** harrow or ripper to aerate soil in preparation for planting – these are similar to chisel plows but rather than shanks, they use saucer-shaped coulters to cut vertically into the soil. There is a growing movement among farmers to adopt "vertical tillage" practices that minimally disturb the soil profile (little or no horizontal disruption). On the most progressive end of the environmentally-beneficial spectrum are **no-till** practices, which limit soil erosion, maximize organic residue, preserve soil moisture, and bring down the fuel and labor costs of farming. Wherever the soil type and climate makes no-till farming possible, the time-consuming traditions of digging up black soil (and allowing that soil to blow away or wash away) are waning.

These days, if tillage is done, it's either in the spring right before planting to loosen the soil for seed placement, or in the fall after a harvest to break up the past crop's residue. In any case, farmers are rarely using tillage as a weed control technique anymore. Historically, farmers used to run a **cultivator** in between crop rows to disrupt mid-season weed development in their fields, or even hoed out individual weeds by hand. Now chemical herbicides can accomplish most of these weed-control tasks, so tillage is mostly a technique for preparing the soil or delivering nutrients deeper into the soil.

Planting – Up to this point in the farmer's task list, nothing had to be too precise. As long as he got all the soil prepared without running his tractor into any fences, it doesn't matter very much what pattern he drove to get the job done. Once he goes to put seed into the ground, however, it becomes crucial to maximize the efficiency of the geometrical placing of each row of seeds. **Planters, air seeders**, and **drills** are implements that are pulled behind a tractor like tillage equipment, and which may have similar coulters and down-pressure to get the parallel rows of seeds the right depth into the soil with the right spacing between each seed. Row crop planters tend to be manufactured in six- or eight-row sections (24-row planters are common), with each row perhaps 30 inches apart (or some other width), to facilitate eventual harvesting by similarly configured equipment.

Once a farmer makes one pass of 24 rows of corn seed, for instance, he could just turn around and try to drive a perfectly parallel next pass. He won't necessarily be able to see where the previous pass of seed was placed, but he can use the wheel-marker to guide him. However, if his driving wobbles even a little, he could leave a few extra inches of unplanted soil, or he could over-seed some areas. Farmers carefully select what **planting population** will optimize the yield in a particular field. Too few plants per acre could underutilize the soil and inputs, but too many plants per acre can compete against each other and draw down total yield. So to get seed perfectly distributed in an efficient geometrical pattern, without any skips or overseeding, the agriculture industry has embraced GPS (Global Positioning System) technology as part of an entire suite of **precision agriculture** techniques.

Precision agriculture can include anything that manages the data for intra-field variations of a crop – does it require more nutrients in the low spots? Does it yield better on the south side of the hill? But it all starts with accurately recording data about what was planted. What variety of seed and at what population was it planted on each square foot of soil? To accurately track that seed's performance throughout a growing season, the farmer must know its exact geographic location on earth so that a planting map can be compared to a mid-season aerial photograph, for instance, and certainly to the eventual harvesting map.

Thus, the development of GPS-guided planters. The system works by attaching a dual array of GPS receivers to the tractor, which can measure not only the tractor's latitude and longitude but also its geometric angle compared to the horizon (so the system can account for seed rows planted on a hill, for instance). Then the whole rig is guided in perfectly parallel passes using hydraulic **autosteer**. Depending on how accurate the underlying GPS guidance is, the passes can be accurate to within 1 inch of the intended path. The planter boxes are a measured distance from the tractor itself, so the system knows exactly where each row of seeds is being planted into the soil and can map each seed's location and depth. If the planter is equipped with independent air clutches for each seed row or each section of seed rows, the in-cab computer can also shut off the flow of seeds as the planter passes back over areas that have already been planted (like at the end of rows or at the corners of fields). This obviously saves the farmer in fuel consumption and seed costs – between 3 and 12% less seed gets used, depending on a field's terrain. But the real "savings" from precision ag planting comes from the increased crop yield that is possible when a farmer can put an ideal seed population onto every square foot of his field.[4] After the first decade of the 21st century, not all farmers have made the investment in these precision ag technologies, but the adoption rate is growing.

Scouting – It may not seem like very hard work for a farmer to get in his pickup truck and drive around the county and look at his fields (and his neighbors' fields), but crop scouting is a very important task throughout a growing season. There are any number of stressors that can limit a crop's yield potential, and the key to managing those stressors is to anticipate or identify them as early as possible.

Aside from weather stressors, which a farmer can't do much to mitigate unless his fields have an irrigation system, crops can also be pressured by weeds (annuals, biennials, perennials, and grasses), insects (bugs, beetles, weevils, flies, moths, grasshoppers), non-insects (slugs, mites, and isopods), or diseases (bacterial infections, fungal infections, viruses, nematodes, and phytoplasmas). Sometimes by the time a farmer notices a stressor in his field, it will be too late to do anything, and sometimes there won't be anything he can do. Goss's wilt, for instance, is a bacterial corn disease with no known treatment, although it can be somewhat managed with pre-planting decisions like crop rotations, residual tillage, and selection of partially resistant hybrids.[5] Similarly, Asian Soybean Rust is a fungus that's difficult to treat if its trademark lesions are identified too late in the disease's development.

If a farmer is unsure of something he's noted in his fields, he may consult an agronomist. **Agronomy** is a branch of science which involves the application of plant science (biology) and soil science to crop production. That consultation may not only help the farmer correctly identify the stressor, but also help prescribe the correct treatment.

    <u>Chemical application</u> – To facilitate crop growth, there are nitrogen-based fertilizers and other mineral nutrients. To control insects, there are insecticides; to control diseases, there are fungicides and nematicides; to control weeds, there are herbicides. In the event that a farmer needs to use any of these chemical substances, rest assured he doesn't want to apply any more of it than he absolutely has to, because the stuff is expensive and cuts into profits.

    The development of herbicide-tolerant crop varieties was a disruptive technology that allowed farmers to abandon mechanical tillage for post-emergence weed control. Now they can plant carefully engineered seed, allow the plants to sprout, and then after the plants have emerged the farmers can spray herbicide directly on the entire field, grain plants and all, but the herbicide will only destroy the non-tolerant plants ... i.e. the weeds. It can only be done with certain chemical herbicides and certain proprietary seed technology (and woe to the chemical applicator who sprays the wrong herbicide on the wrong field), so it's a favorite method for agrochemical companies to sell patented products. But it has truly revolutionized agriculture – beyond saving humankind millions of hours of hoeing, it saves the earth from Dust Bowl-style soil erosion because it allows farmers to grow crops with minimal or no tillage. However, just like some human bacteria have grown resistant to certain antibiotics, the multi-decade usefulness of certain herbicides has allowed some weeds to develop resistances. Agrochemical companies are constantly trying to bring new modes of action to compete in the market for farmers' dollars as they strive to keep yield-limiting weeds and other pests out of their crops.

    There are many different techniques to actually apply these products: fertilizer can be "knifed" into the soil with a disk before or during planting, or it may be "side-dressed" precisely along the rows after the plants have sprouted. Chemicals that need to be widely broadcast across a field may be delivered through an irrigation system, saving a farmer the labor of driving a sprayer back and forth across the field. For the majority of fields which don't have an irrigation system, however, chemicals need to be delivered by spraying equipment that drives between the growing rows of plants or by aerial applicators (a.k.a. "crop duster" aircraft) that fly over them. Here again, GPS precision agriculture equipment can save a lot of time and money, because chemicals can be delivered to each square foot of ground only in the precise rates required – no waste.

Harvesting – Once a crop has made it past all the threats it faced during a growing season and has matured into dry grain, farmers must harvest the crop. Historically, this was a two-step process: first cutting the plants with a header (which was pushed "ahead" of a team of animals), then threshing or flailing the cut material to separate the grain from the stalks and leaves. In the early 1800's, **combine harvesters** were invented, which "combined" the two tasks of cutting and threshing. It's still possible to hear young farmers talk about "picking" corn or "threshing" grain simply because those were the terms passed down to them through previous generations of farmers.

Today's combines, however, are probably the most technologically-advanced pieces of equipment (and certainly the most expensive) a farmer is likely to own or lease. Recently, John Deere's version with an in-cab mini-refrigerator for the operator's beverages made quite a splash at farm equipment shows. However many bells and whistles a combine might have, however well it collects precision agriculture data for each square foot of a field, it still accomplishes the same basic tasks of cutting and collecting plant material with a header, feeding that material into a threshing drum where grain is gleaned out, then blowing out the residue and collecting the harvested grain into a large hopper.

Harvesting is the farm task that requires the most parallel labor. One farmer can probably plant all his fields by himself in series, one after the other. But at harvest, it's more efficient to have multiple people simultaneously operating a combine, a grain cart to collect grain out of the combine's hopper, and trucks to haul that grain either to storage or to a grain-buying facility. The bottleneck can be any one of those tasks: maybe the combine harvesting 1,000 bushels per hour is the slowest part of the operation chain, or maybe the farmer bought a bigger, faster combine but now his grain cart can only get unloaded so fast. Maybe the elevator in town is backed up with other farmers' trucks and it wouldn't matter how fast the grain could be combined because there's no place to take it very quickly.

Rather than hire a bunch of part-time help to get his grain harvested, as he currently does, a farmer today has to start wondering about the time when fully autonomous equipment – which exists! – could become widely adopted. Tractors that pull planters already have GPS-guided auto-steer. Combine headers already have sensors to make sure they're lined up optimally with the rows, at the right height and with the right throughput settings. Grain carts and all other equipment *can* be outfitted with optical remote sensing technologies to prevent these "drone" implements from running into obstacles. Adoption of fully autonomous agricultural equipment seems a much closer reality than adoption of fully autonomous automobiles, for instance, but at this point the benefits of reduced labor requirements generally haven't yet outweighed the costs of implementing such a system. Also, at this point, truly precise GPS feeds aren't reliable enough or widely enough available to instill sufficient confidence in the owner of a $200,000 piece of equipment. Most farmers wouldn't be willing to turn such equipment loose with just a computer driving it and no human operator … yet. For now, precision agriculture adopters are perfectly able to use human labor and are simply satisfied with their savings on input costs and their improved yield potentials from advanced data analysis.

Grain Handling – Once the grain is out of the field and tucked away in storage, the farmer's job isn't done. He can spend much of the "off season" transporting his grain to market, or simply managing its condition. Precision agriculture can play a role here, too, with remote sensors within grain bins to communicate the grain's moisture, temperature, and inventory level. Too-high moisture or too-high temperature can threaten rot and / or heat damage to the grain.

<u>Behind-the-Scenes</u> – If he's not fixing equipment, cleaning equipment, drying grain, unloading grain from a bin to a truck, or driving a grain truck to market ... or if the winter weather is too hostile to support any outdoor grain handling tasks ... a farmer's job *still* isn't done. The decisions of when to market grain, at what price, and to whom, or the decisions of what crops to plant, with which seed varieties on which fields using which inputs, aren't the kinds of decisions that can be made on a knee-jerk hunch. Good farm management requires education, research and communication with a farmer's customers and input suppliers – some of which can be caught up on in those months when the crop isn't actively growing in the field.

Row Crops' Supply and Demand

Many of a farmer's tasks will be specific to the crop being grown. U.S. farmers grow 4 times as much corn, by volume, than the next biggest crop, which is soybeans, so by default most of my discussion of farming tasks was centered on these "**row crops.**" They are so called because they are typically planted in parallel rows. Corn production practices are a pretty good benchmark for discussing most other crops' production techniques, but corn does have its idiosyncrasies. One of corn's most important traits, which has directly led to its prominence and popularity, is **heterosis (a.k.a. hybrid vigor)**. Put simply, heterosis is the word for corn's ability to crossbreed well. Within one generation, the offspring of two cross-pollinated corn varieties can display better genetic traits than the sum of its two parents. Especially in comparison with the time consuming, many-generational process of selectively breeding plant varieties that don't crossbreed so well, the creation of hybrid corn seed has led to an astounding **yield curve** over the past seventy years.

Since the 1940's, widespread deployment of hybrid corn seed throughout the Corn Belt has led the national average corn yield not simply to grow at a linear rate (about an extra 1 ½ bushels per acre per year) but actually to grow at an exponential rate, which means that not only are we adding more than a bushel per acre to the average yield each year, but the amount we add itself increases year after year. The ability of seed companies to sell farmers these profitable hybrid varieties obviously leads to a great deal of excitement for those products, and a subsequent willingness to pay. Market demand then encourages seed companies to keep investing in ever-more advanced traits and ever-quicker techniques for bringing them to market (like seed chipping and DNA sequencing), so the whole circle of developing seed characteristics and creating demand for those seed characteristics is like a self-sustaining fire within the industry. Seed for no other crop is as profitable for a seed company to develop and sell (or for a farmer to buy and grow) than corn seed, and it's all due to heterosis.

But that's a fairly esoteric characteristic of corn, one that most farmers may not spend a lot of time thinking about. Rather, the characteristics they look for when buying seed corn include comparative relative maturity, or some similar metric that communicates how many growing-degree days are needed for the hybrid to mature (regions with shorter growing seasons may need to plant 90-day corn rather than a hybrid with a CRM of 100 or higher). The intended end user must also be considered when choosing corn seed – is the farmer intending to sell into a specialized market, like the white corn market, the popcorn market, or the seed corn market? Is he planting corn with a new enzyme that breaks down and flows through his local ethanol plant better, for which they will pay him a premium? Also, a farmer will consider the characteristics a specific hybrid has been bred to exhibit: root strength, stalk strength, drought tolerance, faster drydown of the grain, higher grain test weight, etc.

All those characteristics can be achieved from simply hybridizing corn, which is just a traditional breeding technique. But actual genetic modification of the corn seed's DNA has allowed seed companies to offer even more exciting, useful, or yield-enhancing characteristics to their products. If a variety of corn seed is "**single-stacked**," that means it has been imbued with a genetic characteristic – usually a protein that may come from a non-corn species – which allows it to resist pressure from a stressor like corn rootworms or corn borers, or which allows it to resist a specific post-emergence herbicide, like glyphosate. Corn seed may also be "double-stacked," meaning it has two of those three resistances, or "triple-stacked," meaning it contains all three genetic modifications.

Indeed, as the seed industry develops ever more genetic modifications to help corn resist other stressors, like drought, we will see an infinite number of "stacks" in our corn seed. Quadruple-stacked corn exists, but isn't widely deployed yet at this time.

Once the seed is planted, no matter what type of seed is planted, corn plants will go through a series of defined growth stages. "VE" is vegetative emergence – when the seed first sprouts and remains below soil. About a week later, the corn plant will display one leaf (V1) or two leaves (V2) above ground, and as the plant gets taller and adds more leaves, the **"V" stages** keep getting higher. Between V6 and V12, the corn plant will need to receive about 2 inches of water per week or it will suffer. Yield reduction can be as high as 2% per day if the corn plant faces drought during these stages. V14-V15 is the most critical time period for the crop, as **silking** starts to occur. The corn plant's silks are effectively its flowers, so their condition and how well they receive pollen will directly determine how many kernels of corn grow on each ear of each plant (field corn typically only sets one ear per plant). During pollination, corn yield reduction can be as high as 6% per day in a drought. "VT" is the term for **tasselling,** when the corn plant sheds pollen from the tassels at its top. At this point, the corn plant will have its maximum height, and all the subsequent development stages refer to the ear of grain itself: R1 is silking, R2 is blistering (kernels start to fill), R3 is milking, R4 is the dough stage, R5 is the dent stage, and R6 is physiological maturity.[6]

Once corn is produced and brought to market, the market's interest in a farmer's work may cease, but its interest in that corn does not. Remember there are two sides of supply-and-demand, and demand is no less important to price than supply is. However, it's nearly impossible to break demand down into discrete tasks and describe in detail, because the ways in which corn can be demanded and used are as varied as human existence. Bits of corn grown by U.S. farmers as described above could end up in the ketchup bottle in your refrigerator (as high fructose corn syrup), could end up in the packing peanuts in your next delivery (as a starch byproduct), could end up in your car's fuel tank (as ethanol), or could be ground up into a highly complex nutrition mixture being fed to livestock.

There is no substance on earth more useful, more capable of being bent to human requirement, than corn. Oil might come close, but you can't eat oil.

To assign all the uses of corn into categories, it's useful to adopt the same categories as the USDA uses each month when it releases its World Agricultural Supply and Demand Estimates (the **WASDE** report). On the supply side, there are either carryover stocks from the previous growing season, imports (not likely for corn in the U.S.), or production. On the demand side for corn, there is:

Food, Seed, & Industrial - When the grain markets talk about "corn" to be used in the human food chain, it's important to distinguish that we're not talking about the sweet corn varieties that you'd buy as whole ears or canned corn. Rather, this describes dry field corn that has been sold with certain characteristics (usually color, usually white) and a high-enough quality to be processed for human food products, like corn meal or the corn flour used to make tortilla chips. For corn of that quality, and for seed corn, the market usually has to pay a significant premium (10% of the price or more) in order to motivate growers to take on the extra production tasks, the extra risk, and the generally lower yield potentials. Seed corn refers to corn, usually hybridized, that isn't grown to be placed into the broader market but will rather be treated with inedible fungicides and saved for the following spring's planting needs.

The "industrial" segment is closely related to the "food" segment, because some corn enters the human food chain by way of high fructose corn syrup (**HFCS**), which is the sugar molecules of the grain, but when those molecules are processed by wet milling, other parts of the grain are simultaneously processed, like starch and oil. Corn starch can be used as a cooking ingredient (a thickener used in gravies), as baby powder, or to produce industrial products like eco-friendly plastics and styrofoams. And corn oil can similarly be used as a food ingredient (cooking oil or margarine) or as the raw material for industrial products.

Ethanol & by-products – The corn used for **ethanol**, a **biofuel** substitute for gasoline, undergoes a similar milling process (either wet milling or dry milling) as the corn used to produce industrial sugars, starches, and oils. Once milled, the sugar solution is just distilled into alcohol like any bootlegger would distill corn whiskey, except on a much larger scale and afterward, ethanol plants "denature" their alcohol with poisonous additives to make it inedible. So you might think an ethanol plant could get away with using lower quality grain or even inedible corn as the raw material for its process. However, the fiber and starches that are left over after corn's sugars have been extracted in an ethanol plant are still marketable – they are called "distillers' grains" or "dried distillers' grains" (**DDGs**) and are used as animal feed. You can't have a bunch of aflatoxin-infested corn running through an ethanol plant and ultimately poisoning some poor steer in a nearby feedlot. Corn that is sold to an ethanol plant is never wasted, and in fact much of it (about 30% by volume) ends up back on the feed market as DDGs, anyway, so although it's hard to account for those bushels in *both* the 'ethanol' and 'feed' categories of demand, the ethanol industry truly doesn't steal away as many bushels from the feed sector as the statistics otherwise imply.

Although the ethanol industry today no longer receives a per-gallon blenders' credit from the government, in the late 2000's, government support of the ethanol industry (for environmental and energy-independence goals) made the corn market itself highly sensitive to politics. This phenomenon may certainly continue as various industry participants, senators, lobbyists, and the Environmental Protection Agency all join the discussion about how much ethanol could or should be blended into the nation's fuel supply. Also, just like the corn market which reflects an entire world's worth of supply and demand, ethanol and DDGs can be and do get exported out of and imported into the United States. That balance itself is subject to the international politics of currency exchange rates and the environmental desirability of biofuels.

Feed – Grain, of course, gets fed to livestock, which in turn produce such agricultural products as beef, pork, poultry, fish, eggs, and milk. In the WASDE reports from the 1970's, before the ethanol industry ramped up and before kids started drinking so much soda pop, the 'feed' category of corn used up more than half the nation's total supply. Now, it accounts for less than 35% of the national corn supply, unless you include 30% of the bushels used in the ethanol crush, in which case animal feed use still accounts for about 45% of the nation's supply. All market data about the livestock sector, including USDA's monthly Cattle on Feed reports, their Hogs & Pigs reports, and all the supply and demand data collected by either the USDA or private analysts about poultry, aquaculture, etc., therefore directly affect the corn market, too.

However, feed demand for corn is more elastic than some traders realize. This is because there are so many substitutes for corn in livestock feed rations. Although livestock producers are careful about animal nutrition calculations and don't usually make sudden switches from ground corn to some other grain, most animals can also process sorghum grain (a.k.a. milo), feed wheat, or soybean meal to receive their daily requirements for energy and protein. There is a different mix of energy, protein, fats, and minerals in every feedstuff, but at the end of the day, all feedstuffs (or mixtures of feedstuffs) can be expressed as some combination of those nutrients. Dried milk pellets, beet pulp, the cast-offs from an Oreo cookie factory ... all these things *can* be used as animal feed instead of corn, although they will typically need to be mixed with other ingredients to reach an ideal nutrient content for the livestock species being fed. The implication for the corn market is that high prices can indeed ration the demand for corn itself, and the wheat market can sometimes benefit from that spillover demand.

Exports – Exports are another demand category that receives its own cluster of market data from the USDA and from private estimators. Weekly, the USDA reports how much grain U.S. exporters have committed to sell to foreign buyers, and from which countries those foreign buyers originate (the Export Sales report). There is a separate weekly report that details how much grain was actually physically loaded out from American exporting facilities each week (the Export Inspections report). But while these are the sources of "official" data, that doesn't stop the market from responding to more timely rumors of big sales or cancellations of previous sales. Sometimes, a foreign buyer's big purchase may be directly observable in the futures market as U.S. commercial grain companies hedge their physical sales with futures buying. Always remember that whoever bought or sold the grain, and wherever the grain is headed, once it gets there it will still have to be either fed to livestock, fed to humans, or turned into some useful product.

The other row crops have their own idiosyncrasies and their own supply and demand situations. Soybeans, for instance, require relatively less nitrogen and water to grow than corn. In fact, young soybean plants are relatively more sensitive to standing water in their field (soybeans don't like "wet feet") and relatively more sensitive to early frost than corn plants are. Their flowering and fill stages occur later in the growing season and stretch out for a longer period of time than corn's stages do, and it's therefore relatively more difficult to predict a soybean field's yield before harvest (although you can calculate the average pods per plant and beans per pod) than it is to predict a corn field's yield (all you have to do is observe the ears per acre and kernels per ear). Other than that, the crop's terminology will seem familiar: VE for emergence, V1, V2, V3 etc. for each subsequent trifoliolate (bunch of three leaves). Flowering starts after V6, followed by full bloom, pod setting, pod fill, leaf-dropping, and maturity.

Obviously, the pests and diseases and related treatments will be different for soybeans than corn, but the same agronomists and ag chemical retailers who provide inputs for corn farmers are also knowledgeable about soybean production. However, corn fields tend to yield 3 ½ to 4 times more grain, by volume, than soybean fields, and harvested soybeans tend to shrink and shatter more than other grains, so farmers, elevators, input retailers, and seed companies all tend to treat their soybean business as an afterthought to their main cash cow: corn. That's indeed what soybeans are; possibly the only reason so many soybeans get planted in the United States now is that it's considered good practice to rotate a field through different crops from one year to the next (rather than planting corn after corn after corn), plus soybeans are a **legume**, which means they actually fix nitrogen into the soil for the next crop, plus their relatively cheaper seeds and inputs sometimes make them attractive to farmers looking to save expenses. Of course, all this disregard for soybeans could change pretty quickly if the global supply and demand situation suddenly changed to make U.S. soybeans more profitable than corn, so the market itself plays a big role in soybeans' popularity or lack thereof.

The demand categories for soybeans will be similar to the ones for corn, except that they are applied not only to soybeans themselves, but also to their crush products: soybean oil and soybean meal. It's uncommon for soybeans to be consumed as whole, dry beans. A very specialized market exists for edamame (soybeans-in-pod, consumed fresh by humans like sweet corn) or for non-GMO or organic or specially-colored, high-quality soybeans that can enter the human food chain after processing into soy-based products, like tofu. But for the most part, the only people who would use a whole, dry soybean out of an American soybean field would be a livestock producer, and even that's rare. More frequently, end users will purchase one of the two soybean by-products (meal or oil) after the beans have been **extruded** in a processing plant.

Soybean meal is used as a very popular livestock feed. Some categories of livestock, like farmed fish, might never consume an ounce of corn in their lives, but soybean meal is a staple of their diets. Soybean meal's demand categories include both domestic use and exports, although exports make up less than a third of total demand. Because the end goal of a soybean processor is to sell a feed product with a certain protein profile with specific amino acids to animal nutritionists, processors need to measure the raw soybeans coming into their plants for their protein and oil contents. There is a market mismatch (and thus, endless arbitrage opportunities) between farmers selling as many *bushels* of soybeans as they can raise, and processors selling as high a *quality* meal and oil product as they can produce. It's common practice for soybean processors to reflect the value of a certain region's soybean quality from any given crop year buried within their posted basis bids, rather than as a premium / discount schedule for soybeans above or below 48% crude protein, for instance. Nevertheless, there are some soybean premium programs that directly pay growers for producing value-added soybeans.[7]

Soybean oil is also produced domestically, then either used domestically (for cooking oil, as a food ingredient, in industrial applications, or as biofuel) or exported, but exports are a relatively small portion of the picture. Soybeans themselves, therefore, are either kept as seed for next year's crop, crushed domestically into soybean meal and soybean oil (at levels reported monthly in the National Oilseed Processors Association – **"NOPA" – Crush Report**), or exported to some other country where the buyers will just do their own crushing. Soybean extrusion is a value-adding process, so politically, most countries would prefer to buy soybeans whole and keep as much of the industry within their own borders as possible. No discussion of soybean demand would be complete without mentioning China, which is by far the world's #1 importer of soybeans (over half the world market). Although China has its own agricultural land, it prefers to direct its resources toward growing feed grains domestically and then effectively "outsourcing" soybean production to the western hemisphere. Warmer regions, like Brazil and the U.S. Delta tend to produce soybeans with a higher protein content, which are then more highly sought-after.

A final row crop to mention is grain sorghum, also known as **milo**. Sorghum may be grown specifically as a hay or silage crop, and "sweet sorghum" is the term for a molasses-like substance that is processed from sorghum cane, but once it is harvested as grain, semantically "sorghum" = "milo." They are not two separate grain crops; there is no difference between them; they are simply two words for the same thing. Milo is directly comparable to corn in almost every way. If you drive past a young, green, growing row crop field, you'd have to look twice to tell whether it was milo or corn. Milo plants tend to be a little shorter and spikier. If you're feeding livestock or running an ethanol plant, you can pretty much directly substitute milo for corn in a 1:1 ratio.

The main differences between milo and corn are evolutionary – the ancestors of modern corn plants developed in Central America while sorghum developed in Africa. The two crops also have cosmetic differences - corn grows in ears that set fruits (kernels) about halfway up each plant's stalk, but like corn's ancestor, the wild teosinte grass, used to do, milo sets its fruits up in the tassels at the top of the plant. Each little kernel of milo is a tiny spherical berry, ranging in color from white to dark red, and quite distinct from corn kernels. I should add that there's no gluten in sorghum, making its flour and sugar products appealing for humans who are allergic to gluten. In any case, it's the production practices that really set milo and corn apart from each other. Milo is somewhat drought tolerant and well suited to arid climates, so even though corn tends to produce about 2 ½ times as much grain per acre (as a national average), the yields and profits from milo can exceed those from corn in relatively dry regions like northwest Kansas. Beyond its established geography in western Kansas, Oklahoma, Texas, Colorado and South Dakota, however, it's not a very popular U.S. crop.

Corn and milo also differ in price, with milo typically selling at a discount to corn, if for no other reason than its relative unfamiliarity and less-established supply chain. But because milo is such a direct substitute for corn, the cash market for grain sorghum can be directly hedged using corn futures. Milo can be bought and sold with basis contracts based on corn futures prices, so the difference in price between corn and milo can actually be expressed as a basis spread. For instance, the nearby bid for corn in Phillipsburg, Kansas may be -20 the May corn futures contract and the nearby bid for milo in Phillipsburg, Kansas may be -45 the May corn contract, so we could say the corn-milo spread was 25 cents at that point, no matter how the international futures market for corn behaves.

There are other crops which are technically grown in rows, like sugar beets, cotton, sunflowers, and tobacco, but they are either fairly far out of the feed grain sector (to my knowledge, nobody feeds tobacco to livestock), or they are a small enough segment of U.S. agriculture to be lumped together with the "specialty crops."

Wheat

Wheat is the world's most widely-grown grain – it can be grown on nearly every continent (with the exception of Antarctica) and in possibly every country. But producing wheat and using wheat is quite unlike dealing with row crops. The order of the tasks are the same – planting, scouting, applying nutrients, harvesting, storing – but as we discovered in the crop calendar above, some varieties of wheat are actually planted in the fall, dormant over the winter, and harvested in the late spring or early summer. Like corn, wheat is technically a grass species, but that's about where the biological similarities end. The growth stages of wheat include: tillering (tillers are the independent leaf-like shafts that make up a grass plant), jointing (the plant develops nodes with fully differentiated spikelets growing out of them), the boot stage (below the "flag" leaf, a future "head" of grain forms), heading (the head of wheat, containing individual berries of grain, ripens), and maturity.[8]

Winter wheat farmers have, by virtue of the crop's very-long growing season, a couple of benefits. For one thing, their crop can rely on roughly ten months of weather to provide sufficient moisture, rather than the seven months corn and soybeans get. For another thing – and this is something which traders should be watchful for – wheat farmers have the ability to completely change their minds about even raising wheat on certain acres halfway through a growing season. If, after a droughty winter, it looks like the wheat crop is going to have a very poor start, a farmer can choose to just graze cattle on the spring or summer wheat grass rather than wait to harvest the mature wheat. Similarly, if a spring frost severely damages the no-longer-dormant wheat crop, a farmer can abandon his whole wheat-growing plan by simply "burning" down the plants with a chemical herbicide and instead planting corn or soybeans in that same field at the usual spring timeframe. A note about frost: even though a region may technically get a "frost" one night, it may or may not actually harm the plants growing in that region. One rule of thumb is to say that temperatures around the plants' growing point (and tall plants can form somewhat of an insulating barrier around themselves) must reach lower than 28 degrees Fahrenheit for two straight hours before damage occurs, or reach lower than 30 degrees for four hours, or lower than 32 degrees for six hours,[9] but even these thresholds are different depending on which stage the crop is in. And even within a field, the results may be variable as relatively cooler air collects in relatively lower areas.

Even spring wheat has some notable differences from our benchmark corn crop, despite being grown in roughly the same seasons. All wheat varieties tend to be more drought-resistant than corn or soybeans, although they will obviously yield better with adequate moisture than they will without it. In very arid climates like eastern Colorado, wheat farmers sometimes "summer fallow" their fields, which is just the practice of leaving a field unproductive perhaps once every three years so the soil's moisture profile can recharge. Weeds must still be managed during that fallow year, however, so the fields must either be tilled (leaving them highly susceptible to wind erosion) or "chemically fallowed." Wheat plants also aren't particularly nitrogen-efficient. A truly great wheat crop will require some extra fertilization, unlike the legumes (soybeans) which can fix their own nitrogen.

The timing and amounts of moisture and nitrogen provided to a wheat field, as well as the temperature that occurs while it's growing, can influence that wheat crop's ultimate protein level. Typically, a wheat field can sacrifice some protein for higher yields or vice versa. Very high-yielding wheat fields usually don't produce wheat with a high protein level, but fields that are stressed by drought (and therefore usually pretty low-yielding) can produce some unusually high protein levels. Farmers can also influence their fields' protein levels and yields by timing their nitrogen applications correctly, but if their local cash market doesn't pay a premium for higher-protein wheat, why would they bother? On the other hand, if there is a small protein premium in the market, what is the optimum mix of protein level and total yield from any given field, if one must be sacrificed for the other? These are the kind of considerations that can make trading wheat more challenging and more interesting than trading most other varieties of grain.

Trading protein spreads is especially interesting from the demand side. Nearly every meal of an American's life may include some kind of wheat flour product – bread, pasta, cookies, etc. Cereal grains, like wheat and rice, have relatively inelastic demand, as compared to meat or sugars, which consumers can abandon if the prices get too high. However, not all wheat is created equal – flour mills seek out specific characteristics of wheat, depending on the ultimate product desired. Durum wheat is a specialty variety of spring wheat with very high protein levels used in bread flours around the world and pasta products here in the U.S. Other varieties of spring wheat tend to have higher protein levels than winter wheat varieties, which makes them relatively better suited to pasta and bread flours, although wheat of all characteristics can be mixed and blended together into flour. If winter wheat has a low enough protein level – and this is particularly true of soft winter wheat grown in eastern states rather than the hard red winter wheat grown in the Plains – it may never enter the human food chain and rather be used as animal feed. However, some soft winter wheat flour is prized for use in cakes and biscuits.

Small Grains

Oats, barley, rice, rye, millet, spelt, amaranth, teff, emmer, triticale, buckwheat, flaxseed, kamut – some of these things you've probably eaten for breakfast or been served in a soup. Others probably seem like made up words, but if you'd like to see what those "ancient grains" look like, you can typically find them in any health food store these days. They are so called because genetically, they are very nearly unchanged from the wild grains our ancestors would have cultivated thousands of years ago. Not even wheat, which is also technically a "small grain," displays heterosis like corn does, so there is relatively less commercial interest in breeding wheat, oat, barley, or rye seed, although they can be hybridized. In the case of those ancient grains, their novel prehistoric-ness actually serves them well in today's niche market.

If you're a futures trader, oats, barley, and rice will be more interesting to you than those other small grains crops, since they are the only ones that are traded on a futures exchange. Supply (acreage, yield, etc.) and demand (food, seed, exports, etc.) data is as easily available for these crops from the USDA as it is for corn or wheat, so a fundamental trader can get a good feel for those markets' relative bullishness or bearishness. In fact, because such a relatively small proportion of North America's acreage gets planted to oats or barley, a person may feel they can truly master the full picture of expected production and demand in any given growing season. It used to be said that, "Oats knows," which implied that price changes in the oat futures market tended to predict or lead price movements in corn and other grain markets. And maybe that was true, but the floor traders who used to populate the open outcry oat trading pit at the Chicago Board of Trade aren't there anymore – there is virtually zero volume of oat futures traded by open outcry anymore, and frankly not much traded by the electronic system, either – the open interest in oat futures is typically less than 1% of the open interest in corn futures, for instance.

That makes them notoriously hard to trade, because there aren't as many market participants to meet your bid with an ask or vice versa. And you have to assume that the folks who are using oat futures are doing so for a reason – they are either growing the stuff themselves or are an end user. The CFTC's weekly **Commitments of Traders report** bears this out: usually about ¾ of the oat market is made up of Producer / Merchant / Processor hedges. That means most of the other participants in the oat market will know more about supply and demand, and know it faster, than a speculator could. This is also true for barley, which doesn't have an open outcry pit at all, but rather trades exclusively on the electronic-only ICE futures exchange.

Furthermore, much of North America's small grains crop is grown on contract, meaning an end user will agree to pay a grower a specific price for the crop, if the grower agrees to raise it for them. The relative bearishness or bullishness of production from acres grown on contract should theoretically have very little influence on the wider market, since those bushels are already assigned a market home at a known price. This is particularly true for the rarer crops like amaranth and triticale; otherwise, why would anyone grow such an uncommon crop without a known, stable market to sell it into? But it is also true for crops like malting barley, which is used by the brewing industry to create the beer in your refrigerator. The price risk for grain grown on contract has already been laid off by both the producer and the end user (they both know what price they will receive or pay), so there is no further financial hedging necessary. That's good ... because if you're growing amaranth, there's no futures market for you to hedge against even if you wanted to.

There's one other thing to keep in mind when observing a small grains market – whatever grain isn't destined to end up in the human food chain or the pet food or birdseed market can still be used as animal feed. In fact, even grain that was originally grown to fulfill a rice contract, for instance, if it ultimately doesn't turn out with a high enough quality level, could still be sold as a livestock feed ingredient. For that reason, even if oat futures and barley futures trail the benchmark corn market by a couple dollars per bushel or more, these markets are still rough substitutes for one another and should display a fairly strong correlation with each other.

Oilseeds

Flax is a rather hard crop to classify; although the production practices and equipment used to grow it are pretty similar to other small grains, and even though it shares some of the same market space in the health food and birdseed sectors, it also has its own specialized market space (fibers from the flax plant's stem are used to make linen), and in reality, it's an **oilseed.** Oilseeds include any crop that can be crushed for oil, so peanuts, palm nuts, coconuts, castor beans, jatropha, etc. can all be considered oilseeds. If you've ever heard of linseed oil, linseed is actually just another name for flax.

Anyway, the real benchmark of the oilseed market is soybeans, but canola is the world's second-largest oilseed crop. There is about 4 ½ times as many soybeans produced, by weight, around the world than there is canola, which is also called rapeseed, and is more commonly grown in Europe, Canada, and Australia than it is in the U.S. What canola is grown in the U.S. is mostly planted in North Dakota or Montana or Minnesota or Idaho as a spring crop or in Oklahoma and a few other southern plains states as a winter crop, with a growing season similar to winter wheat. There is a canola futures market traded on the ICE and denominated in Canadian dollars.

In order of world production quantities, other oilseeds include cottonseed, peanuts, and sunflowerseed. Like flax and canola, sunflowers are an uncommon crop in most areas of the U.S. but experience thriving interest in regions that aren't too humid, like the Dakotas and western Kansas, because oilseeds are susceptible to mold. Specialized varieties of sunflowers experience their own market niches as a human snack food ("confectionary" sunflowers) or as birdseed, but as oilseeds that can be used to produce edible cooking oils, the sunflower, cottonseed, and peanut oil markets are correlated to the soybean oil market, so rough hedges or speculative trades can be made in soybean oil futures to try and capture price movement in this sector.

Specialty crops

I always kind of scratch my head when I walk into a hardware store and see the 10-pound bags of thistle seed for bird watchers to put out for the finches. Who grows entire fields of thistles, and how does that work? Most farmers consider thistles to be noxious weeds and go to considerable expense and effort to eradicate them from their fields. Even with all the farmers I've met over the years, I've never met anyone who could explain to me how thistle seed is produced for market (probably because most of the thistle seed for sale in America actually comes from Africa). I did meet a guy once who worked for a farm that grew wildflower seeds to be sold to state highway departments. Apparently, those seeds were all cultivated and harvested by hand, so I imagine the thistle-growing industry is similarly labor-intensive. But I still wonder what the neighbors with nearby corn and soybean fields think of the guy who intentionally plants a field full of noxious weeds.

Anyway, there is obviously no end to the variety of crops which can be grown on American soil. Hay, edible dry beans, nuts, trees (like Christmas trees), vine crops (like grapes), fruits or vegetables can all be considered **specialty crops.** Where and how they are produced is usually the result of a perfect storm of geographical opportunity and relative profitability. Consider the case of sugar beets:

First of all, because pretty much no one outside of Minnesota, Idaho, or North Dakota even knows what a sugar beet is, let's establish that. Sugar beets are pretty much like the beets you buy at the grocery store or grow in your garden, in that they are a root vegetable of the beet family that grows underground. However, their flesh is white like a potato and they have a very high sugar content, so they can be commercially sliced up like a shoestring potato then cooked in hot water to extract a thick, sugary juice, which can then be stored or distilled down into sucrose – the crystallized sugar you buy at the grocery store to put in your cookie recipe or morning coffee.

The sugar beet industry is very different than the grain industry. First of all, the equipment needed to harvest and handle bulky root vegetables is entirely different than the combine harvesters and grain hoppers used to harvest and haul grain. Secondly, unlike dry store-able grain, sugar beets are 80% water, so they must either be processed into sugar immediately after harvest or piled up, ventilated, and covered with lime for the winter's deep freeze. If you're running a sugar beet processing campaign to cook fresh beets 24 hours a day, 7 days a week for only a portion of the year, you can't be hauling those beets from hundreds of miles away. There are only a few sugar beet processing plants in the United States, and all the sugar beet acreage tends to be clustered nearby around a processing plant. It takes somewhat more than 100,000 sugar beet acres to feed a typical processing plant (about 150 square miles), although those acres will actually be spread out across more like 1,000 square miles because sugar beets are actually planted alongside corn, soybeans, or wheat in a rotation pattern that might only see sugar beets planted on any given field once every four years.[10]

To sell his sugar beets to the local processing plant, a farmer must belong to the farming cooperative (the co-op) which owns that plant. 100% of the sucrose (sugar beet) industry in the United States is owned by farmer co-ops, which sets it quite apart from the fructose produced by large ag processing corporations. However, to participate in such a co-op and have access to its profitable market space, a sugar beet farmer typically has to pay a membership fee based on the number of acres he signs up, which must meet some minimum number of acres, and which he is then contractually obligated to plant to sugar beets for a certain number of years. This ensures the local availability of sugar beets for that plant and thus, the plant's survivability. The co-op markets its sugar and pays its members based on the profits from the sugar.

The profits from growing a field of sugar beets are generally better than the profits from growing a similar-sized field of corn, otherwise no one would go to all this trouble and risk. The University of Minnesota estimates it takes more than 3 times as many human work units to grow sugar beets as it does to grow corn. But on the other hand, the opportunity to even enter this market space is only available to a few people who happen to farm in the regions where sugar beets grow and where sugar beet processors have thrived. Sugar beets require very long periods of sunshine to reach maturity, which is why their market has mostly developed in northern regions where summer daylight hours are very long, or in places like Colorado and Wyoming where cloud cover doesn't disrupt much of the summer sunshine.

This pattern for producing and using sugar beets is pretty much the same pattern as you'd see for most specialty crops – their markets develop in the geographical regions where the crops thrive (cotton in the irrigated fields of Texas with a long growing season; fruits in the mild climate of California) and once the processing facilities are established in those places, virtually no one from outside that region would go to the expense and risk of growing that specialty crop elsewhere. Most of America's farmland *could* be used to produce carrots, for instance, but most of America's farmers *wouldn't* grow carrots unless they had a known, nearby market into which they could sell them.

Anyway, with regard to specialty crops' effects on the markets, cotton has its own futures market, but crops like sugarbeets, tobacco, edible dry beans, and nuts/fruits/veggies/etc. have virtually no substitutability or market influence on the prices of corn, soybeans, or wheat. However, the reason they're included in this book is because in the limited regions where they are grown, they have an immense influence on the price of farmland and the uses to which farmland is put. Sugar beets are not part of a futures-hedgeable or speculatable market. Their prices don't even necessarily correlate to the international cane-based sugar market. But wherever they are grown, their profitability will affect every land investor's and farmer's management decisions.

The incremental changes in acreage use from one year to the next can have a profound effect on a grain market's supply and demand. If market prices motivate America's corn farmers to plant 2% more acres to corn this year than last year, and if yields are normal and demand simultaneously remains unchanged, the ending stocks-to-use ratio of the corn market can increase by more than just 2% (which would be significant), and the overall market sentiment can turn decidedly bearish. That's why each year's planting decisions, including every little 160-acre chunk that gets planted to peanuts or sugar beets, are rabidly analyzed by market participants. At the end of each March, USDA releases the results of their annual **Prospective Plantings** survey. These reports show data collected from actual farmers who respond with how many acres they intend to plant to each crop during the next few months.

USDA and private analysis firms can guess at those figures ahead of time, based on the market's signals (a relatively high price for soybeans may economically motivate farmers to switch some of their wheat acres to soybeans, for instance), and in fact the USDA does make some non-survey-based, long-term projections at their annual outlook meeting each February (called the "Baseline Projections"). Even the direct survey results in the Prospective Plantings report are never set in stone. What a farmer *intends* to plant in March may be significantly different than what he actually gets planted by the middle of June, if weather keeps him out of his fields at critical times or if the futures markets alter his motivations during that timeframe. Not until the USDA releases its **Crop Production** report is there one, official source of data about how many acres were planted to each crop that year and how much of that crop was actually produced. Of course, by the time all that data gets officially collected, processed, and published, the market itself has long since digested the relative bullishness or bearishness of supply, so Crop Production reports tend to be fairly inconsequential to the futures markets.

Organics

From a lifestyle standpoint, it seems to be much "cooler" to purchase **organic** food than non-organic food. But as far as I can tell, the *scientific* basis for consumers to prefer organic agriculture products over conventionally-raised agriculture products is something about organophosphates from pesticides getting into the food system and ... something (it's rarely documented what the consequences are supposed to be. Death? A third arm growing out of your head? Ridicule from the other trendy moms at daycare?). Never mind that "organophosphates" are actually a really broad category of biochemicals, some of which are necessary for life.

I can see why a grocery shopper wouldn't want to buy a tomato or an apple that had recently been sprayed down with some toxic substance, but personally, I trust the FDA to keep any truly dangerous chemicals off our food. Anyway, the manner of "bad" things getting onto grain gets harder for me to conceptualize. One wouldn't want to bathe in anhydrous ammonia or glyphosate or any other mildly toxic, extremely helpful chemical farmers use to nourish their crops or reduce stresses in their crops, but the actual grain kernels, unlike the plants on which those kernels are grown, virtually never come in contact with any modern agrochemicals. Correspondingly, I think grocery shoppers are more likely to seek out organic vegetables than organic cereal. Nonetheless, organic milk, organic eggs, and organic beef, pork or chicken must be produced by cows, chickens, and hogs who have only been fed organic grain, so there is a strong market for organically-produced feed grain.

To receive a USDA Organic seal, a food product has to meet a lot of requirements, including land and water usage requirements. For instance, organic grain can't be raised from genetically modified seed, and it can't be fertilized with any synthetic fertilizers. This obviously makes achieving high yields more challenging from an organic grain field than it is from a grain field that has all the benefits of modern technology.

One could argue that the corn the Native Americans fed to the Mayflower passengers at the first Thanksgiving was already "genetically modified," in the sense that humans had been cultivating certain seed characteristics over others and therefore radically altering the species over time. But what is really meant by **GMO** (Genetically Modified Organisms) today is that the DNA of the grain seed has been altered with DNA from some other species, usually allowing it to produce a specific protein that protects it against some threat, like a rootworm. So our techniques for altering grain species today may be more scientific and yield faster results than the historical selection and breeding practices, but the final products are still grain that tastes the same to a cow today as it would have tasted to a cow sixty years ago.

Although it's not really germane to the topic of organic grains, let me also just say that fructose sweeteners (such as High Fructose Corn Syrup – a.k.a. HFCS, the substance in soda pop that gets the nutrition police so fired up) are nutritionally equivalent to table sugar[11], but neither one of them are particularly good for your waistline. And yet cane sugar, of all unlikely "health foods," has achieved a kind of mystic righteousness as certain activists pursue their quest to throw stones at the modern agriculture industry. Don't even get me started on the demonization of wheat gluten, when over 99% of people have no sensitivity to the gluten itself and could actually use a nice boost of whole grains in their diets, rather than following some superstitious fad.

But I digress. Whether you or I want to purchase organic food products (whether you or I can even *afford* organic food), or whether there really is something inherently evil about modern corn – a substance which up until about six years ago was *just* a grain, *just* the means of pushing thousands of years of human civilization forward and pulling billions of humans out of starvation – doesn't matter much. Obviously *some* people want to purchase those specialized products, and the customer is always right.

The customer, in fact, is willing to pay a premium for being "right" (or "self-righteous" – pick your adjective). A trip to the grocery store will show you the premium for organic products over conventional products could be anywhere from 30% of the sticker price to triple the price, depending on the product. This is a function of both demand and supply. A consumer who believes non-organic milk will turn her children into chemically-altered zombies will have a greater willingness to pay for milk that supposedly won't do that. From the supply standpoint, however, organic ag products can be more expensive to produce. An organic dairy farmer must buy more expensive organic grain to feed his cows, so the market must reimburse him for that expense or else he'll just go back to producing milk conventionally.

In some cases, it can actually be cheaper to produce an organic crop than a conventional crop. USDA's Agricultural Resource Management Survey (ARMS) showed in 2009 that organic wheat producers actually spent $13 *less* per acre on input costs than conventional wheat farmers spent. Presumably, this is because they didn't have to pay for high-priced synthetic nitrogen fertilizers and instead may have used animal manure to fertilize their crops. I will say, as someone who worked at an elevator that handled both conventional grain and organic grain, organic grain is more likely to have weed seeds and other foreign material in it, because organic farmers can't use chemical herbicides to control that threat. It's also more likely to be damaged by insects or mold (same story for pesticides). The quality losses and the expenses organic farmers must undertake to clean their grain need to be reflected by higher market prices.

So the market itself for organic grains is more like the market for specialized crops than it is for typically-traded corn, soybean, and wheat commodities. You *could* express the price for nearby organic wheat as a basis figure compared to the current wheat futures price, but because the supply-and-demand situation for organic grains changes independently from the supply-and-demand situation for feed grains in general, the futures markets aren't always a nicely correlated, ideal hedging tool. In fact, organic grains are more likely to be grown on contract like a specialized crop than they are to be blindly grown by a farmer who intends to just seek out the best nearby market after harvest.

These contracts can be quite lucrative. The organic market displayed more favorable price differentials in some non-recession years than in recent recessionary years, but nonetheless, many business-minded farmers have turned to organic grain farming, attracted more by the profit than the ideology. Of course, there are many organic farmers who choose the path because of a sincere belief they are doing something good for the planet, and I can respect those efforts, even if I think their products can only ever be a niche luxury for a certain subset of the human race.

If I come off as overly defensive of conventional agriculture and overly sensitive about the air of superiority from the organic segment of the consumer market, I think that's because I see too much rhetoric from food bloggers and environmentalists who seem to imply *every* farmer *should* be forced into giving up their present use of technology. Organic food consumption is indeed related to moral licensing[12] - which is to say that I wouldn't put it past some consumers of organic food to try and legislate all farmers from using modern fertilizers and modern pest treatments. As it stands, the consumption of organic food is a luxury and anyone with a sufficient bank account is free to do it, and at this point I don't know of any pending legislation to outlaw GMO seed (in the U.S. anyway – Europe is another story). But if such legislation did occur, and if all American farmers were bound to use only Stone Age organic farming practices, let's consider what would happen.

Sticking only to the benchmark corn market, let's assume yield would drop by about 10%.[13] If the world produced 9/10^{ths} as much corn as it currently does, without a change in demand, the ending inventory of corn at the end of any given marketing year could go from being 15% of the total initial supply to being only 5%, for instance. Or it could go from being 10% to being 0%. In the first instance, rationing would occur and there might be riots as certain countries' populations discovered their favorite food products were no longer affordable, or there simply might be an abandonment of the developing world's recent adoption of more nutritious, higher-protein diets. In the second instance, there would be massive starvation. Neither instance would be good for agriculture; neither instance would be good for humankind. As Robert Paarlberg wrote in his book, *Starved for Science: How Biotechnology Is Being Kept Out of Africa*, "Citizens in wealthy countries are skeptical toward genetically engineered crops, in part because they know they can remain rich and well fed without them." The rest of the world doesn't have that luxury.

In my opinion, the temptation for organic activists to want to handcuff modern farmers from using all the modern technology that has improved our quality of life is, at best, misguided. No one is more motivated to use truly *sustainable* production practices than grain producers ourselves. I say sustainable, as in "capable of being done logically and profitably forever without depleting resources." If GMO grain causes some unknown reproduction malformation in mammals, it is our own cattle and hogs who will be first to eat that grain and suffer that consequence. If a fertilizer damages the long-term fertility of soil, that soil will someday be our own children's soil. So we wouldn't use those things if science convinced us those were the consequences.

There are three reasons why grain farmers are unlikely to use any more agrochemicals than absolutely necessary; why another age of DDT overuse won't occur; why we won't experience a "Silent Spring." First, overuse of specific herbicides or insecticides can lead to resistant weeds or pests, and no farmer wants to incubate those. Farmers are therefore constantly on the lookout for new modes of action that can effectively manage crop stressors without creating the new "superweed," and they're unlikely to use a herbicide or pesticide in any greater quantities or for any other uses than its label prescribes. Secondly, when nitrates or other chemicals are found in human water supplies several decades after their parent chemicals were overused on agricultural land, it's out here in the rural, very agricultural communities where farmers themselves live. Now that the mechanism of that pollution is better understood, no farmer wants to apply an ounce more chemical than his crop needs or can totally absorb. Why would he knowingly threaten the health of his own family and neighbors? Thirdly – and perhaps most compellingly – no farmer wants to apply an ounce of wasted chemical ... because it's *expensive*. Gone are the days of strewing several hundred pounds of nitrogen per acre just because it was cheap – today's ag technologies (side-dressing, foliar-applied nitrogen, application rates prescribed by the square foot) allow farmers to apply less than half the fertilizer rates they used a generation ago. Today's conventional grain farmers are using fewer resources to grow more food that will end up in more human stomachs more spread out across the globe than ever before.

So as for me, when I go to the grocery store, I take pleasure in purchasing conventional, non-organic food products. That's not because I have anything against organic farmers; they tend to put out a good niche product. It's because I know I'm supporting farmers who embrace technology and are at the forefront of solving humanity's real challenge – feeding nine billion hungry people by 2050.

Many of the facts and considerations in this chapter may not have seemed directly associated to the grain *markets* themselves. What does a futures speculator care if the corn price goes up because production goes down due to poor weather or due to poor production practices, just so long as the price goes up? Still, any participation in the grain markets is a form of participation in agriculture, and it should be regarded as one piece of a beautiful, challenging, miraculous whole.

CHAPTER 7
Epilogue

At ten o'clock in the morning on the last Friday of December, Joe Smith slammed the phone down with an almighty thud. He had just been talking to Jason at the Mungus Elevator about setting the basis on some of the corn he had been forced to bring in to the elevator during harvest because he didn't have enough room for it in his own on-farm bins. The little turd had said: "You know, Joe, it's important for you to focus your marketing efforts on achieving a profitable price and not be concerned about basis. Basis is not the producer's opportunity." It sounded like he was reading off a page[1] or something. "When farmers like you start looking at the basis in making your marketing decisions, you tend to lose sight of your real objective – which is selling for a profit. Price is the farmer's opportunity; basis is the elevator's. By keeping the two separate, we both win!"

Meanwhile the latest schmuck who called himself an expert on the ag news website Joe subscribed to was saying: "Farmers don't care about futures – they're either only watching the flat price or they're already hedged and they only care about basis."

"What?" Joe wanted to scream at his computer screen. "How about 'all of the above'?" Nobody was that good at predicting how much grain they could raise before they raised it; nobody was ever perfectly hedged and so no farmer *only* cared about basis. And even if that were so, he'll still care quite a bit about the number on the check he'd be receiving for his grain, whether he looked it as just a flat price or as a function of futures and basis together.

It was maddening enough not only to make Joe's head hurt, but also to flat-out tick him off. True – the flat price could account for 90% of Joe's annual income that year, but every five cents per bushel he saved by not paying the Mungus folks for their latest "DP" (a.k.a. Dumb Producer) scheme on 100,000 bushels was equivalent to his family's much-needed annual vacation. Every ten cents of basis appreciation he captured by watching the seasonal patterns of his local market accounted for two semesters of his daughter's college education. Every fifty cents of carry in the market he was able to capture by storing his own grain and earning the futures spreads was equivalent to a new pickup truck, or the yearly mortgage payments on that quarter of land he'd just bought.

Jason had said that Dale, the elevator manager, was out of the office fixing something at the elevator's dump pit, so Joe decided to just send Dale an email about the basis level he was willing to accept on those storage bushels. He had never sold grain by email before, but what the heck – he just wanted to get the sale over with. After one of the most nerve-wracking growing seasons of his life (the dry spring, the hot pollination weather) and one of the longest harvests he could remember (having to rely on his neighbors' charity had been no picnic), Joe knew his job wasn't done. He had to get the grain marketed. And even once he had all of this year's grain sold, there would always be next year's ... and the year's after that ... and so on and so forth in a never ending pattern. He really just wanted that vacation.

So when he got Dale's emailed response a few hours later, he read it with mixed feelings: "Joe – sure I can write up the contract at that level we'll probably be posting there in a few days anyway. are you coming to the new years eve party" A party ... Joe had the habitual introversion of someone who was used to spending all day every day making his own decisions about what to do, where to go, and who to talk to or not talk to, but ... there would probably be free beer ...

Of course Joe Smith was going to Dale's New Year's Eve party, whether he wanted to or not. His wife would make sure of that. So when Saturday night rolled around, he put on his new khakis (Becky had bought them for him at Macy's on one of her post-harvest shopping sprees) and a nice plaid shirt and helped her carry several trays of devilled eggs out to the car.

When they pulled up in Dale's yard, Joe recognized most of the parked vehicles or the silhouettes of the people he saw walking in the garage door. Like old Leonard Stern and his wife, Ardis, who were just entering the pool of light from the yard lamp. Stern had his leathery, paw-like hand on the small of Ardis' back as she minced toward the door. Those were two people who had spent every day of the past 60 years together, much of it as dairy farmers who both had to feed and milk cows for several hours twice a day ... Every. Day. Together. And they still seemed not only to tolerate each other but to be genuinely fond of each other's company. Sixty years of weaknesses, complaints, and faults, and they still smiled at the opportunity to go to a party together. How do such people even exist? Joe suspected not many big city types would be able to pull that off, no matter how much they thought they loved their spouses.

There were other people already mingling around the keg once Joe and Becky walked in – Dale himself, Lindsey Kearney with her mother-in-law Shirley, Gary Green, the banker Rodney Brune, Jason from the Mungus elevator with some girl who couldn't have been more than 18 years old, and some overdressed tall guy Joe had never seen before. In pinstripe suit pants, he seemed a little hesitant to sit down on any of the dusty folding chairs Dale had scattered around.

As it happened, Dale's mother-in-law, Irene Loomis, had a sister, Dee, who had recently been diagnosed with skin cancer and convinced herself and her whole family that her death was imminent. So she browbeat all of her extended family to coming home to Iowa for Christmas, to be gathered around her one last time. Among those kin was none other than Bob Albany from Chicago, who hadn't been to Springfield, Iowa in forty years and had very little intention of ever returning. He was the guy in the pinstripe pants.

Once he'd reminded himself that it was always better to be overdressed than underdressed, and once he'd negotiated with the host that no, he really preferred to drink the scotch he'd brought along rather than drink the free keg beer, Bob finally settled into the event and decided he should try to get some financial benefit out of the situation. It was unlikely he'd find any new clients here for his antitrust litigation firm on Wacker Drive, but Bob figured he might possibly get an inside line on same great grain trade from one of these farmer-looking guys. Unfortunately, he spent half an hour explaining to his cousin from Jacksonville (who was woefully *underdressed* for a Midwestern winter night in cargo shorts) how those commodity ETFs were a waste of time and that he should be making futures trades instead.

"OK, so let's say I started my account with $20,000 and let's say I just threw all that $20,000 into some grains ETF, right? Some fund that tracks some index of corn, soybean, and wheat prices. I'm guessing your financial advisor told you you oughtta diversify into commodities, right?"

"Well, yeah – you gotta diversify. God knows with this stock market anymore. I don't want my whole friggin' retirement fund stuck in that hole."

"Right. So. Get into commodities, somebody tells ya. So you sink your 20,000 bucks into some grains ETF. Let me tell you, over the past year your 20,000 bucks woulda turned into 15,000 bucks. Return? Bupkis. Non-correlation to the stock market? I guess! But listen here – if you did what *I* did, if you actually *traded* these grains ... you could be rolling in the dough."

It occurred to Bob that he was starting to sound like his own brother-in-law from last year's Christmas dinner, and that, like his brother-in-law, he was about to conveniently leave out all the stories about the stupid trades and uncomfortable losses of his futures-trading adventures, in order to make himself sound cool. But he did it anyway. "So at harvest, right – all these guys standing around here, they harvested their corn a couple-a months ago – and there was just a crapload of the stuff; I'm talking more corn than anybody knew what to do with. Prices took a nosedive. If you had all your cash locked up in that ETF, you were losing money. But if you were *me*, you shorted the futures market. You don't need prices to go up to make money, you just gotta be smart enough to figure out what direction prices are gonna go. Grain prices went down and I made a 20% return on my account this year. Hell, I made that 20% return on that one trade in one month!"

Bob and his cousin had been standing near the keg, where Joe Smith happened to overhear their conversation, and quite contrary to his not-so-extroverted character, decided to speak up. "Oh, so you're *that* guy."

The two out-of-town men looked over at the farmer. Bob said, "Hm? What guy?"

"The guy who's been driving down my grain prices."

Intuiting that he had waded too loudly into a sensitive subject, Bob backpedaled a little, "Well, I mean ... an efficient market is always going to find the true price of an asset, no matter what a little ol' guy like me does on any given day ..."

Joe just laughed and slapped Bob on the shoulder. "I'm just pulling your leg, man. I don't care what the futures market does from this point on; I've got my grain pretty much all hedged."

Bob finally took a full breath and nodded. "OK, so you're a farmer." They all introduced themselves and Gary Green, who had been standing with Joe talking about some tiling equipment, spoke up. "Well it sure as heck bugs the crap outta me! I *know* corn's worth more than $4.50. If you jackass speculators wouldn't make the markets jump around so much, we'd probably get it. And Joe, I know you don't have all your grain priced, neither – I saw you taking the temperature of a bin full of corn just the other day when I was driving past."

"Yeah, but I've got all that hedged. Anything I didn't have sold in March, I hedged it all in the middle of July at $6.50."

Now Gary was just mad. He'd sold all his grain off the combine at harvest for $4.75, except for the 20,000 bushels he put on DP for a 10-cent fee and which had only continued dropping in value, and it ticked him off to think his neighbor was standing around bragging about some mythical price that never existed. He knew Joe had to be lying. Nobody was that good to get within five cents of the futures high, to say nothing of the basis that probably shaved some cents off of that. He saw Jason walking away from the keg with three red cups of beer in his hand and pulled him into the conversation. "Jason! Hey, you tell me – did Joe here sell all his corn at $6.50?"

Jason shook his head. "No way. Not to us anyway. Our bid never got higher than $6.35, and I happen to know that not even Cedar Rapids got higher than $6.45. No way somebody sold corn for $6.50."

"Well I did, and here's how." Joe took a drink of his beer and explained to his little audience how, on July 13 when the crops looked good and he was pretty sure he would raise at least 100,000 bushels of corn, he had called his broker to put in a limit order to sell 20 December futures contracts at $6.50 or better. The market hit that level the very next day, at the same time that the Mungus elevator was bidding $6.30 (a -20Z basis bid) for harvest corn delivery. Over the next few days, the futures contract lingered at or just below $6.50 and the Mungus elevator strengthened its harvest basis bid to -15Z, accounting for the $6.35 level that Jason remembered as their highest cash price of the year. At that time, the Cedar Rapids ethanol plant was bidding -5Z for November corn, representing the best cash bid of the year anywhere in the state. But Joe never locked in his basis level that early, or indeed at any time until the day before the party. Instead, he held onto his short December futures position, which made him a $2-per-bushel hedge profit while the market collapsed, and then he rolled it over to the March futures contract because he had no intention of trucking most of his corn to town until after the month of December had passed. In the process of buying December futures at $4.50 and selling March futures at $4.65, Joe gained an extra $0.15 of carry per bushel to reimburse him for storing his grain a few more months. When he eventually locked in the basis for his spring corn delivery with Dale in late December, the Mungus elevator wrote up the contract at -15H. So ... $6.50 futures - $0.15 of basis - $2.00 loss in the cash market + $2.00 profit in the futures position + $0.15 of carry spread between the futures contracts = a $6.50 per bushel equivalent financial outcome for Joe Smith, even though the Mungus elevator would actually be sending him a check for $4.35 corn ($4.50 - $0.15).

In the telling of his marketing glory, Joe managed to annoy his neighbor Gary (who had predicted the wrong futures direction, and who had given up the carry and paid fees and transportation costs for the 'benefit' of deferred pricing, with no room for basis negotiation). Joe had also confused his new friends from out of town (who had never heard of basis), and flummoxed the young merchandiser, Jason, who considered basis trading and capturing the carry to be his own private domain.

So Joe decided it was a good time to go to the restroom. As he walked through the kitchen to get to the bathroom, he noticed Dale's mother-in-law Irene about to cut an onion at the counter. A few kids were gathered around her and she was explaining: "By tomorrow morning we'll know how much rain will fall each month in the new year." That got Joe's attention. He stopped and watched her bisect the onion down its axis, and pull it apart into 12 little white "cups," setting them in two rows of six along the counter, with the biggest cups on the left. She instructed one of the little girls to stand on a stool so she could reach the counter and put a teaspoon of salt into each cup. Irene smiled and said, "Now the salt will draw some water out of each cup, and each cup represents a month of the new year. If there's a lot of water in one month's cup, that will be a rainy month. If the cup stays dry – no rain that month."

"Huh," said Joe. "That works?"

"Works every year of my life for the past forty years. Well, most of the time. I write it all down in my calendar, just like I write down when it's foggy and ninety days later there will be snow or rain."

"Or the locusts."

"Cicadas, yes. When you hear those ugly insects start to buzz in the summer, frost will be six weeks away."

Joe found himself staring at those onion cups and counting out which ones represented June, July, and August. Even though he didn't believe in such nonsense, he found himself willing some water to pool up in those little white cups. Irene chuckled and patted him on the shoulder as she walked out of the kitchen, following the scattering children. "It'll be ok, Joe. It always rains after a dry spell."

And he knew she was right. When spring came around next year, the smell of the fresh soil would waft up to him from his planter's coulters, and he would have yet another shot at trading the fruits of his labors for the best value he could get. Joe Smith was optimistic that all the years of his life would give him the chance to produce food for the world, and to maybe ... just maybe ... make a living at it along the way.

STUDY QUESTIONS BY CHAPTER

CHAPTER 1: The Philosophy of Commodity Profits

1-1: Why do you think it's important to include a disclaimer at the front of a book about grain trading stating that "the market examples and example trades are NOT RECOMMENDATIONS for trades"?

1-2: Think of as many jobs as you can which are related to the grain markets. List them.

1-3: Investment in The Widget Company has an expected return of 5% per year and an expected standard deviation (volatility) of 14%. Meanwhile, investment in The Doohickey Company also has an expected return of 5% per year, but an expected volatility of 22%. According to the Mean-Variance Rule, which should be the preferred investment? Which would you choose and why?

1-4: As a historical average, soybean prices tend to be 2.45 times higher than corn prices. If the price of soybeans is $9 per bushel and the price of corn is $3 per bushel, which asset is underpriced and which asset is overpriced? How would you arbitrage that? What are the barriers (of market access, funding, or licensing) to making that trade?

1-5: The stock price of The Doohickey Company lingered between $20 and $25 for several years. Then, within three weeks it started streaking higher and is now $57 per share. You hire an analyst to calculate the value of the company, with its known assets and profit stream. How will you know if that stock is experiencing a "bubble"? How will the analyst's valuation prove if it is or isn't in a "bubble"?

1-6: The price of oat futures lingered between $3.50 and $4.25 for several years. Then, within three weeks it started streaking higher and is now $8 per bushel. You start to research the price being paid for physical oats by end users. How will you know if oat futures are in a "bubble"? How will the cash price for oats prove if the market is or isn't in a "bubble"?

1-7: Is it "good" or "bad" when grain prices fall? Why?

1-8: Through the 1990's and early 2000's, it was noted that there was a negative correlation between the stock market's returns and the changes to the price of crude oil futures. What does that mean?

Why might those two markets have had a negative relationship? Why do you think this is no longer true?

1-9:   Let's say it was noted that over the past 5 years, the historical standard deviation (volatility) of weekly crude oil prices was 4.5%. What does that tell you about the probability of crude oil prices to go up, down, or sideways from now until one week in the future?

1-10:   Let's say consumers are widely adopting a diet that completely avoids all wheat flour, and the prices for wheat flour and wheat itself are projected to drop 30% and reach drastically unprofitable levels. What changes could a wheat milling company make to its strategy? What changes could a wheat farmer make? What changes could an ethanol plant make?

CHAPTER 2: Contracting a Fair Trade

2-1:   A bushel of corn weighs 56 pounds. Let's say each little kernel of corn weighs 0.0112 ounces. An average ear of corn has 500 kernels on it. So about how many ears of corn, once shelled, does it take to produce a standard bushel? If the price is $5 per bushel, what is the amount of grain on one ear of corn worth?

2-2:   The Mungus Grain Company stored 100,000 bushels of corn in an open pile on the ground at harvest, but the grain itself and the weather was very wet. Three months later, the corn is now 11% damaged. The ethanol plant to which they will sell this corn charges a three-penny discount for each point of damage above 5%. Assuming they bought the grain with no discounts, how much money has Mungus lost from quality losses on their pile? How could they sell the grain without taking that loss?

2-3:   Give an example of a direct trade from a farmer to an end user. Why might the buyer of an agricultural product need a more efficient system? Why might a farmer not want to sell directly to an end user?

2-4:   In the six months from June 2008 to December 2008, grain of all varieties lost an average of $6.50 per bushel. If a large grain company with 600 million bushels of grain storage capacity theoretically had all their storage full during that time and had all their grain flat priced without any hedges, how much value would that company have lost?

2-5: As a historical average, Minneapolis spring wheat prices (representing milling wheat with higher protein) tend to have a 15% premium over Chicago wheat prices (representing feed wheat with lower protein). Let's say you note that spring wheat's current price is $6.27 and feed wheat's current price is $5.88. Do you think there's an opportunity for a trade here? If so, what trade would you make? When would you know to exit the trade? What might go wrong with the trade?

2-6: One day as you're watching CNBC, you see a stock trader come on the screen and emphatically declare he is bearish on the market. Does he expect to lose money? Why or why not? In the next segment, a grain market trader comes on and says she is bearish on grains. Does she expect to lose money? Why or why not?

2-7: Gary Green is 50 years old and is planning to retire from farming when he's 70. He typically raises 100,000 bushels of corn every year. He does not presently have anything hedged or sold for upcoming years. How long is Gary in the corn market?

CHAPTER 3: A New Dimension –Time

3-1: It was cool and wet all season, with late planting and late maturity of the crop. Now it's late September. If you're a merchandiser who has short commitments in the nearby timeframe (e.g. you have a train load of corn sold, or you're sourcing grain for an ethanol plant that requires 1.5 million bushels of corn every month), how do you anticipate the weather and the schedule of harvest will affect your strategy for the next few months?

3-2: You work for an elevator that has four bins: one is half full of corn, one is half full of soybeans, one is half full of wheat, and one is empty. The corn market's carry structure is offering 13 cents of carry to store corn for the next six months, the soybean market is at an inverse for that same period, and the wheat market is offering 42 cents for the time period. But row crop harvest is about to start and your local farmers are going to expect to be able to deliver corn and soybeans to you over the next two or three months. Describe what your strategy will be for managing your inventory and optimizing profits.

3-3: Before a farmer sells his grain to a buyer, which trading party (or parties) have price risk? After the trade has been made and the buyer owns all the farmer's grain, who has price risk?

3-4: It's presently January. An elevator is bidding $4.12 for old crop corn to be delivered in March and $4.25 for new crop corn to be delivered in November. Does this show a carry market or an inverted market? Is that normal or unusual? For soybeans, the elevator is bidding $12.54 for March delivery and $10.54 for new crop November delivery. Is that a carry or inverse? Normal or unusual?

3-5: Search online or make phone calls to get cash grain bids from two nearby elevators. Assume a truck will hold 1,000 bushels of grain and the trucker will charge you $1 per mile both ways. To which elevator would you prefer to sell one truckload of corn? Soybeans? Wheat?

3-6: What will it cost per bushel to move soybeans (which weigh 60 pounds per bushel) from Faribault, Minnesota to Sioux City, Iowa? A trucking company quotes you $1.35 per mile and can haul 57,000 pounds of dry bulk matter per truck. The truck has a backhaul opportunity, so you only need to pay for one leg of the trip. Be careful and find the shortest mileage!

3-7: Use the most recent Grain Transportation Report from www.ams.usda.gov to find the price of soybeans at the Gulf of Mexico. Assuming that freight would cost $1.25 per mile, what are soybeans worth FOB at your location right now? If you are near an Origin Region listed on the rail rates table, use the table to calculate what soybeans are worth FOB your location and compare your two answers.

3-8: By searching online or calling nearby elevators, can you find a local buyer with a cash bid that is farther out than 1 year? Farther out than two years? Why do you think that is? If you presented a business plan to a banker but couldn't say what the price of your product would be in 5 years' time, how do you think the banker would react?

3-9: Let's say you buy a car off Craigslist, and the seller accepts a personal check from you as payment. What is your counterparty risk? Now let's say you sell a car and accept a personal check as payment. What is your counterparty risk? Compare that to the grain markets' counterparty risks and licensing requirements.

3-10: Warren Buffett once said, "You can't make a good deal with a bad person." Do you think that's true in the grain markets? Why or why not?

CHAPTER 4: Futures Contracts -Everybody's Business

4-1: How would the bankruptcy of one grain buyer affect the entire local market? On the other hand, how would the appearance of a new buyer affect the market?

4-2: Compare and contrast the buying/selling experience of trading one standardized 5,000-bushel corn futures contract versus trading 5,000 physical bushels of corn with 8% damage and 17% moisture.

4-3: Describe how you could set up an exchange for all the buyers and sellers of used cars on a given day in your nearest city. How would the exchange be different if the trades were all done over the internet?

4-4: Once a futures contract goes into "delivery" in the weeks before it expires, short sellers of that futures contract can *choose* to deliver physical grain in a warehouse as settlement for the expiring futures contract. But long owners of the futures contract cannot *compel* someone else to produce physical warehoused grain as settlement for a futures trade. How does arbitrage make cash prices and futures prices converge during the delivery timeframe when futures prices are higher than cash prices? When cash prices are higher than futures prices (which is rare), why doesn't arbitrage work to force convergence?

4-5: By searching the internet, find the Final Settlement language of ICE futures contracts for corn, soybeans, and wheat.

4-6: Consult www.cmegroup.com, www.mgex.com, and www.theice.com to find the daily trading volume of wheat futures on each of those exchanges yesterday. Why do you think the volumes are so different?

4-7: Find a chart of soybean futures prices over the past several months. Just by eyeballing (using no math), decide how much margin money you would ask for from each trader of a 5,000-bushel soybean futures contract if you ran the exchange and you wanted to have cash to cover 99% of all losses within the next day.

4-8: Why don't exchanges and brokerages just demand 100% of the face value of the substitute goods being traded as margin on futures trades? Why is the present leveraged system important for companies who use futures as hedges? Bona fide hedgers have cheaper margin requirements than speculators. Why do you think the CFTC allows that?

4-9: You hear a report that the bid-ask spread for PNW HRW wheat basis prices is +150N/+160N. The July (N) KC wheat futures price is $8.00. If you were a buyer, at what flat price would you try to buy that wheat? If you were a flat price seller, what price would you try for? What's a reasonable price at which you might expect a trade to take place?

4-10: The Teucrium Corn Fund (NYSE: CORN) is an Exchange Traded Fund (ETF) with holdings in "(1) the second-to-expire CBOT Corn Futures Contract, weighted 35%, (2) the third-to-expire CBOT Corn Futures Contract, weighted 30%, and (3) the CBOT Corn Futures Contract expiring in the December following the expiration of the third-to-expire contract." Which contract months would those be today? Why do you think the company designed the fund like that?

4-11: Just off the top of your head (using no math), if you owned some grain bins and I were to offer you 15 cents per bushel to store some grain for an entire year, would that seem like a good deal or a bad deal to you? Why?

4-12: Look at upcoming corn futures prices. Which bid would you rather accept (sell into) at this moment: -5H or -15K?

4-13: Look at upcoming futures prices. How much carry per bushel could the Mungus Grain Company earn by buying corn at -27Z and back-to-back selling those purchases at -15N?

CHAPTER 5: Other Derivatives - Just a Taste of Grain

5-1: How is counterparty risk affected when an elevator holds a futures position (e.g. a HTA contract) or an options position (e.g. a premium offer contract) on behalf of a farmer?

5-2: List the maximum theoretical gain and the maximum theoretical loss for each of the following positions: a long $4 corn call option bought at $0.14, a long $4 corn put option bought at $0.12, a short $4 call option sold at $0.14, a short $4 corn put option sold at $0.12.

5-3: The delta (or price sensitivity) is listed as 0.5794 on a $4.00 corn put option that is priced at $0.12. Predict what the premium of the put option will be if the underlying market goes up 50 cents, or what it will be if the underlying market goes down 50 cents.

5-4: It is possible to trade options on ETFs that track the price of grain futures, and therefore possible to gain short exposure to grain markets without using futures or commodity options at all. List all the derivative layers there are between a physical bushel of corn and a NYSE option on an ETF. Do you have concerns about the structure of this arrangement?

5-5: From <u>websoilsurvey.nrcs.usda.gov</u> (or the SoilWeb app!), find what soil type you are standing on right now.

5-6: On finance.yahoo.com, look up the stocks listed in the *Ag Equities* section of Chapter 5. Which would have been best investment during the past 5 years? Why do you think that is?

5-7: What is the nearest ethanol plant to you? Who owns it? Can you invest in it? Why do you think farmers tend to be heavy investors in ethanol plants?

Chapter 6: Making and Using the Grain

6-1: Search <u>news.google.com</u> or any other news aggregator for stories on "wheat price," "corn price," or "soybean price." Pick three headlines that seem interesting. How do you think the facts of those stories will affect the supply and demand of the market? Are the implications bullish or bearish? Why?

6-2: From an archived USDA Crop Progress report, how much Texas corn tends to be corn harvested by mid-September (use the 5-year average)? How much U.S. corn is usually harvested by that time? Do you think the September corn futures contract should be considered an old crop or new crop contract?

6-3: Look at a 6-10 day local weather forecast. Predict any effect it may have on the grain markets. Can you suggest a trade based on that information?

6-4: Why do you think activists want GMO food to be labelled at the grocery store? How would that affect demand of various food products? Why do you think consumers care so deeply about the food they eat, even if every scientific agency and study tells them a certain product has not been proven unsafe?

ABOUT THE AUTHOR

Elaine Kub has been an ardent participant in the grain markets her whole life. The path from a childhood on a cow-calf operation in South Dakota; to engineering student; to MBA graduate; to market analyst, grain trader, futures broker, and farmer has made her eager to communicate her observations through a column, speaking engagements, and television and radio appearances.

More can be learned at
www.masteringthegrainmarkets.com

ACKNOWLEDGMENTS

"The most essential gift for a good writer is a built-in, shock-proof, bullshit detector."
– Ernest Hemingway

While writing this, my first book, I sometimes doubted my own detector and am therefore extremely grateful to have been able to rely on the kind appraisals of Patricia Hill (the first person I trusted to read my ramblings), Teresa Konda, and Dr. Daniel Davidson. I've also appreciated the encouragement from David Anderson (the first person who really seemed to think this book was a good idea) and Carrie Phair. I'll also thank everyone who, throughout the years, contributed to my understanding of the grain markets. That of course includes Mark Pearson, whose love of the industry was hearty and knowledge of its workings very deep. Every farmer (and every participant in the agriculture industry) owes a debt of gratitude to all the "masters" who have come before her and taught her how plants – and profits – are really made.

SOURCES

CHAPTER 1: The Philosophy of Commodity Profits

Trimble, D. E. (1980). *The Geologic Story of The Great Plains*. Washington, D.C.: United States Government Printing Office.

Morgan, Dan (1980). *Merchants of Grain*. New York: Penguin Books.

1.   Ulrich, H. (1996). *The Amber Waves of History: 200 Years of Grain Prices*. Chicago: Commodity Research Bureau.

2.   Time Inc. (1957, March 11). Agriculture: Drop in Parity. *TIME Magazine* .

Gilmore, Richard (1982). A Poor Harvest: The Clash of Policies and Interests in the Grain Trade. New York: Longman Inc.

3.   Markowitz, H. M. (1959). *Portfolio Selection*. Malden, MA: Blackwell Publishing.

4.   Ulrich, 1996.

CHAPTER 2: Contracting a Fair Trade

1.   Totman, C. (2005). *A History of Japan: Second Edition*. Blackwell Publishing.

2.   The Grain Elevator and Processing Society. (2011, June 03). *GEAPS: The Knowledge Resource for the World of Grain Handling Industry Operations*. Retrieved June 05, 2011, from www.geaps.com

3.   United States Department of Agriculture. (2011, May 26). Grain Inspection Packers and Stockyards Administration. Retrieved May 27, 2011, from http://www.gipsa.usda.gov

4.   McKenzie, B. A., & Van Fossen, L. (1995). Managing Dry Grain in Storage. *Agricultural Engineers' Digest* , http://www.extension.purdue.edu/extmedia/AED/AED-20.html.

5.   The World Bank / Food and Agriculture Organization of the United Nations. (2011). *Missing Food: The Case of Postharvest Grain Losses in Sub-Saharan Africa (Report No. 60371-AFR)*.

6.   Sumner, P. E., & Lee, D. (2009). *Reducing Aflatoxin in Corn During Harvest and Storage*. The University of Georgia Cooperative Extension Service.

7.   Dairyland Laboratories, Inc. (2010). *Feed and Forage Report*. St. Cloud, MN.

8.   National Grain and Feed Association. (2008). *NGFA Trade Rules and Arbitration Rules Booklet*. Washington, D.C.: NGFA.

9.   The Sunday Times. (2009, November 08). I'm doing 'God's work'. Meet Mr. Goldman Sachs. The Times of London.

CHAPTER 3: A New Dimension –Time

1.   Nebraska Public Service Commission. (2011). *Grain Dealers Division.* Retrieved April 2012, from Grain Warehouse Department: http://www.psc.state.ne.us/home/NPSC/grain/graindldiv.html

CHAPTER 4: Futures Contracts -Everybody's Business

1.   CME Group. (2010). *Corn Futures.* Retrieved July 15, 2011, from CME Group: http://www.cmegroup.com/trading/agricultural/grain-and-oilseed/corn_contract_specifications.html

2.   Standard & Poors. (2007). *S&P GSCI Highlights and Definitions.* The McGraw-Hill Companies.

3.   Fama, Eugene. (1965). Random Walks in Stock-Market Prices. *Selected Papers No. 16 of the Graduate School of Business University of Chicago.*

4.   Sanders, D. R., Irwin, S. H., & Merrin, R. P. (2010, Spring). The Adequacy of Speculation in Agricultural Futures Markets: Too Much of a Good Thing? *Applied Economic Perspectives and Policy* , pp. 77-94.

   Ennis Knupp & Associates. (2008). *The Role of Institutional Investors in Rising Commodity Prices.*

CHAPTER 5: Other Derivatives - Just a Taste of Grain

1.   Cook, J. (2009). *An Introduction to Cattle Feeding Spreads.* Chicago: CME Group.

2.   Wisner, R. (1997, March). *Hedge-to-Arrive Contracts.* Retrieved September 2011, from Iowa State University - University Extension: http://www.extension.iastate.edu/agdm/crops/html/a2-74.html

   Cocheo, S. (1997). Has HTA Set Back Farmers' Thinking? *ABA Banking Journal, Vol. 89 .*

   Wisner, R. (1997, January). *Understanding Risk in Hedge-to-Arrive Contracts.* Retrieved May 2012, from Iowa State University Extension: http://www.extension.iastate.edu/Publications/PM1697B.pdf

3.   Fuglie, K. O., Heisey, P. W., & al., e. (December 2011). Research Investments and Market Structure in the Food Processing, Agricultural Input, and Biofuel Industries Worldwide. *ERR-130 .*

4.   Nickerson, C., Morehart, M., Kuethe, T., Beckman, J., Ifft, J., & Williams, R. (February 2012). Trends in U.S. Farmland Values and Ownership. *USDA Economic Research Service - Economic Information Bulletin* , Number 92.

5.   Nickerson, Morehart, Kuethe, Beckman, Ifft, & Williams, February 2012

Duffy, M. (2011, January). *Estimated Costs of Crop Production in Iowa - 2011*. Retrieved August 2011, from Iowa Stat University - University Extension: http://www.extension.iastate.edu/agdm/crops/html/a1-20.html

6. Lascano, R., & Sojka, R. (2007). *Irrigation of Agricultural Crops*. Madison, WI: American Society of Agronomy, Crop Science Society of America, Soil Science Society of America.

7. USDA National Resources Conservation Service. (2012, February 17). *Web Soil Survey*. Retrieved May 12, 2012, from websoilsurvey.nrcs.usda.gov/app/

8. U.S. Small Business Administration. (2007). *Guide to SBA's Definitions of Small Business*. Retrieved May 2012, from U.S. Small Business Administration - Services.

Hurst, Blake. (2009, July 30). *The Omnivore's Delusion: Against the Agri-intellectuals*. The American Magazine. Retrieved August 2009 from theamerican.com.

9. Hoppe, R. A., & Banker, D. E. (July 2010). Structure and Finances of U.S. Farms. *USDA Economic Research Service - Economic Information Bulletin* , Number 66.

U.S. Environmental Protection Agency. (2009, September 10). *Demographics*. Retrieved June 05, 2010, from Ag 101: www.epa.gov/agriculture/ag101/demographics.html

10. Comstock, G. (1987). *Is There a Moral Obligation to Save the Family Farm*. Ames, IA: Iowa State University Press.

11. Diller, R. (Reprint 1979). *Farm Ownership, Tenancy, and Land Use in a Nebraska Community*. Chicago: University of Chicago Press.

12. Koopman, R. B. (1989). *Efficiency and Growth in Agriculture: A Comparative Study of the Soviet Union, United States, Canada, and Finland*. Washington: USDA Economic Research Service.

CHAPTER 6: Making and Using the Grain

1. Alesina, A., Giuliano, P., & Nunn, N. (May 2011). *On the Origins of Gender Roles: Women and the Plough*. Cambridge, MA: Harvard University Department of Economics.

2. Rundquist, D. C., & Samson, S. A. (2005). *University of Nebraska - Lincoln CASDE*. Retrieved May 21, 2012, from A guide to the Practical Use of Aerial Color-infrared Photography in Agriculture: www.casde.unl.edu/activities/cir-uses/index.php

3. Wilcox, Tom, & Ebmeier, Pat. (2011, June 20). Farmers, Phelps County Nebraska. (E. Kub, Interviewer)

4. Lucas, Dan. (2012, May 10). Precision Ag Account Manager at Heartland Technology Solutions. (E. Kub, Interviewer)

5.   Jackson, T. (n.d.). *Goss's Bacterial Wilt and Leaf Blight*. Retrieved May 2012, from University of Nebraska Lincoln CropWatch: http://pdc.unl.edu/agriculturecrops/corn/gosswilt

6.   D.A McWilliams, D. B. (1999, June). *Corn Growth and Management Quick Guide*. Retrieved May 2012, from ag.ndsu.edu: http://www.ag.ndsu.edu/pubs/plantsci/rowcrops/a1173/a1173w.htm

7.   *SoybeanPremiums.org*. (n.d.). Retrieved December 21, 2011, from soybeanpremiums.org

8.   Miller, T. D. (1999, August). *Growth Stages of Wheat: Identification and Understanding Improve Crop Management*. Retrieved May 2012, from Texas Agricultural Extension Service: http://varietytesting.tamu.edu/wheat/docs/mime-5.pdf

9.   Davidson, Daniel, PhD. (2008, May). Agronomist. (E. Kub, Interviewer)

10.   Watson, Curt. (2011, November 9). Farmer, Renville MN. (E. Kub, Interviewer)

11.   American Medical Association. (2008). AMA finds high fructose syrup unlikely to be more harmful to health than other caloric sweeteners. *American Medical Association* .

12.   Eskine, K. J. (May 2012). Wholesome Foods and Wholesome Morals? Organic Foods Reduce Prosocial Behavior and Harshen Moral Judgments. *Social Psychological and Personality Science* .

13.   Delate, K., Cambardella, C., Burcham, B., & Friedrich, H. (2002). *Comparison of Organic and Conventional Crops at the Neely-Kinyon Long-Term Agroecological Research (LTAR) Site-2002*. Retrieved May 2012, from Iowa State University Extension: http://extension.agron.iastate.edu/organicag/researchreports/nk02ltar.pdf

      Steven D. Savage, P. (2009). *A Detailed Analysis of U.S. Organic Crops*. USDA National Agriculture Statistics Service.

      Paarlberg, Robert. (2008). *Starved for Science: How Biotechnology is Being Kept Out of Africa*. Harvard University Press.

      Carson, Rachel. (1987). *Silent Spring: 25th Anniversary Edition*. Houghton Mifflin.

CHAPTER 7: **Epilogue**

1.   Lorton, S., & White, D. (2002). *Merchant's Edge: A Complete Guide to Grain Merchandising, Fourth Edition*. Champaign, IL: Stipes Publishing Company. Page 347.

GLOSSARY

acre – p. 185 – A unit of area measurement used to describe land, equal to 4,046.8 square meters (approximately the size of a football field), or traditionally the amount of land that could be plowed in one day with an ox.

agronomy – p. 222 – The study and practice of various sciences which improve crop production: biology, chemistry, soil science, et al.

alternative investments – p. 113 – Investments in any asset other than traditional stocks, bonds, cash, or real estate; i.e. the universe of hedge funds, commodity futures, private equity, credit derivatives, etc.

American options – p. 179 – The traditional category of option contracts which settle their payoffs based on the difference between the strike price and the underlying asset's price when exercised, and which can be exercised at any time before the expiration date.

AP – Associated Person – p. 101 – Anyone who must be registered with the National Futures Association to solicit funds or solicit trading orders in U.S. futures and options markets.

arbitrage – p. 2, 5, 13, 37, 46, 96 – The practice of simultaneously buying and selling related assets in order to profit from the difference between their prices. Perfect theoretical arbitrage should have no risk of loss.

Asian options – p. 179 – A category of "exotic" option contracts which settle their payoffs based on the average price of the underlying asset during a period of time called the discovery period. Compare to **American options**.

at-the-money – p. 166 – A description of put or call options when the underlying asset's price is equal to the option's strike price.

autosteer – p. 221 – Mechanical technology (usually hydraulic) that allows a piece of farming equipment, like a tractor, to steer itself on an intended path (usually using GPS guidance).

back-to-back – p. 138 – In trading, when a purchase is immediately offset by a sale (or vice versa), at a known profit margin, to limit the risk of the market changing over time.

backwardation – p. 93 – The opposite of **contango**. When nearby futures contracts have higher prices than deferred futures contracts. In the grain markets, this is known as an **inverted** structure.

bar chart – p. 106 – A market chart with, for each discrete time period, a vertical line with its top at the highest period price, the bottom at the lowest price, and a horizontal tick on the left side at the opening price, and a horizontal tick on the right side at the closing price.

barge – p. 40, 130 – A freight-carrying water vessel, usually used on canals and rivers to haul dry goods, like grain.

basis – p. 125 – The difference between the price of a physical commodity and the price of the futures contract for the same commodity. May be either negative or positive (premium).

bearish – p. 48 – A market "bear" is one who expects the price to move lower. Any factor that could cause prices to fall may be described as "bearish."

bid-ask spread – p. 130 – The difference between the price where willing buyers are willing to buy (the bid) and where willing sellers are willing to sell (the ask).

biofuel – p. 229 – A fuel produced from biological raw materials (e.g. corn or plant matter), rather than from petroleum.

Black-Scholes model – p. 170 – A mathematical model used to determine the theoretical price of an option contract, given the underlying market's volatility and other assumptions.

bonded – p. 40 – Under a legal agreement with pledged surety for contingencies which may cause a trading partner financial loss.

bubble – p. 10 – A market is said to be in a "bubble" when its price rises above its true value and it becomes susceptible to a sudden "burst" that will bring the price equivalent to the true value.

bullish – p. 48 – A market "bull" is one who expects the price to move higher. Any factor that could cause prices to rise may be described as "bullish."

bull or bear flag formation – p. 108 – A technical chart pattern, with a nearly vertical rise or fall forming the 'flagpole,' followed by a rectangular period of price consolidation forming the 'flag.'

butterfly spread – p. 175 – A trading strategy using four options contracts to simultaneously create both a bull spread and a bear spread.

calendar spread – p. 156 – The simultaneous purchase of a futures contract with one delivery month and the sale of a futures contract with a different delivery month (of the same commodity on the same exchange), meant to profit as the difference between the contracts' prices changes.

call option – p. 164 – A financial contract that bestows the right, but not the obligation, to buy an asset at a specified price at a certain time. The buyer of a call pays the seller a **premium** for this right.

carry – p. 61, 92, 143 – The cost of storing, insuring, and financing a physical commodity over a period of time. The prices of grain in forward months typically reflect the cost of carry by being relatively higher than the nearby price of grain.

center-pivot irrigation (circle irrigation) – p. 183, 218 – A method of distributing water to plants with sprinklers mounted on overhead trusses that are motorized to rotate around a well hub.

CFTC – Commodity Futures Trading Commission – p. 78 – The independent federal regulatory agency that oversees U.S. futures and options markets.

Chicago Board of Trade (CBOT) – p. 75 – The world's oldest exchange of futures and options contracts, offering grain and oilseed contracts, now part of the CME Group.

CME Group (formerly the Chicago Mercantile Exchange) – p. 75 – The company that owns and operates the largest U.S. financial securities exchange with a wide array of products, and that provides market services and information.

CIF (Cost, Insurance and Freight) – p. 127 – A trading term that obligates the seller of a physical commodity contract to pay the freight costs of getting the goods to their destination and to procure marine insurance against the risk of loss or damage to the goods during carriage. Colloquially in the grain industry, "CIF" grain is the market segment that is traded on barges.

collar – p. 174 – A strategy of buying one type of option (e.g. a call) and simultaneously selling the opposite type of option (e.g. a put) to reduce the net premium cost of the strategy.

combine harvester – p. 224 – Most commonly called a "combine." A machine used to harvest grains and oilseeds by cutting the plants then separating the grain from the non-grain material.

commercial trader – p. 116 – A futures market participant whose primary business is in the underlying physical commodity market (e.g. an elevator, an ethanol plant, a grain exporter).

Commitment of Traders report – p. 116, 239 – A weekly report provided by the CFTC to show a breakdown of the open interest in futures and options markets.

commodity – p. 21 – A widely-available, unspecialized economic good or substance that is interchangeable (and therefore trade-able) with all other samples of the same grade of the same substance.

container shipping – p. 37 – A method of transporting freight in truck-size intermodal containers, which can be used to ship dry bulk cargo, like grain, in standard unit sizes by road, rail, and sea.

contango – p. 92 – A futures market structure when deferred months' contracts are priced higher than nearby prices. The opposite of **backwardation**. More commonly called **carry** in the grain markets.

convergence – p. 118 – The movement of the price of an expiring futures contract toward the price of the physical, underlying cash commodity.

cooperative (co-op) – p. 49, 65 – An organization owned and operated by those who use its services. In agriculture, co-ops frequently buy grain from and sell inputs to local farmer owner-customers.

Corn Belt – p. 39 – A region of the United States that has soil and climate well-suited to growing agricultural crops (especially corn). Generally, Ohio is considered to be the eastern boundary; Nebraska the western; Minnesota the northern; and Missouri the southern but there are no hard-and-fast geographical limits.

correlation – p. 121 – A statistical relationship that measures how similarly two data sets behave; interdependence of variable quantities.

cost of carry – p. 144, 157 – See **carry.**

counterparty risk – p. 69 – The risk of one's trading partner not performing on the other side of a contract; i.e. credit risk.

CPO – Commodity Pool Operator – p. 102 – Trading entity that combines funds from multiple participants to invest in commodities futures and / or options contracts.

crop insurance – p. 72 – Indemnity contracts which compensate agricultural producers for financial losses (caused either by forces of nature or by market losses), usually subsidized by the federal government to promote stability of national food production.

Crop Production report – p. 244 – A monthly or annual summary of data objectively surveyed by USDA's National Agricultural Statistics Service, including the area planted to all crops in all states, the yield per acre, and the total production.

Crop Progress report – p. 213 – A weekly summary of subjective evaluations for all currently growing crops in all states, released by USDA's National Agricultural Statistics Service.

crop rotation – p. 204 – The practice of using a sequence of different crops during a series of growing seasons on any given field.

crush margin – p. 150, 154 – In any processing industry, the profit margin that results from buying raw materials, turning them into refined products, and selling those products. In grain markets, the profit margin from crushing soybeans into meal and oil or the profit margin from processing corn into ethanol and distillers' grain.

CSR (Corn Suitability Rating) – p. 185 – An index procedure that rates soil types for their ability to produce row crops, and which can be used to calculate a weighted rating for a field with many soil types and characteristics.

CTA – Commodity Trading Advisor – p. 102 – Trading entity that makes recommendations or manages accounts for clients to invest in commodity futures and options, and which receives a fee for these services.

cultivator – p. 220 – A piece of agricultural equipment used to break through soil and disrupt roots.

DDGs (Dried Distillers Grains) – p. 230 – A byproduct of ethanol production which is used as animal feed. May also be wet.

day order – p. 105 – A trading order to buy or sell an asset only on the day the order is made; if the order isn't executed by the end of the day's trading session, it's automatically cancelled.

deferred contract – p. 90 – Any futures contract with an expiration date later (more distant) than that of the **front-month** contract.

delta – p. 169 – The ratio of how much an option's price changes with respect to the change in price of the underlying asset, i.e. the "price sensitivity" of an option.

derivative – p. 76, 165 – In finance, a contract whose value is set or derived from the price of an underlying asset. Derivatives can be used as financial proxies to hedge against specific outcomes.

designer contract – p. 163 – In grain trading, any exotic cash grain contract that transfers ownership of physical grain from a seller to a buyer with conditional pricing.

disk harrow – p. 220 – A piece of agricultural equipment used to aerate soil with vertically-mounted, saucer-shaped disks.

double-cropping – p. 207, 212 – The practice of growing two crops in sequence on one field within one growing season.

DP contracts – p. 163 – Cash grain contracts that transfer ownership of physical grain from a seller to a buyer, but give the seller the privilege to set the price on the grain at a later point in time. May be officially called "deferred price," "delayed price," or "price later" contracts.

dryland – p. 183 – Non-irrigated farm land.

elevator – p. 28 – A grain-storage structure and the related weighing, testing, receiving, and load-out facilities. Traditionally a concrete or steel tower with a bucketed-belt grain leg to "elevate" dry bulk material and gravity-fed paths to direct the material into silos. Also used to describe the organizations that purchase grain and store it in such facilities.

ethanol – p. 229 – The grain alcohol product of grain fermentation, which can be used as a **biofuel**.

ETFs (Exchange Traded Funds) – p. 14 – A financial security that can be bought and sold through an exchange, with a value that is set or derived from the price of some underlying asset, e.g. a stock index or a basket of commodities.

European options – A category of "exotic" option contracts which can only be exercised on the expiration date. Compare to **American options** and **Asian options.**

exchange – p. 22, 74 – A marketplace for fair and efficient buying and selling of financial contracts. An exchange can either be a physical location where traders gather, or an electronic platform to handle traders' orders.

Exchange for Physicals (EFP) – p. 149 – A transaction between two bone fide hedgers who trade futures positions as representation of a physical grain trade. Also known as "Exchange of Futures for Cash," or "Versus Cash," or "Against Actuals."

extrusion – p. 155 – In agriculture, the process of either mechanically or chemically turning raw soybeans into soybean meal and crude soybean oil.

facilities operators – p. 33 – The employees who operate the unloading and loading facilities of an **elevator**, as well as its mix & blend and other grain handling and general maintenance tasks.

FCM – Futures Commission Merchant – p. 102 – A trading entity that solicits and accepts orders to buy or sell futures and options contracts, and that accepts payment from traders, subject to the rules of the exchange where the contracts are traded.

forward contract – p. 54 – A non-standardized, non-exchange-traded contract that transfers ownership of physical grain from a seller to a buyer, with a delivery date some time in the future.

flat price – p. 125 – The net price per bushel paid for grain by a buyer to a seller. Mathematically equivalent to the **futures** price at the time of the trade, plus or minus the **basis**.

floor broker – p. 53 – A member of an exchange who executes futures and options buy or sell orders on behalf of customers, directly on the physical floor of the exchange (i.e. in the "pit").

front-month contract – p. 90 – The futures contract with the most imminent (the "nearest") expiration date.

fundamental analysis – p. 108 – A method of evaluating an asset's intrinsic value by considering economic influences on supply and demand. Compare to **technical analysis.**

fungibility – p. 73 – The state of being interchangeable. A fungible asset can be replaced by any other equal asset, and is therefore capable of being efficiently traded.

futures contract – p. 74 – A legally binding contract to buy or sell an asset (e.g. a commodity like corn or wheat) of a standardized quantity, quality, and delivery mechanism, at some point in the future, for an agreed-upon price. The price is typically traded through an **exchange**.

futures broker – p. 76 – A sales agent that accepts customers' orders to buy or sell futures contracts, in return for a commission.

GMO (Genetically Modified Organism) – p. 245 – An organism that has been altered using genetic engineering techniques, such as giving it altered genes or genes that originate from a different organism and are therefore novel to that original organism.

Good Till Cancelled order (GTC) – p. 105 – A trading order to buy or sell an asset, which remains valid until it is either filled or cancelled. May also be called an "open order."

grain – p. 21 – Technically, the seed of a cereal grass, but for the purposes of the markets, "grain" may refer to any commodity seed used for its energy and therefore include oilseeds.

grain marketing – p. 215 – Grain producers' practice of choosing when to sell their grain, at what price, and via what mechanism.

Greeks – p. 169 – Mathematically derivative variables of options pricing. They are the quantities that describe certain parameters of an option's price sensitivity with respect to the underlying price of the asset, the volatility, etc. See **delta, vega, theta, rho.**

growing degree days – p. 206 – A unit system to measure the cumulative heat needed to grow a crop.

gut slot – p. 132 – The point in time during grain harvest when throughput is heaviest, or when it is constrained by a bottleneck, usually the filling of all available storage space.

head-and-shoulders formation – p. 108 – A technical chart pattern, with a peak forming a 'left shoulder,' followed by a higher peak forming a 'head,' followed by a peak forming a 'right shoulder' (or valleys instead of peaks), signifying a potential reversal in trend.

hectare – p. 185 – A unit of area measurement used to describe land, equal to 10,000 square meters or 2.47 **acres**.

hedge fund – p. 13, 116 – Private investment vehicles, formed as partnerships of multiple high net worth individuals or other funds, which may be subject to relatively flexible regulations and which may use relatively aggressive techniques to pursue high returns.

hedging – p. 59 – The practice of making offsetting investments that reduce the net financial risks of an entity's core business. For instance, a livestock feeder can "hedge" his future needs to purchase grain by making substitute purchases of grain futures contracts, which, if the price of grain increases, will financially reimburse him for the increased cost of running his business.

heterosis (hybrid vigor) – p. 226 – The tendency of a crossbred hybrid to exhibit better qualities than its parents.

HFCS (High Fructose Corn Syrup) – p. 229 – A byproduct of corn processing used as a sweetener in many food products.

HTA contracts – p. 161 – Hedge-to-arrive contracts that set a benchmark futures price for a forward cash grain trade, but which leave the basis and flat price un-set.

IB – Introducing Broker – p. 102 – A brokerage firm that solicits customer business and accepts orders to buy or sell futures and options contracts for a commission, but whose customers' money is actually held by a clearing futures commission merchant.

in-the-money – p. 167 – A description of an option contract which could be exercised profitably; i.e. a call option with a strike price lower than the underlying market's price or a put option with a strike price higher than the underlying market's price.

index fund – p. 92, 119 – A passive category of mutual fund with its value set or derived from the price of an underlying index, such as a stock index or a basket of commodity futures.

Intercontinental Exchange (the ICE) – p. 76 – An exclusively electronic-based trading exchange, offering futures, options, and OTC swaps contracts for grains and other markets

intermarket spread – p. 156 – A trading strategy using a simultaneous purchase in one market and an offsetting sale in another market; e.g. a long and short position in corn futures and soybean futures, respectively.

intramarket spread – p. 157 – A trading strategy using a simultaneous purchase and sale within the same market; e.g. a long position in March corn futures and a short position in May corn futures.

intrinsic value (of options) – p. 166 – The difference between the strike price of the option and the price of the underlying asset, if positive. Also called "inherent value." Together with time value, a theoretical portion of the **premium** price of an option.

inverted – p. 62, 94 – See **backwardation.**

investment – p. 4 – The expenditure of money with the expectation of receiving a greater return of money at some point in the future.

irrigation – p. 184, 219 – The application of water to farmland with the intention of promoting healthy plant growth.

Japanese candlestick – p. 106 – A market chart with, for each discrete time period, a vertical line with its top at the highest period price and its bottom at the lowest price, and a wider bar or vertical "body" with its top at the opening price and its bottom at the closing price (or vice versa, as the case may be).

legume – p. 232 – Any plant of the legume family, with nodules on its roots which foster nitrogen-fixing bacteria. Bean varieties, pea varieties, and clover varieties are common legumes.

leverage – p. 81, 85 – In finance, the use of borrowed capital to increase potential returns. With futures and options contracts, investors are only required to "**margin**" a fraction of each contract's value and effectively borrow, or leverage, the rest of the value of their investments.

LTM – Leverage Transaction Merchant – p. 102 – A trading entity with permission from the CFTC to trade certain futures instruments outside commodity exchanges.

limit order – p. 104 – A trading order to either buy an asset at or below a specified price level or to sell an asset at or above a specified price level.

line chart – p. 106 – A market chart that connects the series of an asset's past prices with a continuous line.

liquidation – p. 84 – The closing out of trading positions. Typically refers to selling previously-established long positions ("long liquidation") but short positions may also be liquidated for cash ("**short covering**").

liquidity – p. 73 – The degree to which an asset can be quickly and easily traded or converted into cash.

managed futures – p. 113 – A category of **alternative investments,** with professional portfolio managers or **CTAs** directing an investor's funds into futures and options contracts.

margin – p. 82 – In futures trading, the 'good-faith' collateral an investor must deposit with his brokerage against the risk of financial loss; usually some percentage of the market value of the asset being traded, as determined by the exchange.

marked-to-market – p. 122, 139 – A method of accounting the realistic price of assets in a portfolio by attempting to approximate the current market value of those assets, rather than the book value at which they were purchased.

market maker – p. 74 – A trading entity that agrees to facilitate efficient trade in a certain market by owning and offering those assets to the broader market, or perhaps by always posting a willing bid and a willing ask in that market.

market neutral – p. 154, 174 – The term for any trading strategy which doesn't seek to profit from the underlying market price moving either up or down, but which may instead seek to profit from changes in the market's volatility or time to expiration, for instance. Alternatively, a strategy may be "market neutral" if it seeks to profit from an individual asset's price movement independent from the price movement of the broader market.

market order – p. 104 – A trading order to buy or sell an asset at the best possible price as soon as possible.

marketing year – p. 94 – For grains, the annual cycle of buying and selling each discrete national production of a crop. The USDA considers September 1st to August 31st the marketing year for corn and soybeans, and June 1st to May 31st the marketing year for wheat.

merchandiser – p. 28, 36 – In the grain markets, someone who is involved in the buying and selling of physical grain.

milo – p. 234 – A feed grain. Also known as grain sorghum.

mini-contract – p. 122 – As compared to a standard 5,000-bushel grain futures contract, a futures contract that represents only 1,000 bushels of physical grain.

mix & blend – p. 32 – The opportunities to improve a grain trading position's net value by virtue of better quality grain being commingled together with cheaper grain.

moving average – p. 107 – An average of a fixed number of a subset of values (e.g. the past 10, 20, or 50 data points), which shifts forwards to include the same number of data points after each new data point is created.

naked puts or calls – p. 173 – A term to describe any stand-alone options position; i.e. an option contract with no underlying options, futures, or physical market position to offset it.

National Futures Association (NFA) – p. 98 – The self-regulatory agency in the commodities futures industry that enforces the regulations of the Commodity Futures Trading Commission (CFTC), and with which most participants are require to register.

National Grain and Feed Association (NGFA) – p. 43 – The non-profit trade association which represents and provides services for all categories of commercial businesses involved in the grain markets.

new crop – p. 61 – A term for grain trading contracts which represent the upcoming, yet-unharvested crop of grain.

no-till – p. 220 – The practice of planting grain without disturbing the soil or leaving it susceptible to erosion. Similar to vertical tillage.

NOPA Crush Report – p. 234 – A monthly report from the National Oilseed Processors Association detailing the number of bushels processed by member firms and their byproduct inventories.

Normal distribution – p. 16 – A bell-shaped statistical distribution of data, with the area of a vertical section of the curve representing the probability that a variable lies at that value (i.e. a vast majority of data points lie at the center of the range, with predictably decreasing likelihoods of them lying farther out from the center).

oilseeds – p. 21, 240 – The seed of a plant grown specifically for oil extraction.

old crop – p. 61 – A term for grain trading contracts which represent the already-past, most recent crop of grain.

open interest – p. 90 – At any given moment, the total number of futures or options contracts which have not yet been closed out or delivered on.

option (1) – p. 164 – In finance, a derivative financial contract which confers upon its owner the right, but not the obligation, to buy (or sell) an asset at an agreed-upon price at a certain period of time.

option (2) – p. 131 – In grain trading, a term for "zero over" or "zero under" **basis,** i.e. when the local cash price for a physical commodity is exactly equal to the futures contract price for that commodity in that time period.

organic – p. 245 – Literally, anything derived from living matter (carbon-based). In marketing terms, foods may carry an "organic" label if no genetically modified **(GMO)** seed or synthetic fertilizer was used in its production, and if it meets other land and water usage requirements set forth by the **USDA**.

originator – p. 33 – In the grain markets, someone who is employed to purchase physical grain from producers and thereby increase the number of bushels in a company's cash grain position.

out-of-the-money – p. 166 – A description of an option contract which couldn't be exercised profitably; i.e. a call option with a strike price higher than the underlying market's price or a put option with a strike price lower than the underlying market's price.

outside reversal formation – p. 108 – A "key" outside reversal is a technical chart pattern that occurs when the prices within a discrete time period trade both higher than the previous period's high and lower than the previous period's low, then the price closes either higher or lower than previous period's close, signifying a reversal in the market trend.

over-the-counter (OTC) contracts – p. 176 – Any financial contracts traded through a dealer network rather than through a centralized, anonymous exchange.

overbought / oversold – p. 110 – A market condition when participants' willingness to buy or sell an asset is unjustified by real economic conditions, or alternatively, occurring beyond the price level dictated by some technical analysis technique.

Panamax – p. 37 – A category of ocean-going freight vessel, traditionally limited by the dimensions of the Panama Canal, which would typically hold a deadweight tonnage greater than 65,000 metric tons (about 2.5 million bushels of corn).

pit – p. 53, 80 – The physical location at an exchange where open outcry trading occurs.

planters, air seeders, drills – p. 220 – Pieces of agricultural equipment used to place grain seed into the soil.

plow (moldboard, chisel, etc.) – p. 219 – A piece of agricultural equipment used to break up and aerate soil to prepare it for seed placement.

PNW – p. 131 – Abbreviation for the Pacific Northwest, which has ports from which a large quantity of American grain gets exported

position limits – p. 78 – Rules established by trading exchanges that prohibit any one trader from owning net long or net short positions that would be large enough to manipulate prices in any given futures or options market.

precision agriculture – p. 221 – The suite of farm management practices focused on detailed imagery and data-gathering tools which allow grain producers to manage each square foot of farm land to minimize inputs and maximize production.

premium – p. 166 – In options or insurance contracts, the fee paid by a contract's buyer to its seller to compensate for bearing the risk of a payout, given a potential financial outcome. In markets, the positive spread between two assets.

pressure / support – p. 150 – In futures markets, "pressure" is the effect of selling activity to limit price rises and "support" is the effect of buying activity to limit price losses.

profit taking – p. 119 – In futures markets, "profit taking" may either occur as selling when market bulls close out previous long (buying) positions, or as buying when market bears exit previous short (selling) positions.

Prospective Plantings report – p. 243 – An annual report released each March by USDA's National Agricultural Statistics Service to summarize a survey of which crops farmers intend to plant that year.

put option – p. 164 – A financial contract that bestows the right, but not the obligation, to sell an asset at a specified price at a certain time. The buyer of a put pays the seller a **premium** for this right.

quarter section – p. 185 – One-fourth of one **section** of land, equivalent to 160 **acres.**

Relative Strength Index (RSI) – p. 107 – A technical analysis metric which describes the momentum of past rises or falls in a market's price.

reportable positions – p. 114 – Trading entities who hold a specified number of net long or net short positions in a given commodity futures or options market must report those positions to the CFTC.

rho (interest rate sensitivity) – p. 170 – The ratio of how much an option's price changes with respect to the change in the underlying risk-free interest rate, i.e. the "interest rate sensitivity" of an option.

risk premium – p. 215 – In grain markets, the proportion of a futures contract's price which is due to the uncertainty of upcoming supply. Alternatively, in any market, the proportion of a specific asset's return above and beyond the expected return of the broader, risk-free market.

rolling futures – p. 90 – The practice of switching a long or short position in a futures contract with a specific expiration date to a similar futures contract with a more-deferred expiration month.

round turn – p. 115 – A complete trading unit of entering and exiting a trading position, involving both the purchase and the sale (or the initial sale and the offsetting purchase) of a financial asset.

row crops – p. 226 – Agricultural products grown with common equipment and technology, e.g. corn, soybeans, milo, or cotton planted in 24" or 30" parallel rows.

scale ticket – p. 30 – A document which records the quantity and quality of each load of grain delivered to a buyer.

section – p. 185 – A unit of area measurement used to describe land, equal to one square mile or 640 acres.

short covering – p. 119 – The practice of exiting previously-established bearish (short) positions by buying future contracts. When done in sufficient quantities, a mass of buying activity may act to **support** a futures market's prices.

short squeeze – p. 111 – When there is a scarcity of a physical commodity or a scarcity of willing previous long futures positions owners, those who own the remaining physical stocks or the remaining long futures positions before expiration can "squeeze" traders with pre-existing short positions to pay exorbitant prices to meet their needs.

shrink – p. 144 – The tendency of physical grain to lose its volume as it dries and ages over time. If a sample of stored grain loses 1% of its volume (and/or weight), for instance, the owner correspondingly loses 1% of its market value.

silking – p. 228 – The reproductive stage of the corn plant when it produces a "flower" of thin, string-like "silks" that accept pollen to fertilize a cell which will mature into a grain of corn.

specialty crop – p. 240 – Any horticultural agricultural product which isn't part of the widely-traded, commoditized grain market, but which may compete with the grain markets for farmland availability or producer attention.

speculator – p. 75 – An investor who hopes to make a profit by anticipating a price change and risking capital based on that prediction, without actually consuming or producing the asset being traded.

spot price – p. 28 – In the grain markets, the free market price of a specific category and quality of grain at a specific location *right now*. Colloquially, "spot" prices may refer to grain within a 30-day shipment timeframe, but **NGFA** rules detail "immediate" shipment within 3 days, "quick" shipment within 5 days, or "prompt" shipment within 10 days.

spread – p. 61, 92, 130, 154, 156 – Broadly, the mathematical difference between any two market prices (e.g. a geographical market spread, or the spread between a location's milo and corn prices). Specifically to futures market speculation, the "bid-ask spread" may refer to the difference in the price proposed by an asset's willing buyers and the price offered by an asset's willing sellers; or the "**calendar spread**" may refer to the difference between a futures contract with one expiration date and a futures contract with a different expiration month.

spread trade – p. 154 – An arbitrage trading strategy involving simultaneously buying and selling related assets in order to profit from a change in the difference – i.e. the spread – between their prices.

"stacked" seed (single-stacked, double-stacked, etc.) – p. 227 – A term for genetically modified organism (**GMO**) seed, denoting how many non-native characteristics the seed exhibits, such as glyphosate resistance or corn rootworm resistance.

Stochastic Oscillator – p. 107 – A technical analysis metric which describes the market's momentum as a function of the most recent closing price in relation to the price range of the recent past.

stocks-to-use ratio – p. 109 – A measure of comparative supply and demand; the remaining inventory of a commodity expressed as a percentage of the total demand.

stop order – p. 104 – A trading order to buy or sell an asset at the market price if and only if the market hits a certain price trigger.

stop limit order – p. 105 – A trading order to buy or sell an asset at a specified limit price if and only if the market hit s a certain price trigger.

straddle – p. 174 – The simultaneous purchase and sale of a put and a call at the same strike price, in the same market, with the same expiration date, with the goal of profiting as the volatility portion of the premiums increases.

strangle – p. 175 – The simultaneous purchase and sale of a put and a call in the same market with the same expiration date, but with different strike prices, with the goal of profiting if the market makes a large jump in one direction or the other.

strike price – p. 164 – The price at which a call option's underlying asset may be purchased, or a put option's underlying asset may be sold, if the option is **in-the-money.**

structural analysis – p. 110 – The study of supply and demand of a derivatives market, rather than the supply and demand of its actual underlying physical market; i.e. the intersection of **technical analysis** and **fundamental analysis.**

support / pressure – p. 150 – In futures markets, "support" is the effect of buying activity to limit price losses, and "pressure" is the effect of selling activity to limit price rises.

swap dealers – p. 118 – A category of futures and options traders who traditionally act as market makers for **over-the counter** hedgers, in return for a fee.

"T" account – p. 141 – A colloquial term for a bookkeeping practice with one side of transactions offset with another side of transactions recorded across a vertical 'T' line. For disciplined hedgers, every purchase in the cash or futures market is offset by a sale in the futures or cash market on the other side of the 'T' account.

tasselling – p. 228 – The reproductive stage of the corn plant when it produces a pollen-producing "tassel" at its top.

technical analysis – p. 106 – A method of predicting future market activity by evaluating patterns of past market activity, such as price and volume. Compare to **fundamental analysis**.

terracing – p. 187, 195, 218 – A farmland management practice, creating "steps" of ground up a hillside, reducing potential erosion or making it possible to cultivate land that would otherwise be too steep for crop planting.

terminal elevator – p. 41 – A grain warehouse facility with the ability to accumulate and load out large-scale shipments of grain to domestic or international markets.

test weight – p. 30 – A density metric for grain, usually expressed in pounds per bushel (standard 56 lbs/bu for corn; 60 lbs/bu for soybeans and wheat).

theta (time sensitivity) – p. 170 – The ratio of how much an option's price changes with respect to the change in the time before the underlying asset expires, i.e. the "time-value sensitivity" of an option.

tiling – p. 187, 218 – A farmland management practice, placing drainage pipes under the soil to remove excess moisture from the roots' zone.

time-value of money – p. 142 – The theory that any unit of money has an inherent potential to earn value over time and is therefore worth more in the present than the same amount of money is worth in the future, determined by the assumed interest rate.

trailing stops – p. 153 – A series of stop orders placed between a trade's entry level and the current market price, designed to close out the trade at a profit if it starts to backslide.

trend – p. 106 – The general direction of a market's prices – higher or lower. A trend may exist on a short-term, intermediate-term, or long-term basis.

USDA – p. 32, 184, 213, 229, 231, 243 – The United States' Department of Agriculture.

"V" stages – p. 228 – The vegetative stages of a grain plant.

value-added product – p. 22 – A product with unique value above and beyond its raw material inputs; distinct from a **commodity.**

vega (volatility sensitivity) – p. 170 – The ratio of how much an option's price changes with respect to the change in the volatility of the underlying asset's prices; i.e. the "volatility sensitivity" of an option.

volume – p. 80 – The quantity of trades made in a market.

warehouse receipt – p. 77 – A document that guarantees the availability of a physical commodity in a specific storage location

WASDE (World Agricultural Supply and Demand Estimates) – p. 229 – A closely-watched monthly report summarizing estimates from USDA's Office of the Chief Economist, Agricultural Marketing Service, Farm Service Agency, Economic Research Service, and Foreign Agricultural Service, including both supply and demand categories for all major crops produced in the U.S.

yield curve – p. 226 – In the grain markets, the mathematical expression of how much a crop's average yield per acre has grown over time.

Index

10-34-0 ammonium phosphate 190
4-H 176
accumulated swing index 111
accumulator contract 163
acre 185
ADM (Archer Daniels Midland) 37, 138, 187
aeration of soil 220
aerial imagery 206
aflatoxin 35
Africa 34
AgLeader 201
agriculture industry 194
agronomy 222
air seeder 220
alfalfa hay 23
algorithmic trading 170
alternative investment 113
amaranth 21, 238
American option 179
ancient grain 238
anhydrous ammonia 190
anti-money laundering 100
AP (Associated Person) 101
arbitrage 2, 5, 13, 37, 45, 47, 66, 96, 122, 130, 147, 157, 171, 182
arbitration 43
Argentina 212
Asian option 179
Asian Soybean Rust 222
at-the-money option 166
autosteer 221
Available Water Holding Capacity of soil 183

backhaul 128, 148
backtesting 110, 176
back-to-back transaction 138, 189
backwardation 92
backyarditis 213
banking 142
bankruptcy 68, 71, 137
barge 40
barley 21, 88, 238
BASIC (Background Affiliation Status Information Center) 98
basis 125, 129, 133, 139, 146, 161, 210, 250
bear spread / bull spread trade 156
bearish / bullish 48, 109, 215
Berkshire Hathaway 102
bid-ask spread 130
Bill of Lading 42
biofuel 229
biotechnology 191
Black-Scholes equation 170
Blankfein, Lloyd 47
blistering 228
Bohemia 1
bona fide hedge 116

boot stage 236
bottleneck 210, 224
Brazil 212, 234
broker 75, 81, 97
brokerage 75, 81, 98, 113
bubble 10, 118
buckwheat 238
Buffet, Warren 102, 109, 187
bull or bear flag formation 108
bull spread / bear spread trade 156
bullish / bearish 48, 109, 215
Bunge 138, 188
bushel 30
butterfly spread 175
buying acres 203

calendar spread trade 156
California's Central Valley 184
call option 164
call spread or put spread 173
Canadian prairie 184
canola 21, 240
Cargill 37, 138, 188
carry 61, 92, 131, 143, 157
Case IH 200
cash grain contract 29
casino 117
cattle feeding margin 155
CBOT (Chicago Board of Trade) 53, 75, 96
CDS (Credit Default Swap) 177
cellulosic ethanol 21
center-pivot irrigation 183
Certificate of Deposit 4
CFTC (Commodity Futures Trading Commission) 78, 83, 100
charts: bar, line 106
chisel plow 219
CIF (Cost, Insurance, Freight) 127
CME Globex electronic platform 87, 95
CME Group 75, 106
collar 174
combine harvester 189, 224
commercial trader 116
commission 90, 115
Commitments of Traders report 79, 116, 239
commodity 14, 21, 70, 79
communal farming 195
compaction 219
Comstock, Gary 193
condition report 213
contango 92
continuous chart 90
contract 28, 73, 136
contract growing agreement 239, 247
contract symbol 89
convergence 77, 118
cooperative / "co-op" 49, 65
corn 21, 184, 205, 226
Corn Belt 39, 183
corn borer 227